Global Inequality: Political and Socioeconomic Perspectives

Westview Replica Editions

This book is a Westview Replica Edition. The concept of Replica Editions is a response to the crisis in academic and informational publishing. Library budgets for books have been severely curtailed; economic pressures on the university presses and the few private publishing companies primarily interested in scholarly manuscripts have severely limited the capacity of the industry to properly serve the academic and research communities. Many manuscripts dealing with important subjects, often representing the highest level of scholarship, are today not economically viable publishing projects. Or, if they are accepted for publication, they are often subject to lead times ranging from one to three years. Scholars are understandably frustrated when they realize that their first class research cannot be published within a reasonable time frame, if at all.

Westview Replica Editions are our practical solution to the problem. The concept is simple. We accept a manuscript in camera-ready form and move it immediately into the production processs. The responsibility for textual and copy editing lies with the author or sponsoring organization. If necessary we will advise the author on proper preparation of footnotes and bibliography. We prefer that the manuscript be typed according to our specifications, though it may be acceptable as typed for a dissertation or prepared in some other clearly organized and readable way. The end result is a book produced by lithography and bound in hard covers. Initial edition sizes range from 400 to 600 copies, and a number of recent Replicas are already in second printings. We include among Westview Replica Editions only works of outstanding scholarly quality or of great informational value, and we will continue to exercise our usual editorial standards and quality control.

Global Inequality: Political and Socioeconomic Perspectives

edited by D. John Grove

Redistribution of the world's wealth, not only among nation-states but among cultural, class, and sexual groups, has become increasingly a major issue of concern. This book examines existing inequality in both the domestic and international arenas. Its multidisciplinary approach facilitates an understanding of the complex structure of global distribution patterns and allows a comparison of redistribution patterns at different levels and in different political, social, and economic contexts. A key question is explored: to what extent are domestic inequalities a function of the international structure?

D. John Grove is assistant professor in the Graduate School of International Studies, University of Denver, and director of the University's Center of International Race Relations.

Global Inequality: Political and Socioeconomic Perspectives
edited by D. John Grove

Westview Press/Boulder, Colorado

0949845

A Westview Replica Edition

Published in 1979 in the United States of America by
Westview Press, Inc.
5500 Central Avenue
Boulder, Colorado 80301
Frederick A. Praeger, Publisher

Library of Congress Catalog Card Number: 78-21437
ISBN: 0-89158-252-5

Printed and bound in the United States of America

Contents

Contributors

Elise Boulding, Professor of Sociology, University of Colorado

Raymond R. Corrado, Assistant Professor of Political Science, Simon Fraser University

Raymond Duvall, Associate Professor of Political Science, University of Minnesota

D. John Grove, Director of the Center of International Race Relations, and Assistant Professor, Graduate School of International Studies, University of Denver

Satish Raichur, Associate Professor of Economics, University of Denver

Bert A. Rockman, Associate Professor of Political Science, University of Pittsburg

Edward Thomas Rowe, Associate Professor, Graduate School of International Studies, University of Denver

Bruce Russett, Professor of Political Science, Yale University

Baldave Singh, Research Associate, Office of Minorities, University of Minnesota

William K. Tabb, Associate Professor of Economics, Queens College of the City, University of New York

Fred von der Mehden, Professor of Political Science, Rice University

Preface

One central issue of the twentieth century is a greater
redistribution of global wealth--not just between rich and poor
nations, but among cultural, sexual, class, and gender groups.
Although the extent of global inequality between and within nations
has now become an area for serious research, there is still a great
deal to be learned about "who gets what." Systematic research on
distributional patterns is of very recent origin, and there remain
uninvestigated areas. This book brings together a wide range of
original papers which examine the conceptual, theoretical, and
empirical problems of global inequality.

The papers were originally presented at the Conference on
Global Inequality at Estes Park, Colorado, June 8-9, 1977. The
purpose of the conference was to relate research being conducted at
the Center on International Race Relations[1] with other research
projects on inequality studies. The papers present a broad
approach to the global problem of skewed distribution of wealth.
The conferees were grouped into three areas which became the basis
for discussion: 1) issues in inequality studies, 2) linkages
between international and domestic inequality, and 3) strategies for
change.

The starting point for the conference discussions on issues in
inequality studies revolved around the impossibility of determining
the extent of inequality in the Jack Sprat social system. Jack Sprat
and his wife value different goods. One values lean meat, the other
values fat. Who is to say which is more desirable? To measure
social inequality, one would, therefore, have to identify the inherent
and intrinsic social goods valued by each group.

It could be argued, however, that every political system tends
to socialize its different groups to accept the inequalities of that
system. This not only means that socialization plays an important
role in the definition of acceptable inequality, but it can also mean
that socialization defines the preferences of groups: do they prefer
lean meat or fat?

There was also considerable debate on the levels of analysis
issue. Some felt that class was the only legitimate group for
comparative studies. Others felt that cultural or sexual groups
could not be subsumed under a class analysis. How the various
levels are defined will partly determine whether economic exploitation
or social discrimination is a major factor in the allocation process.

In an early conference discussion on linkages between international inequalities and communal distributional patterns, the levels of analysis issue was addressed: should the world be defined 1) in terms of nation states, or 2) in terms of subnational groups linked to a global system of allocation? The conference participants agreed that domestic and international levels are a meaningful and useful distinction; sovereignty is very much bound up in the determination of socio-economic inequality. The political boundary around the nation-state is largely coterminus with the set of processes that determine the extent of inequalities among groups. Put another way, sovereignty largely defines how the problem of inequality is sliced. This is especially true of multi-ethnic societies where the socio-economic gap between groups is almost always defined within the political boundary.

Two arguments relate the extent of the linkages between the international economic system and communal or sexual groups. The two approaches are: 1) the Marxian one world system, and 2) the domestic contextual approach. The Marxian argument begins with the classic Leninist-imperialist position that the world operates as a single global economy. The distributional decisions are made so that the spatial patterning of both human capital and physical resources is done on a world scale. In other words, the primary decisions concerning production, investment, and economic growth yield the initial distribution of wealth or the international division of labor. Redistribution of wealth, therefore, is confined to a secondary procedure at the sovereign level.

The second argument begins at the nation-state level where distributional patterns are largely defined by such factors as prejudice, ethnocentrism, or repressive policies. The inequalities are largely dependent on long-standing historical factors, and it is necessary to understand the specific contexts or situations in which they occur. Some would even argue that the central government does not have much influence on the inequalities among subnational groups, and that to understand the differences one must study the values and cultures of each group. This school of thought readily admits that existing global inequalities exacerbate communal and sexual disparities, but that these disparities existed long before colonial regimes or multi-national corporations began to penetrate the economies of nation-states.

The two schools of thought were well represented at the conference and are the underpinnings of much of the research presented in this book. The papers are organized along four subjects areas: 1) issues in inequality: exploitation and discrimination, 2) international inequality, 3) domestic group inequality, and 4) strategies for change.

Support for this project came from the Ford Foundation; from the Center on International Race Relations, University of Denver; and from a comparative studies grant from HEW.

For her invaluable editorial work, I would also like to thank Mary Jane Lewis, without whose help this book would have been immeasurably the poorer.

NOTES

1 The Center on International Race Relations is collecting basic socio-economic and political data on seventy-five ethnic and racial groups in twenty-five multi-ethnic societies. The inequality study is part of a larger project designed to systematically examine different groups in culturally heterogeneous societies.

D. John Grove
June 16, 1978

Part I
Major Issues: Inequality
and Discrimination

1. Issues in the Theory and Assessment of Social Inequality

Raymond Duvall

INTRODUCTION

At least since the publication of The Widening Gap by Barbara Ward and others in 1971, we have heard arguments about contemporary inequality among national societies. Many scholars now claim that over the last several decades rich nations have become more advantaged while poor nations have become worse off.[1] Other scholars reject these claims and argue that social and economic inequality among nation-states has not changed. I do not want to venture into this debate here. But putting aside its substance, I find it noteworthy that scholars are talking about inequality among such social aggregates as nation-states or whole societies at all.

As it turns out, however, the global inequality debate is not unique in this respect. On the contrary, students of inequality within national societies frequently base their assessment of the actual extent of inequality (and changes therein) on the income (or some other value) of households.[2] Others base their judgments of intra-national inequality on differences among social classes or ethnic/identity groups.[3] And less macroscopic are studies of inequality in particular markets based on comparisons of some attribute of firms (e.g., sales, capital stock).[4] All are instances of inequality among social aggregates.

But what is meant when one talks of inequality among nation-states, groups, classes, firms, or households? And how is one to make empirical assessments of such inequality? These questions are too frequently ignored in the now extensive literature that discusses international or intranational inequalities. Too often, scholars proceed as if these were irrelevant questions with little or no consequence for research on the real nitty-gritty of the subject of inequality. The position expressed in this paper is the opposite. It is an attempt to demonstrate that conceptual and methodological issues can make a tremendous difference, and to highlight some of the relevant issues that are generally ignored in discussions and analyses of inequality among social aggregates.

The paper is organized in four sections. In the first, I address the issue of the general meaning of the concept of social inequality. To what is one basically referring when using the concept in the analysis of some social system? Focusing on one of

3

two general meanings, I move in the second section to deal with the problem of social aggregates as the units among which inequality is said to exist. I ask what the conditions are under which the concept can be meaningfully applied to differences among aggregates. In the third section, my concern is the valued things or conditions that are unequally distributed. What do social aggregates have in unequal amounts that creates a situation of social inequality among them? Finally, in the fourth section, I deal with the problem of empirical assessment and attempt to provide part of an answer for the question, how does one measure the extent of social inequality among social aggregates?

THE CONCEPT OF SOCIAL INEQUALITY

Social inequality has been widely used to refer to two analytically distinct phenomena with the result that there are two general meanings for the concept. In some scholarly traditions, especially those of sociology, social inequality is often virtually synonomous with social stratification.[5] In this sense it refers to aspects of how a social system is organized, to structural features of the system. Call this the structural meaning of inequality. In other traditions, such as in economics, it often refers more restrictively to distributions among elements of the system with no direct implications for structural or organizational properties. Call this the distributional meaning of inequality.

Unfortunately, it is far too frequently the case that scholars use the concept imprecisely, slipping back and forth between the two general meanings. But assessment of inequality and, in turn, fruitful empirical-theoretical dialogue about it, are dependent on reasonably precise conceptualization. What, then, is structural inequality? How does it relate to distributional inequality? And where do the two lead the discourse on social inequality in different directions?

Let us begin by reflecting on social stratification as a synonym for structural inequality. My impression is that in the sociological literature there is general consensus that social stratification entails four constituent processes: 1) the differentiation of actors or elements in the system; 2) the social evaluation of differences; 3) the allocation of rewards or goods according to different social evaluations; and 4) the crystallization of categories of positions in the social structure according to the allocation of rewards.[6] Now the number of constituent processes and their exact definition are of no real importance here. But what is important is the general feature that each process directly involves both attributes of actors and relationships among actors in the social system. For example, in speaking of the first constituent process, Eisenstadt says:

Social differentation usually refers to (1) the situation that exists in every social unit, large or small, by virtue of the fact that people with different characteristics perform different tasks and occupy different roles, and (2) the

4

fact that these tasks and roles are closely interrelated in several ways (1971:45).

In short, social differentiation is the process through which actors with different attributes regularly do different things and relate to one another in distinct ways. Similarly, evaluation means making invidious distinction, or assigning to various roles different places on a scale of value (Tumin, 1967:24). This attribution of value is clearly relational, and results in the creation of an actor attribute--the social value of the actor's role. The allocation of rewards is likewise relational in the flow or exchange of social goods, and involves actor attributes in the possession of goods prior to and subsequent to exchange or transfer. Finally, the crystallization of categories of positions is essentially the temporal stabilization of the rewarding process. It is the creation of a hierarchical system structure according to positions in the network of exchange.

The point is that social stratification and its synonym, structural inequality, have two basic aspects. On the one hand, socially valued objects or conditions (which I refer to as social goods) are unequally possessed or realized by actors in the system. Structural inequality entails distributional inequality. On the other hand and in addition, social interaction is asymmetrically ordered. The system is structured hierarchically to some degree. It is the inclusion of this latter aspect--hierarchy of interactional structure--as a part of the concept that distinguishes structural inequality (or social stratification) from distributional inequality.

I am, of course, implying that distributional inequality and hierarchical structure or its manifestation, relational asymmetry, are conceptually and empirically distinct phenomena. I do not claim that the two are empirically independent; they can be expected to covary. But covariation is imperfect. Rather, each of the two is in some part determined by different variables.[7] Consider three contrived, but revealing, examples.

(1) Schwartz concluded that strong processes operate to restrict and reduce distributional inequality in Israeli kibbutzim. Strict adherence to the allocational principle "from each according to his abilities, to each according to his needs," and socialization into a community norm which attributes no particular value to many human and social differences are two such processes. At the same time, according to Schwartz, job rotation is "largely symbolic, having run into competition with the economic necessity for effective co-ordination" (1955:427). Managerial positions, for example, regularly are occupied by the community's best managers. The result is that processes operate in some kibbutzim to reduce distributional inequality while others operate to increase or maintain hierarchy by fostering the crystallization of asymmetric relational positions for actors. Relational position (and hence status) in these communities has no intrinsic social value, hence does not itself constitute a form of distributional inequality.

5

(2) Sahlins (1958) investigated the social organization of "primitive" Polynesians and found that cultural groups of islands differed markedly in the degree to which distributional inequality was associated with hierarchical social structure. In each of his three cultural groups inequality was apparent. Some members regularly realized more social goods such as leisure or food consumption. One group, however, was marked by a distribution system of reciprocal exchange, no insignia of rank, and communal regulatory and punitive decision-making processes (Mayer and Buckley, 1970:21-22). That is, hierarchy was essentially absent, although distributional inequality was marked.[8]

(3) Finally, one can conjure examples of a negative correlation between possessions and position in a hierarchy. Beneficence and altruism, such as in the giving of one's life to save another's life, are but extreme examples of situations in which an actor with greater possession of a social good (e.g., safety or life chance) relates to another actor with less of that good in a reverse asymmetric fashion. An example with greater temporal stability, which is, as a result, more appropriate to a discussion of hierarchy as structure, is found in Olson and Zeckhauser's analysis of NATO (1966). Assuming that the social system defined by the NATO organization produces and distributes two social goods, one of which, security, is public or indivisible, and the other of which, wealth, is private or divisible, and assuming that the public good is most important to the actor which possesses the greatest amount of the private good (the most to lose argument), Olson and Zeckhauser demonstrate that the relationships among the actors must be asymmetric, with the wealthiest actor being systematically and disproportionately disadvantaged to the benefit of the poorer actors as they work together jointly to produce security.

If one accepts this argument that the two are conceptually distinct phenomena and if one has an interest in social stratification or structural inequality, the task is to specify the conceptual relationship according to which structural inequality is defined by distributional inequality and structured relational asymmetry conjointly. In general, the connotation is clear that the relationship involves more than a simple aggregation of the two variables.

The three examples above shed light on this issue. If taken to the limit, the first two examples could be characterized as situations in which one of the two conceptual components is absent while the other is present to some degree, and if the general consensus would be, as I believe it would, that social stratification is absent in such situations, then an interactive relationship between the two concepts is implied in specifying stratification or structural inequality. In addition, if the third example of inverse correlation between possessions and relational position is also characterized as an unstratified system, then the implied interaction of the two concepts is of a very particular nature. It involves a positive conjunction, or covariation, between distributional inequality and relational hierarchy. In particular, social stratification, or social inequality in the broad sense, refers to the extent to which a social system is organized such that interrelationships among distributional unequals are systematically structured in a hierarchical form. Equals occupy similar positions (define strata) in the relational hierarchy and actors with less social value occupy lower positions in the relational hierarchy. Moreover, stratification refers to the degree of congruence among strata that are defined according to different goods or social values. The more that the inequality of distributions and the hierarchy of relationships are congruent across different social values, the more stratified the system, or equivalently, the greater the social inequality of the system in the broad sense.

The implication of this discussion is that the student of social inequality must begin by determining and making clear the basic conceptual nature of the subject of study, inequality. If implicitly a defining aspect of the phenomenon of inequality is some feature of the organization of the social system, then the appropriate assessment of inequality is a very complex and difficult task indeed. It involves the assessment of three things: distributional inequality; relational asymmetry (i.e., interactional hierarchy); and covariation or positional congruence between the two. This is the case if one includes as part of the concept of social inequality the extent of social mobility across social positions or rank categories, for example. It is also the case if social inequality refers in part to the degree of unequal exchange, or the regularly asymmetric flow of value such as through labor exploitation, between and among social "positions". Similarly, if differences in the extent of dependence of various actors on one another is implicitly a part of the concept of social inequality, then reference is to organizational features of the system and hence to inequality in the broad, structural sense. Said conversely, if one restricts empirical assessment (i.e., measurement) to distributional inequality as is typically the case, one is not reflecting directly on social inequality in the broad structural sense even though conceptual/theoretical discussion might be cast in those terms. That is, measures of attributes, possessions, or realizations alone cannot be relied upon to determine social stratification. Because distributional inequality of possessions can be expected to covary only imperfectly with relational asymmetry, measures of the former do not adequately inform about aspects of the organization of the system, such as mobility, unequal exchange, or differential dependence within it. Strata, as relational or structural phenomena, cannot be determined by measuring inequality in wealth, health, education, or any other attribute. This is an important point because all too frequently verbal theoretical discussion focuses on hierarchy or relational asymmetry while measurement focuses on distributions of goods. And all of this is mixed under the heading of the study of social inequality.

I do not want to convey the impression that I think structural inequality to be a less useful or less important concept than distributional inequality because of its conceptual complexity. On the contrary, I believe that in general there is an important positive empirical relationship between distributional inequality and hierarchy. The structure of relations that compose a social system certainly can

7

be expected to be bound up with the distributions of goods that actors in the system realize or possess. But because the two are bound up only imperfectly and because they are analytically distinct phenomena, it is important that the student of social inequality be clear and consistent about whether reference is to distributional inequality or to social stratification. Otherwise, empirical assessment may be meaningless and empirical theoretical dialogue may be vacuous.

In the remainder of this paper, attention is restricted to distributional inequality. Again, this is not because I regard it as the more important concept but rather because it is important in its own right and because it is a constituent component of structural inequality, as I have shown above. An analysis and assessment of that latter, broader concept necessitates a coming to grips with distributional inequality, and hence has a clear basis in what is said in this paper. But it goes beyond this paper to an analysis and assessment of hierarchy and positional congruence. Nothing is said about those here. Nevertheless, some important implications for the study of social inequality are brought out.

To facilitate analysis, I offer a formal definition of the concept of distributional inequality. It is the extent of differences in the realization of (some) social good(s) by social entities. As social actors differentially realize things and conditions that are socially valued, there is greater or lesser inequality among them. This definition is intentionally general in order to provide the fullest opportunity to explore theoretical and methodological implications. I will focus, in this order, on three aspects of the definition in an attempt to develop some of these implications: social entities; the realization of social goods; and, the extent of differences.

SOCIAL AGGREGATES AS SOCIAL ENTITIES

Typically, definitions of social inequality specify or imply individuals as the entities to which the realization of goods is differentially attributed (Wrong, 1964; Tawney, 1964:57-58). If the implication is that individuals are the only entities to which the concept of social inequality is applicable, then the notion of social entities is not a problem. Indeed, if the concept of social inequality were taken to be applicable only to individuals, one could increase the simplicity of my definition by replacing the term social entities by the term individuals. But in doing so, one would unnecessarily restrict the scope of the concept. In fact, while formal definitions are typically given in terms of individuals, I do not believe that most authors who offer such definitions actually intend the implied reduction in conceptual scope. A perusal of one conventional collection of readings on social inequality (Thielbar and Feldman, 1972) reveals articles that utilize the concept to apply to groups (van den Berghe; Billingsly), organizations (Knudsen and Vaughan), and whole societies (Horowitz), with no apparent reaction from those who explicitly define the concept in terms of individuals. I assume, then, that the analysis of social inequality among social aggregates

8

can be a legitimate application of the concept. This paper proceeds on that basis.

There are two distinct ways in which students of social aggregates can and do treat inequality among them. In the first case, the social aggregate is merely an analytical convenience with which to organize and simplify an investigation of inequality among individuals. In this case, the relevant social entity is the individual, and the question of inequality is the question of differences in the realization of goods for members of one aggregate relative to members of another. The concern is whether the defining characteristics of the aggregate constitute bases for, or at least are associated with, inequality among individuals. The social aggregates have no special status except to organize the analysis of individual-level data, and to provide a theoretical basis for the explanation of individual inequality. Sexual, racial/ethnic, and class inequality are commonly treated in this way.

Inequality among social aggregates in this first sense poses no special conceptual problems and leads to no particular theoretical implications. However, it can be the basis of sloppy and inappropriate empirical research. In particular, one must keep in mind that the assessment of inequality among social aggregates in this sense is based necessarily on individual-level data. If aggregate measures are employed they must contain sufficient information to enable safe inferences about separate members of the aggregate. This means that the aggregate measures must reveal the features of the distribution of the members of the aggregate. This point is far too frequently overlooked because analyses of inequality among aggregates often are based only on group averages and composites (means, medians, modes, amounts per capita, etc.), whereas to inform about individual-level data it is at least necessary to know average and dispersion within the group. It is not simply that it would be nice to have measures of within-group variation; it is entirely necessary to have those measures (or to be able to infer them safely) if one is using the social aggregates merely as constructs to facilitate the analysis of inequality among the individual members of those aggregates.

An example should help to make the point. Typically, students of international inequality are interested in the realization of goods or attainment of well-being by individuals rather than nation-states, per se. Their concern is the extent of inequality between Brazilians and Americans, for example, and not between Brazil and the United States. But also typically, these students assess that inequality by reference only to indicators of "averages" for the separate aggregates, such as GNP per capita, percent of households with running water, or proportion of adult population that is literate. They claim that it would be nice to have measures of intra-national distribution to include in the analysis, but maintain that the aggregate indicators are the best available and must suffice. Unfortunately, they do not suffice because they provide information only about whether a Brazilian can be expected, on average, to be less well off or better off than an American. They do not provide

9

information about inequality between Brazilians and Americans as sets of individuals, which is purportedly the concept at issue. Thus, there is considerable slippage between concept, namely inequality between members of social aggregates, and the alleged assessment of concept. In fact, assessment by means of group averages and composites comes as close to being appropriate for the concept of inequality between the social aggregates as entities themselves, as it does for the concept of inequality between members of the aggregates. I doubt that most scholars who employ group averages for the assessment of sexual, racial/ethnic, class, or international inequality recognize that.

The second way in which scholars view social inequality among social aggregates is to treat the aggregates themselves as the units or entities among which inequality is the subject of investigation. Common examples of this include inequality in household or family wealth, market shares of business firms (generally labelled industrial concentration), and national power, national wealth, and national level of technological development. In this case, conceptual problems and theoretical implications are greater, if only because whenever one treats supra-individual aggregates as entities, critics invariably raise a flag and charge reification. The analyst is allegedly guilty of attributing essence and substance to a mere abstraction. According to this line of argument, General Motors is not real. Rather, the people who work together and call themselves employees (or is it the owners?) of General Motors are real. Those people engage in activities with certain manifestations and effects; what each does affects what others do, and the set of activities is organized. But General Motors as a concept is merely a convenience to stand in or substitute for the sum of the individuals and their activities. And all the more so for "entities" such as nation-states!

The issue here is the questionable necessity of a methodological individualism. Must the student of social inequality adopt the perspective of methodological individualism, as the critics caricatured above would have it, or are there conditions under which it is meaningful to talk of inequality among social aggregates as entities rather than as mere aggregations? Is it meaningful, in principle, to talk about differences in the realization of goods by Brazil and the United States where the concern is something other than inequality between Brazilians and Americans as individuals? Two considerations should affect our answers to these questions, I believe.

First, the position of the methodological individualist that rejects descriptive emergents (i.e., accepts as meaningful only those concepts which are ultimately definable in terms of individuals), and hence that leads automatically to a charge that references to supra-individual aggregates as entities, are instances of reification is a specious position. This is because it fails to specify criteria for determining "realness," principles to ascertain whether reification occurs. Methodological individualists provide no explicit criteria by which to conclude that in simply moving to a supra-individual level of conceptualization, one is inherently engaging in reification. This might be because firm criteria are elusive. In the words of a noted astronomer,

10

> I am afraid of this word Reality, not connoting an ordinarily definable characteristic of the things it is applied to but used as though it were some kind of celestial halo. I very much doubt if anyone of us has the faintest idea of what is meant by the reality or existence of anything (Eddington, 1929:282).

Moreover, "we have no idea what the supposed qualification would consist in, nor in what way the prestige of the world would be enhanced if it passed the implied test" (Eddington, 1929:285-86). A possible exception, of course, is the criterion of direct sensory perceptibility, which often is implicit in the reification argument. But I doubt that if pressed on this criterion most scholars would want to defend its logical implication that the particular sensory mechanisms that have evolved and now characterize the human species are the sole bases by which to determine if something is an entity, or real. The limited range of phenomena humans can directly perceive is surely not all that is thought to be real. Or, "to quote Heraclitus: 'He who does not expect the unexpected will not detect it; for him it will remain undetectable, and unapproachable'" (Popper, 1962:147).

This line of argument can be and has been extended to an extreme that denies the ultimate existence of entities at all. According to this position, which is currently quite popular among physical scientists, all "things" are intellectual constructs because ultimately everything is in flux, being composed of processes interacting with one another over different spatial and temporal domains. Heisenberg, famous for the uncertainty principle, makes the argument:

> The elementary particles of modern physics are determined by mathematical symmetry requirements, rather like the regular bodies mentioned in Plato's philosophy, they are not constant and unchanging and can therefore scarcely be considered as real in the usual sense of the word. They are rather to be considered as simple representations of the fundamental mathematical structures at which we arrive if we attempt to divide up matter into sections of ever decreasing size, and which form the content of the fundamental natural laws. We therefore see that in modern natural science it is not the thing but the form, the mathematical symmetry, that is the beginning of all things (Heisenberg, 1959:58).

The implication of this latter position is that the defensive burden is shifted to the methodological individualist because reference to any social entity, even the individual, is seen to be something of an act of reification. The problem then becomes showing why a reification of the individual is acceptable while a reification of supra-individual aggregates is not, in principle. This is not easy to do. After all, we refer quite naturally and meaningfully to social aggregates in everyday discourse. If we insist on breaking them down to constituent descriptive concepts, where do we stop? What are individuals, if not, in part, features and creatures of a social whole? Systems of social relations do provide a critically important part of the very definition of individuals.

On these grounds, I believe that one does not have to accept the position of methodological individualism. It is a sophistical position.

The second consideration that should affect how one approaches the concept of inequality among social aggregates as entities goes more directly to the heart of the matter than did the first. It is a pragmatic consideration that one must refer to entities of some kind if one is to make knowledge claims at all, even if one accepts the position that reference to entities is always something of a reification. Purely process theories are impossible, since one cannot focus on processes without a referent background which includes the more stable processes with which the process in question interacts and the lower-order processes which give rise to it and to which it applies. That is, to know processes it is necessary to distinguish between these and the process packages, or "entities," on which these processes occur (Campbell, 1966; Parsons, 1961). Entity is shorthand for the process package. It is a more than convenient shorthand, for to require reasonably full specification of the entire process-package in any knowledge claim would contribute so many terms and variables that knowledge processes would be impossible. One, then, needs entities. So one needs criteria for evaluating the appropriateness of referring to process packages or relational systems as entities in specific instances. This is true whether one is referring to individuals or to social aggregates.[9] Two criteria are: (1) scientific utility; and (2) empirical tenability. These two principles may lead to different conclusions, so it is helpful to view them as distinct.

Scientific utility is a dispositional criterion in that it is concerned with the potential for aiding in the understanding of phenomena. It becomes in effect an ex post facto test of descriptive and explanatory import. Does treating some process package or relational system as an entity enable one to better organize rigorous theoretical understanding of some observable phenomena? If so, reference to that as an entity is appropriate, according to this criterion.[10]

But what does this mean for the student of inequality? It means that if one speaks of inequality among social aggregates as entities, one bears the burden of showing explanatory import by accounting for some range of observables that would not be accounted for otherwise. This is a tough standard to say the least. To my knowledge, it is not met with much frequency. A rare instance is the ability of students of "industrial concentration" to account for pricing behavior by referring to firms as social entities to which inequality in market shares is attributed. Others may

12

include an ability to account for war by referring to nation-states as entities with unequal power or wealth, or an ability to account for the level of well-being of individuals by referring to national societies as entities with unequal levels of technological development.[11] And so on. But otherwise the criterion of scientific utility may make one less than optimistic about the prospects for meaningful discussions of inequality among social aggregates.

The second criterion, empirical tenability, is dealt with creatively by Campbell (1958), who acts on the logic employed in referring to individuals as entities. He sets, thereby, the criterion of multiply-confirmed boundaries. Boundary is, of course, imperfect in any instance (including the individual) but is indicated, Campbell claims, through instances of spatial/temporal proximity of components, attribute similarity of components, shared or common fate among components, reflection or resistance to intrusion by components acting together, and internal diffusion or communication among components. In giving these indicators operational specifications (as Campbell attempts to do in some cases), one is establishing the observational cues to entities. In the present context any of Campbell's tests might be adopted and prove worthwhile in the determination of the empirical tenability of the assumption of some social aggregates as entities. Such tests, of course, would not prove that they are entities in any ultimate sense. Rather, they would serve only to distinguish those aggregations which meet the definitional criteria from those which do not.

It is important to realize that how one defines and measures an entity has direct implications for the theoretical questions about that entity that can be addressed. Concepts and indicators used in defining an entity have restricted theoretical utility since the definition narrows the range of variation the data can assume and limits the degrees of freedom on theoretical outcomes. In adopting Campbell's tests one would be in a poor position to include (the degree of) boundary--or any other concept indicated by his tests such as integration (through communication and internal diffusion indicators)--as a theoretical concept. The conclusion to be drawn is simply that there is an integral relationship between how entities are defined (generally implicitly) and the processes or phenomena concerning those entities that can be included in theoretical statements, either as explanatory or explained phenomena. In order not to define away the world, one needs to be careful to select definers that are not of theoretical interest. Since processes that are the relatively most stable are apt to be those of least theoretical interest (there is little variation, hence, little to explain), the suggestion is often made to utilize these as definers (Parsons, 1961:67-70; Teune, n.d.). Nation-states, for example, might be treated as those social entities defined by stable land areas (or more precisely, by the physical processes sustaining those) to which a political/legal boundary is attributed by some other actor. But that strategy has its weaknesses. It leaves one open to the charge that what one is defining is not an entity in any important experiential sense (that is, one essentially has abandoned the criterion of

13

empirical tenability), and hence leaves scientific utility as the sole criterion. This brings one back to the logic of Campbell's argument--a recognition of the necessity, at some point, of tests for the "boundedness," in some specified sense(s), of the aggregation of lower level processes and entities. Only to that extent does the concept of social inequality among social aggregates as entities take on meaning.[12] Thus the necessity is to balance somewhat opposing principles--on the one hand the need for a definition of the entity and indicators or empirical criteria for that definition, and on the other hand, the realization that such definitions and indicators restrict theory. A once-and-for-all linkage of social entities to defining characteristics is impractical and potentially harmful. The linkage must be theory-specific in part.

An obvious example is social class. In some traditions class is treated less as an aggregation of individuals and more as a social entity in its own right. In these traditions the entity is typically defined by the social relations of production of its constituent members (e.g., owners of the means of production constitute a class entity, the bourgeoisie, etc.). But because social relations of production are used to define the entities, these social relations cannot be employed also as part of a theoretical argument to explain social inequality among classes as entities.[13] The explanation would not be distinguishable from the conceptual definition for the entities in terms of which the explanation was offered. This problem of course is not limited to class inequality.

To summarize this discussion of social aggregates as entities among which social inequality may be a subject of concern, I have said that in purporting to measure or to develop an explanation or theory of social inequality among them, one bears the burden of demonstrating that these aggregates as entities (e.g., nation-states, institutions, or households) are definable and identifiable apart from those processes involving them which are incorporated in the theory of social inequality, and of demonstrating that the entities so defined contribute to greater descriptive and explanatory capabilities of some observable phenomena. This is because social entities are not simply given in reality. Rather, they are constructs of the analyst, and as such, they must satisfy reasonable criteria for good concepts. But if these criteria are met, the arguments of the methodological individualist are misguided. One can, under these restrictive conditions, talk meaningfully of inequality among social aggregates as entities.

The Realization of Social Goods

The problem here is the determination of what the relevant social goods are for any analysis of inequality among social aggregates. More particularly, it is the issue of how a theory of social inequality is affected by the way in which this determination is made. What are the consequences for theory if the theorist stipulates the goods over which there is inequality? And what if the theorist relies on actors in the referent system to reveal the goods?

In this section, I deal with these questions.[14] Note that what I say here is intended to be of relevance to any study of social inequality among social aggregates in either of the above two senses. That is, it bears on theory of inequality among individual members of social aggregates as well as on theory of inequality among the social aggregates themselves as social entities.

I begin by assuming that social inequality is in terms of things of worth or value. That is the connotation of the word goods in the formal definition. Valuation is somehow tied up with any theory of social inequality, then. It is theory about differences in the realization of worthwhile things, desirables. But just how is valuation linked to theory? Clearly, there are two alternatives--either evaluation is performed outside of the theoretical and empirical referent system, or it is performed within it.

Evaluation outside of the referent system is almost certainly evaluation that is sanctioned by the theorist regardless of the language according to which the evaluative claim is justified and rationalized. In this circumstance, a theory of social inequality is a theory based on what is that the particular theorist holds to be good or believes that acts in general to be good. This is the case with most work in moral philosophy or normative theory where the good is often rationalized as "primary," "natural," or "universal." An appropriate example is found in the recently popular book, A Theory of Justice (Rawls, 1971). In that book Rawls offers an analytical theory of justice based on inequality in terms of "primary social goods."

> Now primary goods . . . are things which it is supposed a rational man wants whatever else he wants (sic). Regardless of what an individual's rational plans are in detail, it is assumed that there are various things which he would prefer more of rather than less. With more of these goods, men can generally be assured of greater success in carrying out their intentions and in advancing their ends, whatever these ends may be. The primary social good, to give them in broad categories, are rights and liberties, opportunities and powers, income and wealth (a very important primary good is a sense of one's own worth. . .) (Rawls, 1971:72).

Although it has plausibility and some appeal, this kind of justification is of no real scientific utility. That is because it is based either on obviously invalid assumptions (every rational person prefers X, where rationality means having a preference for X), or on a non-falsifiable assertion (Barry, 1973: 27-33). In the latter sense, it could be either or definitional truism (every rational person prefers X, where rationality means a preference for X), or a metaphysical proposition (X is good by its very nature). I am aware of no other possibilities for the type of argument offered by Rawls. But none of these possibilities contributes to an empirical theory of social inequality.

15

An additional problem with theories of inequality based on stipulation by the theorist of "primary," "natural," or "universal" goods is that "the list of natural rights varies with each exponent. . . . [It] seems difficult to account for the wide variations in the lists of these 'rights' if they have all been deduced from a fixed human nature or essence, subject to an absolutely uniform 'natural law'" (Macdonald, 1946:239-240). (For a discussion of deductive inconsistency in the specification of primary goods by Rawls, see Barry, 1973:56-58.) There is no criterion at the stage of postulation and definition, other than emotional or intellectual appeal, by which to judge the relative scientific utility of a theory based on Rawls' seven primary goods as contrasted with a theory based on Lasswell's eight universal goods of power, wealth, respect, well-being, rectitude, skill, enlightenment, and affection (1958:202). The two sets (and many others) are not coextensive; they can be expected to yield different theoretical implications. Thus we could have as many different theories of social inequality as there are theorists stipulating a set of "primary," "natural," or "universal" goods. That is not a happy state of affairs for the development of social science.

For these reasons, I conclude that when evaluation is (implicitly) performed outside of the referent system and when the goods of relevance to social inequality in the referent system are justified as natural or universal, the contribution to an empirical theory of social inequality is necessarily limited at best. But a rejection of such a priori justifications of the good or goods of relevance to inequality does not entail a necessary rejection of the postulation of those goods that are so justified. Rather, it leaves the conclusion simply that the theorist is functioning as evaluator. The justification is irrelevant--the claim becomes, in effect, "It is assumed that X, Y, and Z are goods." On its face, a postulation of this kind is perfectly reasonable and admissible. But I believe that on closer examination, any formulation of social inequality that entails the theorist as primary evaluator can be seen to be lacking in scientific utility.

Now there are two possiblities open to the theorist acting as evaluator. The first is to specify a single good; the second is to specify more than one good. The potential outcomes for the former case can similarly be dichotomized although less sharply. Either the single good is a general concept of a relatively high level of abstraction or it is a relatively concrete concept.

Probably the most common strategy employed in seeking to construct and/or test empirical theory of inequality is to deal with a single concrete good such as wealth, health, education, or income (implicitly) defined as a good by the researcher. But where does this strategy lead? Unfortunately, it leads to a theory of inequality that is either of very limited generality or of very limited empirical validity. If the theory is intended to be general, i.e., in reference to social inequality in general, it will be valid only with regard to the specific contexts in which the particular concrete good is a singularly important variable or is a marker variable, very highly

16

correlated with other goods. So, if there is an attempt to construct or test a theory of inequality (or stratification) by examining the distribution of income or education for example, the effort will reflect validly on theory only in contexts in which income or education is the key to inequality in general. Unfortunately there is not much information about the precise nature of those contexts, i.e., about how to determine when a situation is one. Conversely, if the theory is intended to be about a restricted concept of inequality (e.g., income inequality), it may be highly valid, but we do not know what it reveals about social inequality in general. There is not adequate knowledge about the linkage from that type of inequality to other types. The result is that scholars tend to vacillate between generality and validity by speculating on implications for inequality in general from findings about inequality in some single concrete good. The conclusion is warranted, then, that perspectives on inequality in terms of a single concrete good (implicitly defined as a good by the researcher) leave us wanting in our efforts to develop empirical theory of social inequality.

Moreover, a definition of inequality in terms of a single concrete good (and hence a separate inequality for each good) renders other concepts vacuous. I have in mind social stratification (or inequality in the broad sense): do we have a distinct stratification system for each good? And what does that say about the structural configuration of a system? Another concept that would be in trouble would be imperialism, which involves the interaction of inequality, dependence, and exploitation (Caporaso, 1973). If inequality is defined separately for each good, must we conclude that there are a multiplicity of imperialisms? And so on, for other similar concepts.

Alternatively, the theorist might stipulate as a single good some general abstract concept such as utility, happiness, or welfare. However, if theory is to have empirical content, an abstract definition of the good must be given a more precise meaning at some point. This entails defining utility or welfare in terms of more concrete goods. In this way, a seemingly single-good formulation is directly equivalent to a multiple-good formulation.

The problem with employing multiple goods in the development of theory of inequality is, in a nutshell, that the theory must provide a means by which to aggregate the several goods. Lacking these means, the theorist has a concept of social inequality defined as "the extent of differences in the realization or possession by social entities of n social goods, X_1, X_2, . . ., X_n," which is so imprecise a concept as to be unobservable in principle because there is no statement of the relative "goodness" of X_1, X_2, . . ., X_n. One could not definitely say that a situation in which one actor held all of X_1 and another all of X_2 was one of greater social inequality than a situation in which both actors held one-half of each. Many alternative statements about inequality would be equally admissible and such "disagreements in evaluation. . . (would) turn not on any difference in principles but rather on one person's giving a number of agreed principles different relative weights from another person"

17

(Barry, 1965:13). Statements of the form, if Z, then greater social inequality, or, if greater social inequality, then Z, would be non-falsifiable because greater social inequality would be a fully imprecise term. Using something of a different line of argument, but with the same purport, Harsanyi points to the necessity of choice. In most social situations, all goods are not realized simultaneously, necessitating a choice by the evaluator (in this case the theorist) of the various values if a meaningful statement about social inequality is to be made.

> However, the traditional attitude among social scientists in general has not been very favorable to facing such facts. Rather, the implicit assumption usually has been that "all goods things come together," all desirable factors have positive correlation with one another. . . . We shall call this implicit assumption the Positive Correlation Fallacy. It has been one of the main obstacles to clear thinking among social scientists (Harsanyi, 1969:537-38).

But how does one make the concept of inequality precise and make theoretical statements about it falsifiable while developing theory that is both tractable and generally valid? One needs inter-good substitution statements which are likely to be either infinitely numerous or context specific. To be of wide scope or applicable to many contexts, the theory must contain statements to the effect that in contexts of such and such a type, good X_1 is evaluatively equivalent to good X_2 in a different context. This argument is based on the seemingly realistic assumption that distributions in one good, for example wealth, do not in all times and in all places have the same consequences or causes. Rather it is assumed that consequences and causes of distributions of particular goods vary according to context. One trivial but informative example concerns the good self-respect, common to Rawls, Lasswell, and others in the tradition of "theorist as evaluator," and distributions of which would be expected to have very different bases and consequences in the context of a communitarian or organicist culture than in an individualistic culture. There is, then, an assumed relativity of values, where "'(r)elative' in this sense means related to surrounding conditions, and carries with it no necessary reference to subjectivity, or to the mental make-up of the person or persons judging" (Ginsberg, 1956:238). It is the assumption, and I think the patently obvious one, that "although two principles need not be reducible to a single one, they may normally be expected to be to some extent substitutable for one another" (Barry, 1965:6), Given this assumption, it is obvious that the contextual substitution principles are potentially as numerous as the contexts to which the theory is applied. Since each contextual substitution principle requires at least one theoretical statement, the extreme conflict between tractability and scope (or generality) is apparent.

In sum, statements of "the good" by a theorist are problematic. They have an inherent tendency to give rise to theories of very limited scope, or of a non-falsifiable character, or of analytical intractability. For this reason, I conclude that the theorist acting as evaluator is not performing a scientifically useful role, but is embarking on a dead-end venture. The contribution of persons like Lasswell has not been, in this vein, a scientifically useful one, whatever the value in other ways. Finally, for this reason, I conclude that the term social goods, and hence social inequality, is usefully employed only in theory that incorporates the notion that entities in the referent system themselves act as evaluators in determining the goods according to which inequality is defined. The attribution of evaluative activities to referent actors, however, has additional implications for theory. At the most basic level, it implies that the concept of social inequality is not usefully employed in a purely objectivist, or strict behaviorist, theory; rather, it has empirical meaning only in the context of a theory in which meaningful (i.e., intentional, purposeful) behavior has significance. Purpose has two rather broad meanings, each of which has given rise to a somewhat distinct tradition in theorizing about purposeful behavior. The first meaning is roughly equivalent to function and is exemplified "as when the 'purpose' (i.e., the function) of kidneys in the pig is said to be that of eliminating various waste products from the bloodstream of the organism" (Nagel, 1961:402-03). The second meaning is roughly equivalent to goal and is exemplified in the statement that Smith's purpose (i.e., goal) in studying hard is to graduate with honors (Rudner, 1966:85). The first meaning of purpose is concerned with behavior that is governed or regulated by some "goal-state," but which is not consciously intentional behavior. Such is the purposeful behavior underlying much of organismic biology and functionalist social science. The second meaning of purpose is concerned with consciously intentional behaviour in regards to a "goal-state," and underlies much of micro-economics and other disciplines in the tradition of rational decision-making. Evaluation involves both a "goal-state" and conscious intentionality in relation to that "goal-state" (see Dewey, 1939). The logical implication, then, is that the purposeful behavior underlying a theory of social inequality must, at some level, entail the notion of conscious goal, or intent. Social inequality cannot be adequately explained by purely functionalist theory.

This is an implication of some importance, although it may seem that I am emphasizing a trivial point. An examination of much of the literature on social inequality and social stratification, however, reveals quickly that the emphasized statement is far from obvious. Most of the literature in sociology on these subjects is entirely functionalist in perspective, as is evidenced by the long debate on the functional or dysfunctional nature of social inequality (see Davis and Moore, 1945; Tumin, 1953; Wrong, 1959; Moore, 1963; and in the form of empirical tests, Abrahamson, 1973). In this literature, the implied purposeful behavior is that of social systems; its nature is

19

entirely non-intentional. The results are ambiguity, lack of theoretical rigor, and little, if any, progress in accumulating knowledge on the subject.

The problem, however, is that theories of consciously intentional action are often criticized on the grounds that they are of non-casual and/or tautological form. To deal with these criticisms requires: (1) a determination of the logical relationship between intention and the behavior (or resulting phenomenon) which is to be explained in using intention as an agent; and (2) a specification of the form or structure of the explanation offered.

On the first, the question is whether the two are conceptually distinct or whether one entails or implies the other. One line of thought has it that the adequate description of an action (or other phenomenon that is meaningful to the actor in the previously discussed sense) must contain a statement of the intent of the actor, otherwise the action is not described as action, but instead is described as act (Hampshire, 1959; Peters, 1958; Winch, 1958). Since the intent is necessary for the description of the act as an action, the intent and the action are not logically distinct; hence, one cannot be offered as a cause of the other.

The response to this line of argument involves an acceptance of the generally intimate relationship between the two in description but a rejection of the conclusion that the two are therefore not logically distinct. In particular, where the intent is part of the direct referential meaning of the action, the intent and the action are not logically distinct, but where the intent is not itself part of the referential meaning, it can provide the basis for non-tautological explanation (Brodbeck, 1963; Davidson, 1963). This presupposes intentions at multiple levels of abstraction for a single action. An example from Meldon (1961) is the case of an automobile driver approaching an intersection, raising his arm, and turning the corner. The context enables the description of the act of arm raising as signalling, an action. But it is argued, to describe the action as signalling entails the (implicit) statement of the driver's intent, to signal. Otherwise it can be described only as arm-raising. But to signal is not the only intention; rather, to avoid an accident, to avoid a ticket, to permit other drivers to move along safely, or to do what is legal are all possible non-tautological causes as intentions. The referential meaning of signalling does not entail any one of them.

For theory construction, the implication is clear; to be a potential explanation of an action or other phenomenon, an intent must not be entailed in the referential meaning of the action (or phenomenon). To describe an action as signalling means that it cannot be explained because of an intent to signal or, more generally, to communicate about future behaviors. The intent must be cast in terms of some aspect or consequence of the action not entailed in the referential meaning of the action. "We cannot explain why someone did what he did simply by saying the particular action appealed to him; we must indicate what it was about the action that appealed" (Davidson, 1963:685). I call such non-entailed aspects or

20

consequences of action the meta-intents of the actor. What is important to recognize is that these meta-intents, as variable properties of action outcomes, are the "goal-states" of action, the "goods" for the intending actor. Non-tautological, causal explanation of intentional behavior requires a specification of meta-intents, and, because they are the goods, so does an adequate assessment of social inequality require their specification. It is necessary, then, that we come to grips with the specification of the meta-intents, or goods, pursued by actors in the empirical referent system for which inequality is a subject of concern.

The basic character of an explanation of conscious intentional action, given as a formal model in skeleton form is:

> X is a rational actor
> X is in a situation of type C
> In a situation of type C, any rational actor will do Y
> ∴ X does Y (Hempel, 1965:471),

where a rational actor is defined as one who does what he believes will most probably enable a realization of his meta-intent, and where C involves: (1) the meta-intent of the actor; (2) the beliefs of the actor concerning the actions available; and (3) the beliefs of the actor concerning the probabilities for each action enabling realization of the meta-intent. This is the standard model of micro-economic theory, game theory, and other traditions in the analysis of rational action. In spite of the popularity and alleged success of those traditions, I maintain that in this form and, in the abstract, the model is unacceptable. The reason is that the theory is not falsifiable as it stands. To be testable the theory must contain a specification of the components of situation C, components which are mentalistic, or non-observable, variables. Clearly there are two options: (1) to attempt the indirect measurement of meta-intents and beliefs; or (2) to attempt a stipulation of them by the theorist.

In previous paragraphs, I argued that the second is not a useful option.[15] At the same time, the first strategy in general is not apt to be a viable option because measuring the goals or desired goods for a set of actors in a system is apt to be prohibitively difficult.

So what remains if intentional behavior must be an element of theory? An alternative that has not characterized any literature with which I am familiar is available, and, I will argue, is potentially adequate on scientific grounds. That alternative is to retain the basic rationality model, and to add assumptions which contain intersubjective, observable concepts, thus providing an empirically-grounding nomological net. The added assumptions will be to the effect of postulating the (observable) conditions, B, under which actor X will be in (mentalistic) conditions, C. The resulting model is given formally and in abstract form as:

21

X is a rational actor
If X is in a situation of type B, X will be in a situation of type C
In a situation of type C, any rational actor will do Y
X is in a situation of type B
.˙. X does Y.

In the abstract, the modification is slight. In practice, it is more extensive, as we shall see. In effect, it is highly significant because it directly renders the theory falsifiable without distorting the meaning of meta-intent, depending on indirect measurement of meta-intent and belief, or requiring theorist specification of the value or state of mentalistic concepts. Rather, the theorist explicitly conjectures about the observable conditions under which the mentalistic concepts will take on different values, or be in different states. The theorist avoids the problem of personal evaluation, retains falsifiability, and has the hopes of constructing a general and valid theory of intentional behavior (and, in turn, of social inequality).

Putting enthusiasm aside momentarily, I feel compelled to provide greater detail to the formalized model of theory. The first axiom assumes actor rationality, a dispositional concept defined as doing that which the actor believes will most probably result in the realization of the meta-intent. Social inequality has been defined in terms of goods--it is by implication a multi-dimensional, or multi-aspected, concept. For that reason, I have spoken throughout of meta-intents in the plural. There are multiple aspects, multiple goals, that are assumed to underlie intentional behavior. An important implication is that the concept of rationality must be redefined--there is not a singular meta-intent about which probability beliefs are held. Rather, any behavioral situation might be expected to have implications for a plural set of meta-intents. Rationality clearly must be defined in terms of believed probabilities of effect on the total set of meta-intents. By implication, a postulation of rationality in the context of a theory of social inequality assumes that actors have organized the meta-intents so that they stand as a coherent whole. The organizing principle can be referred to as the actor's welfare function--it is a statement, or rule, relating the several meta-intents to one another in terms of their respective relative values to the actor (e.g., the rate of which one would be traded off for another). Rationality can, then, be redefined as doing that which the actor believes will most probably result in the realization of the greatest personal welfare, where the greatest welfare involves trade-offs among multiple goods.

The necessary elements of the intentionalist theory of social inequality have merged and can be summarized. The elements are: (1) observable determinants of the set of meta-intents, or goods; (2) observable determinants of the ordered relationship among the meta-intents, or welfare functions; (3) observable determinants of actor beliefs about possible actions; and, (4) observable determinants of actor beliefs about the probabilities of "success" of possible actions. Together, these determinants are specified as

22

condition B in the previously formalized model. With them, the theory is made falsifiable in principle. Whether with them the theory is tractable and falsifiable in practice is another question.

Clearly if a separate statement is required for each possible meta-intent and each possible belief, the theory is not tractable because the range of meta-intents and beliefs is infinite. The theorist must establish a boundary around the set of possible meta-intents and beliefs. To conclude that the theorist must establish a boundary around possible meta-intents and welfare functions is, of course, to conclude that the theory must suffer from a priori or arbitrary specification. It entails some of the problems previously discussed about the theorist acting as evaluator. In this light, it seems impossible to avoid the necessity of evaluation by the theorist at some point in any theory of social inequality. But drawing a conceptual boundary and detailing the elements of a concept are two distinct enterprises. The boundary drawn may be inadequate, but drawing a boundary is certainly less demanding and less risky to the validity of theory than is the direct specification of the goods and the specification of a precise relationship among them. This issue of precise specification was raised previously in rejecting the possibility of the theorist acting as evaluator, and it constituted part of that rejection because it was held to underlie an irreconcilable controversy. The controversy was between scope on the one hand--a precisely specified relationship among the goods cannot be assumed to be valid for many actors in many contexts--and parsimony on the other--a separate specification for each actor in each context would render the theory intractable. But it is in offering a solution in principle to precisely this problem that the rational decision-making model developed here is an attractive (and, I think, virtually imperative) option for theorizing about social inequality. The validity problem is handled by assuming that meta-intents (goods) and welfare functions are variables, changing with actor and context. The parsimony problem is handled, in principle, by abandoning the requirements of a separate statement for each actor and each context, and replacing it with a set of law-like statements that specify the general conditions under which particular kinds of meta-intents and particular kinds of welfare functions will be part of an actor's mental makeup. However, to offer even general statements that determine meta-intents and welfare functions is to include in theory as many statements as there are distinct and meaningful combinations of these variables. Clearly, even in drawing conceptual boundaries the theorist is impaled on the horns of a dilemma, albeit a lesser one than the above. Namely, the tighter the boundary is drawn, the more the theorist is threatening the validity and utility of theory (precisely because of the factors discussed in the section on evaluation by the theorist), whereas the looser the boundary is drawn, the more the theorist is threatening the tractability and, in turn, the falsifiability of the theory. Nor can the theorist opt for imprecision in the specification of meta-intents and welfare functions to the degree that social inequality is to be an empirical or measurable concept.

23

Goods are given as the related set of meta-intents for an actor, the related set of variable properties of situations, objects, and events which the actor values. They are given by the actor, and they imply, at some point, intentional behavior on his part. But none of this discussion should be read as implying that intentional behavior, or even purposeful behavior in general, is a sole explanatory basis. On the contrary, non-purposeful behavior such as reflex, habit, or learned response may well be expected to play a central role in a theory of social inequality. Certainly not all, nor even most, of the behaviors that affect the distribution of social goods are purposeful. Of importance is a determination of the conditions under which actors do behave purposefully, which, in the present context, means to exhibit the disposition of rationality. The theory must capture those conditions explicitly; otherwise, the actors cannot be said to engage in valuation, the concept of goods is meaningless, and a theory of social inequality is impossible. But it should be obvious that goods are not only realized intentionally. While they must be defined intentionally by the actors, they can be realized unintentionally. Some of the latent functions of social behavior can be the differential realization of social goods.

Two problems remain. First is one for which I have no ready solution. That is the problem of "false consciousness," the problem of some actors having the "wrong" meta-intents because of a failure to recognize what is in their "real" interest. Now, if a claim of false consciousness were simply a justification for enabling the analyst to act as evaluator, the charge should be dismissed just as any other instance of the latter. But it does not appear always to be just that. Rather, it can be an empirical claim that the observable determining conditions B in the above model are of a "peculiar" kind, which, if changed slightly, would result in a substantially different set of mentalistic conditions C. That is, false consciousness might be appropriately claimed, and could be a real problem for what I have proposed in this paper, if the referent actors' definition of the "good" differs from what it would otherwise be because of some special or extraordinary conditions in the social system of which they are parts. The only reasonable solution of which I am aware for this problem is to have an empirically well-confirmed theory of the "otherwise" circumstances, which would be employed as a counterfactual model to generate "true" meta-intents and welfare functions in the context of false consciousness. To my knowledge, we lack such well-confirmed theories, and so false consciousness remains a potentially severe and irresoluble problem for the student of social inequality.

Second, there may be special problems for the student of inequality among social aggregates, because it is the case that notions of intent, belief, or other mentalistic concepts may be inappropriate if they are attributed to social aggregates. It is not immediately apparent that the attribution of intentional behavior to supra-individual actors has any meaning. Social organizations do not have minds, but they are composed of individuals who do. The issue is whether the composition or aggregation of a set of minds enables the attribution of mentalistic concepts to the whole. In question form, under what conditions, if any, is a model of a social aggregate sufficiently similar to a model of the human mind that the concepts appropriate to the latter are appropriate to the former? Rather than attempting to develop and justify a model of the human mind, I want simply to develop an important implication[16]. In particular, no theory of intentional behavior of whatever type (and by extension no theory of social inequality) is meaningful except to the degree that the referent (social) entities are co-ordinated, integrated, communications systems. My previous concern with the ontological status of social entities can now be seen to have been more than mere philosophical discourse. Moreover, the often articulated strategy of ignoring the issue of realism by simply defining referent entities according to a priori criteria can be seen to be problematical for theories involving intentional behavior. The advocate of such a strategy, I believe, has not adequately thought through the illogical connection. Moreover, because consciousness is a complex informational process by which the actor represents itself vicariously in alternative future scenarios, social entities lacking decisional units and control centers with such symbol manipulating capabilities are inappropriate referents for a theory of social inequality.

* * * * *

We began this section on social goods several sentences ago. In all that has been said, I have discussed implications only of the term goods. Let me turn more briefly to the modifier, social.

Tumin claims that "(t)o say that stratification is social is to imply, first, that one is not talking about biologically caused inequalities" (Tumin, 1967:14). According to this perspective, goods are social goods if they are socially created rather than the result of non-social, physical processes. Social goods are aspects of society rather than aspects of nature. But there are problems with this perspective. First, it presupposes that the causation or creation of goods can be easily classified as either social or physical in nature. Tumin includes in his list of goods that are not social both strength and intelligence. But would he be confident in his classification if the goods were recast as destructive capability and intellect? I doubt it. Second, on its face it seems too restrictive. Goods that are often of interest to students of inequality but which are predominantly biological or physical in nature would be unnecessarily eliminated from consideration. Assuming that health and nutrition are largely physical and that their provision is a good, are they not important aspects of social inequality? If, as I believe, they are, another perspective is required.

The alternative is to speak of goods that are socially defined. That is to say that social goods are commonly regarded as goods by the members of a social system. There is a general agreement that they are desirables rather than idiosyncratic or private commitment to them as goods. In the form of a trivial but revealing example, if

0949845

one were to take Jack Sprat and his wife as a social system, and given the information that is generally available about Jack Sprat and his wife, one could not make statements about social inequality in the system. That is due simply to the fact that each actor has a single good (lean and fat respectively), and the good is unique to each actor. There is for them no social good.

But while "commonly defined as good" is the meaning of the term social goods as that term is conventionally used in relation to social inequality, it is not a meaning without problems. In particular, it excludes purely personal goods from consideration in the assessment of social inequality. While that is not necessarily a problem, it does mean that social inequality as a concept has no necessary relationship to the set of goods which are of greatest importance to the referent actors individually or separately. Social inequality does involve things which are held as goods by the actors, but it does not involve all of those things. Two implications seem worthy of note. First, the "significance" of the concept of social inequality is a function of the cultural, or value, homogeneity of the total system to which it is being attributed. The more homogeneous a social system is (in terms of actor values), the more meaningful is the concept of social inequality. Conversely, the greater the number of personally important goals that actors pursue, the less important is the concept of social inequality. Second, social inequality is not, in any sense, a concept about the total well-being, personal satisfaction, or "utility" of referent actors. Most writers on the subject lose sight of that fact and tend to use the term in such a way that it connotes that one actor is worse off than another by possessing less of one, or all, of the social goods. To the degree that "worse off" implies something about total personal utility, welfare, or satisfaction, the use of the term is inappropriate. One hardly needs to belabor examples about cultural deviants to make the point that social inequality does not necessarily refer to inequality in happiness, or even to inequality in most-valued goods.

The reader might respond that I have twisted things, that social inequality does not simply refer to distributional differences in the restricted set of common, or social, goods. Rather, it might be argued, social goods are any goods that are desired by actors in the social system. Inequality, in this light, refers to distributional differences in the total set of goods. The problem is that this would necessitate the development of an individualized metric of total value for any package of goods for each actor. This would be an intensity of valuation or "utility" metric, permitting inter-actor or interpersonal comparisons. The notion of social goods as developed in this paper, by contrast, avoids that difficult if not impossible task.

It does that, to summarize this section, through two modifications to the general model of intentional action. First, comparison is limited to the set of socially defined goods, those states of affairs commonly valued by members of the social system. Second, use is made of a common, theoretically defined welfare function to organize and aggregate the separate social goods into a

26

single metric by which to compare the social well-being of members of the social system (and thereby to assess social inequality among them). This theoretical welfare function may not correspond exactly to the personal welfare function of any individual member of the system. Instead, it is "characteristic" of members in a given context.

It is the contention of this section that the development of adequate empirical theory of social inequality depends necessarily on a willingness and ability to make these two modifications. To analyze and theorize about inequality among social aggregates, it is necessary, then, to identify: states of affairs commonly desired by the various aggregates; and, a "characteristic" evaluation of each of these goods relative to one another in a given context. If social aggregates are so different that social goods and a characteristic ordering of the goods in similar contexts does not exist among them, the analysis of social inequality among them is meaningless.

INEQUALITY AS THE EXTENT OF DIFFERENCES

In the two previous sections, I attempted to develop some implications for a theory of social inequality by considering major definitional elements of the concept. I developed implications about the types of referent systems to which the theory can appropriately be applied, the type of theory which must be developed, and the types of phenomena to which the concept and theory will refer. In considering this, the third definitional element, I shift gears somewhat and direct my attention more to questions of measurement than to substantive implications. The phrase, the extent of differences, is the part of a definition of inequality that connotes principles of assessment or observation. Substance and measurement are so intimately related, however, that in focusing here on measurement principles some of the more interesting substantive implications are derived for theory. And although the discussion in this section is about measurement, it does not touch upon the technical issues of measurement. The reader will not find here a discussion of the latest or best inequality indices. Instead, this is an analysis of measurement issues that are prior to index construction.

Let me begin by reviewing what I have said, thus far, of relevance to a determination of the extent of realization or possession of social goods by separate social entities. Of particular relevance, it was argued in the discussion of evaluation by the theorist that a problem is the need to specify the relative "goodness" of each of the goods. Lacking such a specification, the observer is incapable of distinguishing between a multitude of distributional configurations as to degree of inequality. This principle was extended by showing the need for a welfare function for each actor, a systematic, ordered relationship among the goods. I argued that this welfare function is best given as a theoretical argument, and hence specified as characteristic of referent entities, because of the general impossibility of directly and empirically determining the relevant welfare function for each referent entity. In short, the measurement of social inequality, as a multi-good concept, is impossible without some theoretical rule for relating the goods to one another as goods.

The measurement issue of concern here, then, is the theoretical specification of characteristic welfare functions. In particular, should one specify a fixed and common welfare function for all referent entities or should one permit variation among actors and for an actor in different contexts?

Clearly, the first option is the simpler and more convenient. And for that reason it is the one more apt to be used by the student of inequality. To the extent that researchers focus on multiple-good inequalities, then, they generally utilize the same rule for all actors in aggregating the multiple goods in order to make comparision of the differences in well-being among the actors. This often is implicit in analysis rather than explicit as a measurement criterion. To see how pervasive is this strategy, the reader need only reflect on the typical sociological research based on income, education, and occupational status, for example, as three goods entailed in social inequality. In what are frequently only verbal analyses of the composite inequality in a referent system, the sociologist generally treats these three goods (and/or others) as of equal weight. That is, no effort is given to take into account their relative "goodness" or value for the separate referent actors. By implication, this is to say that the researcher assumes (or specifies) a "universal" unweighted linear additive rule for aggregating the goods. Indeed, I have done just that, but as an explicit measurement criterion, in a previous attempt to assess inequalities in terms of multiple goods cross-nationally (Gurr and Duvall, 1973).

But what are the consequences of this nearly universal practice by researchers of multiple-good inequality? First, the specification of equivalence is tantamount to saying that, regardless of context, all actors will pursue a good with the same determination, and that, regardless of actor and context, the possession of a particular amount of a good will have the same effect on actor behavior. This implication is likely to make any test of theory based on a measurement of inequality invalid because it is an implication that is not consistent with what are apt to be explicit assumptions of the theory. (Refer to the previous section of this paper.) But beyond that, and even if this implication is consistent with a researcher's theory, there are other noteworthy consequences.

One rather strange theoretical outcome involves the types and extent of social interaction among the set of actors with respect to a set of social goods. In particular, under the assumption that the actors not only value the same things, but also value them in the same ways (i.e., have identical welfare functions), it can be shown that mutually advantageous exchange of social goods cannot occur according to the theory. In simple verbal form, if actors value the same things to the same degree, they will not exchange with one another if they are rational actors, regardless of how much of any of the goods each actor possesses. A simple example in the style of an economist will suffice to show this, because it would do no violence to the example to extend it to more than two actors and two goods.

Suppose a world in which apples and oranges are the social goods, and suppose that actor A has six apples and six oranges while actor B has nine apples and nine oranges. Also suppose that under these conditions, each actor thought that an orange was equivalent to two apples. Then, if the actors are rational, and even though they possess different amounts, they will not trade apples and oranges. This can, perhaps, be seen most easily in graphic form. Figure 1 is a representation of this exemplary situation in the form of an Edgeworth Box, named for a mathematical statistician who developed it as an analytical tool in the late nineteenth century (Edgeworth, 1881). The four co-ordinate axes of the box represent the amount of each of the two goods for each of the two actors (the origin for actor B is in the upper right corner). Point C is the current position of each actor translated onto the co-ordinate axes by the straight dashed lines. The solid straight line through C, line 0A, represents the relative value of the two goods at point C. The slope of the line is the relative value of the goods in ratio form (i.e., one orange for two apples), and understandably it is called the rate of exchange. That is, since one orange is equivalent to two apples for actor A, he would be willing to exchange apples or oranges at any ratio that exceeded that (give one orange, get two and one-half apples; or, give two apples and get one and one half oranges). Since both actors have the same rate of exchange at point C, they share the same line 0A (a circumstance that is represented by the subscript AB).

Generally, the student of rational behavior and mutually advantageous exchange utilizes curved lines of the form A_1, A_2, B_1, B_2 in the Edgeworth Box to represent each actor's welfare functions, or "indifference" curves. The lines curve because it is assumed that at each different combination of goods, an actor will have a slightly different rate of exchange--that is, the relative values of the goods to one another is assumed to change with changes in the amounts of each of the good possessed. The curves are smooth convex surfaces because it is assumed that the ratio of the goods possessed is inversely related to the ratio of the values of the goods, an assumption of "decreasing marginal utility." With these normal assumptions, the Edgeworth Box permits an easy determination of the final distribution of goods after rational actors have exchanged to the point of greatest value for each. That is done by finding the point(s) at which the actors' welfare functions are tangent to one another, which in Figure 1 is point C. From that point it is impossible to move without one of the actors moving to a lower, or less valued, welfare function. They cease to exchange with one another until something changes.

But when researchers assume a fixed and universal welfare function by implying a single aggregation rule for the multiple goods, they are assuring that actors will <u>always</u> be at point C from the outset. This is because that assumption makes each actor's indifferent curve a straight line (like $0A_{AB}$), and makes the slope identical for all actors' indifference curves. Welfare functions, then, are tangents everywhere, so the initial distribution of goods remains

FIGURE 1

AN EDGEWORTH BOX REPRESENTATION OF THE NO-EXCHANGE SITUATION UNDER CONDITIONS OF INEQUALITY

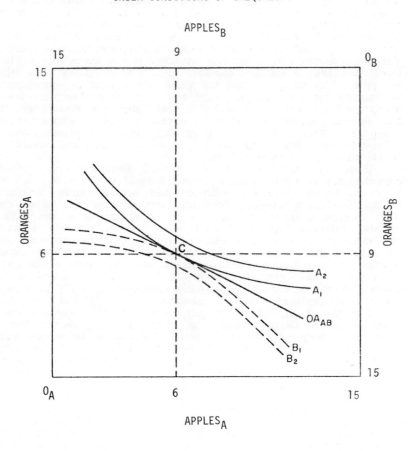

the final distribution, assuming that there are some (however small) transaction costs. Actors will never exchange social goods. The anomalous implication of all of this is obvious. Given that in reality there will generally be differences among the actors in welfare functions, there will normally be some mutually advantageous exchange of social goods among them. But, the greater the extent to which actors share the same values (have common goods, or meta-intents) and the greater the extent to which they value them in the same way regardless of context (have similar, nearly straight welfare functions), the less likely is mutually advantageous exchange to occur among them, and the more restricted the range of that exchange. There are a set of derivative principles of considerable importance that can be enumerated. First, if increased rates of interaction among actors in a system tend to increase the similarity of actor goals and goal-structures in different contexts, then increased rates of interaction tend to reduce the possibilities for mutually advantageous exchange. Second, if similar contexts or conditions tend to make goals and goal-structures similar, then increasing the similarity of conditions for actors reduces the possibilities for mutually advantageous exchange among them. Third, in a nascent system, if the initial distribution of goods is more dissimilar than the distribution of goals and goal-structures, or if the latter tend to converge more rapidly than do the former, then the initial distribution of goods will be relatively fixed, or permanent. The more rapid the convergence of actors' goals and goal-structures, the less rapid the change in inequality of distribution of goods. Each of these derivative principles are of importance to a substantive theory of social inequality. But a fourth principle is of more immediate importance because it involves the conceptualization of social inequality. The principle is simply that the more rigorous the conceptual criteria for social inequality (that the same goods be interrelated in the same way across actors), the more restricted the type of system to which the concept can be meaningfully applied. These are systems lacking "normal" exchange and marked only by degenerative forms of interaction, by which is meant: (1) robbery or stealing; (2) exchange involving irrational action (and here is where the nonpurposeful forms of behavior become relevant); (3) interaction developing out of some action which resulted in externalities for other actors (the set of goals which they pursue was affected by the action of some other actor); or, (4) interaction involving public goods. It may be the case that some social systems, such as the international system, are of just such a degenerative form because actors have highly similar goal-structures--it may be largely inappropriate to assume or speak of mutually advantageous exchange in international relations, for example. But, and this is the important point, it certainly must be the case if the actors in that system are made to have identical welfare functions by concept formation. It would seem wise, then, to avoid this nearly universal research strategy and instead to permit variation across actors in welfare functions, in spite of the fact that the meta-intents of social inequality are those that are the

31

same across actors. Said differently, social inequality as a concept can be applied most meaningfully to systems in which actors value the same things but value them differently in different contexts.

The alternative strategy is to specify expected or characteristic welfare functions for actors. This involves a statement of the conditions under which welfare functions are expected to be held by an actor, which is precisely what the acceptable model of a theory of rational action contains. In this light, the measurement of social inequality is integrally related to the development of theory about social inequality. Such measurement through theory has not been characteristic of the social sciences, in which theory testing and concept measurement have generally been distinct enterprises in practice. But what I suggest here is that the testing of a component of a theory of social inequality (the theory of rational action) goes hand-in-hand with an adequate measurement of the concept which the theory is about. As we conjecture about the test for the determinants of welfare functions, we come to know those relationships through the validity of deductions from theory. We come, then, to know what are the determinants, and, in turn, what are the expected welfare functions under different conditions. As the accuracy of deductions from theory improves, so does knowledge of actors' value structures, and so, in turn, does our ability to measure social inequality. In this light, social inequality is a theoretical concept in the fullest sense, and cannot be adequately measured except through the development of theory of valuation and action.

Unfortunately, even this strategy is not entirely without problems. The major problem is that we buy increased realism and accuracy at the expense of complexity. Complexity is a problem in that it necessitates a large number of observations in the process of theory confirmation. In particular, because the theory of rational choice is held to be applicable only under certain conditions, many behavioral situations must be excluded from the set of tests of that theory, and because choice is theorized as a function of both beliefs and values, or goals, the number of theoretically appropriate behavioral situations must be large enough to permit estimation of the effect of each. A mitigating factor is of importance, however. That is the fact of theory. The relatively untheoretical basis of direct measurement strategies means many separate estimates for many contexts for many actors. Determination of value structures through the confirmation of theory requires only the testing of that theory in a few distinct contexts. Moreover, because the adequate theory will contain statements of expected welfare functions, the researcher has estimates of the latter prior to any empirical work. Theory testing and confirmation serves to increase the validity of those estimates, but a separate measurement procedure need not be adopted prior to the testing of theory. For this reason, and although the ultimate number of observations may be very large if highly valid estimates are desired, I encourage students of social inequality to adopt this strategy for the measurement of actors' value structures.

32

Finally, and in summary, let me reiterate that there is <u>not</u> the possibility of ignoring welfare functions if social inequality is meant to be a multiple-good concept. Ignoring the ordered relationship means either treating inequality separately for each good, or implicitly making the goods equal to one another in worth. In previous paragraphs, I argued that each of these options leads to a dead end for the construction of theory. Here I have extended that to argue that ignoring the ordered relationship of values for an actor is disastrous for the measurement of social inequality.

The first phase in the measurement of social inequality, then, entails three sub-phases. That is, to assess the extent of realization or possession by each actor in the system entails: (1) the determination of the quantity of the goods that the actor currently possesses or realizes; (2) the determination of the characteristic welfare function; and (3) the aggregation of the two into a composite value score for the actor. The first two sub-phases can be thought of as the creation of two data matrices when the process is extended to all the actors in the system. The first is the matrix of actual possessions, the second is the matrix of ordered valuations. The third sub-phase can, then, be thought of as the creation of a vector of composite value scores, one for each actor. This is obtained by summing, for each actor, the products of amounts possessed and relative value weights. In formal terms:

$$S_i = \sum_{j=1}^{m} (P_{ij}V_{ij}),$$

where S is actor i's relative social value score, P is the amount of good j possessed by actor i, V is the relative value of good j from the characteristic welfare function, and there are m social goods.

A final point should be made about welfare functions here. It is the obvious methodological point that differences in welfare functions create differences in actor composite value scores. But contained in that obvious methodological point is an interesting theoretical one, that <u>an actor's relative social welfare position can change with changes in his goal structure, even with constancy in the amount of the goods he possesses. Social inequality is as much a function of the relative values that actors attach to goods as it is a function of the amount of goods possessed.</u> The variable social determinants of goal structures are causes of social inequality, and must be included in an adequate theory of social inequality. (Consider Jack Sprat and his wife under conditions of changed welfare functions.)

The second phase in the measurement of "the extent of differences" is using the relative social value scores to assess the degree of inequality in the total system. Where the system consists of more than two actors, this phase is also somewhat problematic because one must represent a complex configuration simply. It might be labelled the "many body problem" of social inequality. The issue is one of moving from a vector of relative social value scores, one for each actor, and deriving a meaningful summary measure, a scalar, of the extent of differences in those scores among the set of actors in the system. Of all of the important issues in the measurement of social inequality, it is this one alone which has received reasonably adequate attention in the social sciences. That is, most pieces on the measurement of inequality begin with the assumption that each actor has a relative social value score, and that the measurement procedure is simply one of manipulating those scores. Alker, for example, begins his work on the measurement of inequality by saying,

> Let us imagine a universe $\underline{U}$ consisting of values and individuals. Let us label each individual out of a total population of $\underline{N}$ members by an integer $\underline{i}$ (where $\underline{i}$ may equal k, 2, . . ., or $\underline{N}$). The values held by each individual will be denoted v_i and assumed to have the properties of either interval or ratio scale. We shall also assume that the total values in the universe (symbolized by $\underline{V}$) equals the sum of the values held by its individual members. . . . this assumption can be stated as a symbolic equation:

$$\sum_{i=1}^{N} \underline{V}_i = \underline{V}_1 + \underline{V}_2 + \ldots + \underline{V}_N = \underline{V} \text{ (Alker, 1965: 32)}$$

The multi-good language of the paragraph (i.e., values held by each individual) and the symbolic equation, which contains one element for each actor, conjoin to make it clear that Alker assumes that we have already created a composite value score for each individual. He bypasses all of my previous discusssion in getting to that point. But I am not criticizing Alker so much as indicating the imbalance in measurement literatures. In regard to social inequality, much more of our attention has gone to measurement as the manipulation of data than to measurement as the rules and assumptions by which data are obtained. For this reason, I have addressed only the latter on this paper.

CONCLUSION

The development of sound empirical theory of social inequality depends on one's giving careful attention to some conceptual, philosophical, theoretical, and methodological considerations that do not generally occupy our thoughts. To ignore these considerations is likely to embark on a largely futile effort. One may become caught in a trap of conceptual vagueness and ambiguity by slipping back and forth between meanings of inequality as a social structural or distributional concept. Beyond that, one may mistakenly decide a priori that certain social aggregates are or are not appropriate referent entities for a study of distributional inequality, and thereby misdirect empirical validation efforts. And beyond that one may attempt to construct a theory without reference to the definition of goods provided by referent actors and/or a theory in terms of distributions of a single good. If so, one will find that the general validity of theory is very limited indeed.

Each of these problems has been raised in this paper. Each pushes toward the conclusion that the construction of theory and the empirical assessment of social inequality are difficult tasks. They will not be accomplished simply by plunging into the nitty-gritty of empirical research. Rather they are tied up with one another, theory and measurement. And this because social inequality as a theoretical concept is based in the referent actors' relative valuation of each of the goods commonly valued in different contexts.

ACKNOWLEDGEMENTS

I want to thank James Farr for useful comments on a previous draft of this paper.

NOTES

1. This argument has become so widely accepted among the world's disadvantaged peoples that it provides the unchallenged basis for the clamor for a "New International Economic Order." The most important early proponent was probably Raul Prebisch.
2. For example, refer to Muellbauer (1974) and Broom (1977).
3. See, for example, Wright and Perrone (1977), Hogan and Featherman (1977), and Stern, et al. (1976).
4. In this tradition, the phenomenon is generally referred to as industrial concentration, but the nature of the concept is really no different from inequality. See Blair (1956) and note the similarity of his measures of concentration to standard measures of inequality.
5. Indeed, one noted sociologist defines stratification as "the process by which scarce values are distributed" (Lenski, 1966:x). According to such a definition, social stratification and social inequality become virtually interchangeable terms. And consider the title of Tumin's classic textbook, Social Stratification: The Forms and Functions of Inequality. For an example of this sense of the term social inequality as applied in analysis, see Dahrendorf (1969).
6. This enumeration of constituent processes comes fairly directly from Tumin (1967) and Eisenstadt (1971).
7. If the social goods that are realized or possessed are entirely relational, then distributional inequality and hierarchy are the same. This might be the case for a good such as prestige or social status. Were analyses restricted to such goods, structural inequality would be equivalent to distributional inequality. But normally our interest is in goods that are not entirely relational such as wealth, income, health, security, knowledge, and skill. With reference to such goods, the two types of inequality are not equivalent. This is true even of such goods as rights and opportunities which clearly have important social structural bases.

35

8.   We need not look to Polynesia to justify an assumption of social systems marked by distributional inequality with little or no relational asymmetry. Indeed, the whole of neo-classical economic theory is based on essentially that assumption--members of a competitive market possess different amounts of various goods and interact through arrangements of reciprocal, mutually advantageous exchange.

9.   This line of argument is acceptable to the methodological individualist because it is based on pragmatic considerations. Brodbeck, for example, accepts as meaningful only those concepts which are ultimately definable in terms of individuals. But at the same time she recognizes the convenience and even utility of aggregate descriptors. Her reasons are two: (1) current conceptual open-endedness or vagueness prevents a precise definition of terms that are in principle definable (hence, potentially scientifically meaningful to Brodbeck). The elimination of such terms would be premature and harmful. (2) The composition rules in social systems that would be required to define supraindividual concepts are apt to be so complex that any completeness and closure of definition (and theory) will be highly imperfect (Brodbeck, 1958).

10.   This argument is essentially the one provided by Maxwell (1962).

11.   Note that here I am saying that inequality among individuals as members of social aggregates may be best accounted for by referring to inequality among the aggregates as entities. Because the two are conceptually distinct, one can be used to explain the other in meaningful, non-tautological terms.

12.   This means that one cannot rely simply on the nominal stipulation of social entities. If aggregates are entities only because one says they are, or only because they have formal labels, they fail to satisfy the criterion of empirical tenability. As a result, they do not provide the basis for theoretical statements about inequality among them (or about anything else) that are meaningful in any sense.

13.   I am saying that the structure of social relations may be the basis for defining social entities. This, of course, has clear implications for the previous argument that distributional inequality and structural inequality are conceptually distinct. If the entities that are of relevance to the student of distributional inequality are defined in terms of hierarchical structural relations among them, then the conceptual distinction is blurred, to say the least. This is certainly true of the concept of social class. It may be true of ethnic/identity groups in some contexts (but not most).

14.   This section may strike the reader as an instance of what Popper calls methodological essentialism, a tradition that he criticizes in favor of methodological nominalism. Essentialism is not my intent however. I talk of conceptual requirements but those derive more from the logical consequences of nominal definitions than from conceptual truths or essentials. I am very much concerned with the issue of how concepts, as they are defined, imply things for theories which can be developed incorporating those concepts, as well as for

the measurement of those concepts themselves. I do not believe that nominalism means that conceptual sloppiness or ambiguity should be condoned, nor that theory is unrelated to concept. For those reasons, this discussion may (incorrectly) seem to be an exercise in essentialism.

15. It might be said that micro-economists and game theorists depend almost entirely on the second option, specifying a single meta-intent for an actor (e.g., maximizing profit, minimizing cost, minimizing risk, etc.) and indirectly postulating actor beliefs by assuming a one-to-one correspondence between information and belief, and by assuming perfect information. If micro-economics offers empirically valid theory, which, I think, is subject to some question, it is due either to a reactive effect of theory (that is, the scientific enterprise itself modifies how economic actors behave), or to a very simple world, the key elements of which (profit maximization, perfect information, etc.) economic theorists happen to have been fortunate enough to know and specify a priori. It is not due, as is often alleged, to the existence of a simple quantitative variable, money, around which theory can be constructed. Lacking the confidence of the typical economist, I shun adoption of the second option for the construction of theory about social inequality.

16. This discussion is based on Deutsch (1951), Ashby (1970), and others in the tradition of general systems theory. See, for example, Buckley (1967).

REFERENCES

Abrahamson, Mark (1973). "Functionalism and the Functional Theory of Stratification: An Empirical Assessment," American Journal of Sociology, 78(5): 1236-1246.
Alker, Hayward R. Jr. (1965). Mathematics and Politics. New York: Macmillan.
Ashby, W. Ross (1960). Design for a Brain: The Origin of Adaptive Behavior, Second Edition. New York: John Wiley.
Barry, Brian (1965). Political Argument. London: Routledge and Kegan Paul.
Barry, Brian (1973). The Liberal Theory of Justice: A Critical Examination of the Principal Doctrines in "A Theory of Justice" by John Rawls. Oxford: Clarendon Press.
Blair, John M. (1956). "Statistical Measures of Concentration in Business: Problems of Compiling and Interpretation," Bulletin of the Oxford University Institute of Statistics, 18(4): 351-372.
Brodbeck, May (1958). "Methodological Individualisms: Definition and Reduction," Philosophy of Science, 25(1): 1-22.
Brodbeck, May (1963). "Meaning and Action," Philosophy of Science, 30(4): 309-324.
Broom, Leonard (1977). "Groups in the Distributive Process," Social Science Quarterly, 58 (June): 151-155.
Buckley, Walter (1967). Sociology and Modern Systems Theory. Englewood Cliffs: Prentice-Hall.

37

Campbell, Donald T. (1958). "Common Fate, Similarity, and Other Indices of the Status of Aggregates of Persons as Social Entities." Behavioral Science, 3(1): 14-25.

Campbell, Donald T. (1966). "Pattern Matching as an Essential in Distal Knowing." The Psychology of Egon Brunswick, ed., Kenneth R. Hammond. New York: Holt, Rinehart and Winston: 81-106.

Caporaso, James A. (1973). "Inequality, Dependence and Exploitation: An Approach to the Measurement of Three Central Concepts of Imperialism," paper presented to the Peace Science Society, Cambridge, Mass., November.

Dahrendorf, Rolf (1969). "On the Origin of Inequality Among Men," Andre Béteille, ed. Social Inequality. Hammondsworth, Middlesex, England: Penguin Books: 16-44.

Davidson, Donald (1963). "Actions, Reasons, and Causes." The Journal of Philosophy, 60(23): 685-700.

Davis, Kingsley and Wilbert Moore (1945). "Some Principles of Stratification." American Sociological Review, 10(2): 242-249.

Deutsch, Karl W. (1951). "Mechanism, Teleology, and Mind." Philosophy and Phenomenological Research, 12(2): 185-222.

Dewey, John (1939). Theory of Valuation, Vol. II, No. 4 of Foundations of the Unity of Science, eds., Otto Neurath, et al. Chicago: University of Chicago Press.

Eddington, Arthur S. (1929). The Nature of the Physical World. New York: Macmillan.

Edgeworth, Francis Ysidro (1881). Mathematical Psychics: An Essay on the Application of Mathematics to the Moral Sciences. London: Kegan Paul.

Eisenstadt, Shmuel N. (1971). Social Differentiation and Stratification. Glenview, Illinois: Scott, Foresman and Company.

Ginsberg, Morris (1956). On the Diversity of Morals, Vol. I of Essays in Sociology and Social Philosophy. London: William Heinemann, Ltd. Page references are to the bound volume of Essays, Baltimore: Penguin Books, 1968.

Gurr, Ted Robert and Raymond Duvall (1973). "Civil Conflict in the 1960s: A Reciprocal Theoretical System with Parameter Estimates." Comparative Political Studies, 6(2): 135-169.

Hampshire, Stuart (1959). Thought and Action. London: Chatto and Windus.

Harsanyi, John C. (1969). "Rational-Choice Models of Political Behavior vs. Functionalist and Conformist Theories." World Politics, 21(4): 513-538.

Heisenberg, Warner (1959). "Planck's Quantum Theory and the Philosophical Problems of Atomic Physics." Univeritas, 3(2). Page references are to the reprinted article in Science: Men, Methods, Goals, eds. Borich Brody and Nicholas Capaldi. New York: W.A. Benjamin: 45-58.

Hempel, Carl G. (1965). "Aspects of Scientific Explanation," in Aspects of Scientific Explanation and Other Essays in the Philosophy of Science. New York: The Free Press: 331-496.

Hogan, D.P. and D.L. Featherman (1977). "Racial Stratification and Socio-Economic Change." American Journal of Sociology. 83(1): 100-126.

Lasswell, Harold D. (1958). Politics: Who Gets What, When, How? with Postscript. Cleveland: Meridian Books.

Lenski, Gerhard E. (1966). Power and Privilege: A Theory of Social Stratification. New York: McGraw-Hill.

Macdonald, Margaret (1946-47). "Natural Rights." Proceedings of the Aristotelian Society, 47: 225-250.

Maxwell, Grover (1962). "The Ontological Status of Theoretical Entities." Scientific Explanation, Space, and Time, eds., Herbert Feigl and Grover Maxwell. Vol. III of Minnesota Studies in the Philosophy of Science. Minneapolis: University of Minnesota Press: 3-27.

Mayer, Kurt B. and Walter Buckley (1970). Class and Society, Third Edition. New York: Random House.

Melden, Abraham I. (1961). Free Action. London: Routeledge and Kegan Paul.

Moore, Wilbert E. (1963). "But Some are More Equal Than Others." American Sociological Review, 28(1): 13-18.

Muellbauer, John (1974). "Inequality Measures, Prices and Household Composition." Review of Economic Studies, 41 (October): 493-504.

Nagel, Ernest (1961). The Structure of Science: Problems in the Logic of Scientific Explanation. New York: Harcourt Brace and World.

Olson, Mancur, Jr. and Richard Zeckhauser (1966). "An Economic Theory of Alliances." The Review of Economics and Statistics. 48(3): 266-279.

Parsons, Talcott (1961). "An Outline of the Social System," in Theories of Society, eds., Talcott Parsons, et al. New York: The Free Press: 30-80.

Peters, Richard S. (1958). The Concept of Motivation. London: Routeledge and Kegan Paul.

Popper, Karl R. (1962). Conjectures and Refutations: The Growth of Scientific Knowledge. New York: Basic Books.

Rawls, John (1971). A Theory of Justice. Cambridge, Mass.: Harvard University Press.

Rudner, Richard S. (1966). Philosophy of Social Science. Englewood Cliffs: Prentice-Hall.

Sahlins, Marshall (1958). Stratification in Polynesia. Seattle: University of Washington Press. (Especially Chapter 5, "The Degree of Stratification in Pukapuka, Ontong Java, and Tokelau": 92-106).

Schwartz, Richard D. (1955). "Functional Alternatives to Inequality." American Sociological Review, 20(4): 424-430.

Stern, Robert, et al. (1976). "Equality for Blacks and Women: Essay on Relative Progress." Social Science Quarterly, 56(4): 664-673.

Tawney, Richard Henry (1964). Equality, Fourth Edition. London: George Allen and Unwin Ltd.

Teune, Henry (n.d.). "Measuring Characteristics of Complex Social Aggregates," draft manuscript, University of Pennsylvania.

Thielbar, Gerald W. and Saul D. Feldman (1972), eds. Issues in Social Inequality. Boston: Little, Brown and Company.

Tumin, Melvin M. (1953). "Some Principles of Stratification: A Critical Analysis." American Sociological Review, 18(4): 387-94.

Tumin, Melvin M. (1967). Social Stratification: The Forms and Functions of Inequality. Englewood Cliffs: Prentice-Hall.

Winch, Peter (1958). The Idea of a Social Science. London: Routledge and Kegan Paul.

Wright, E.O. and L. Perrone (1977). "Marxist Class Categories and Income Inequality." American Sociological Review, 42 (February): 32-55.

Wrong, Dennis H. (1959). "The Functional Theory of Stratification: Some Neglected Considerations." American Sociological Review. 24(6): 772-782.

Wrong, Dennis H. (1964). "Social Inequality Without Social Stratification." Canadian Review of Sociology and Anthropology, 1(1): 5-16. Page references are to the reprinted article in Thielbar and Feldman (1972): 91-104.

2. Class and Race Stratification in the U.S.

William K. Tabb

If ever America undergoes great revolutions, they will be brought about by the presence of the black race on the soil of the United States; that is to say, they will owe their origin, not to the equality but to the inequality of conditions. Alexis de Tocqueville, Democracy in America

Most race relations literature in the U. S. draws on one of the following perspectives: (1) individual attitudes, the Myrdal-Alport tradition, (2) ethnicity-integration group socialization, or (3) the colonial analogy (Blauner, 1972). While the first of these may seem rather passé to sociologists used to looking at group interactions, mainstream economic analysis (e.g., Becker, 1957; Thurow, 1969) is based on just such a view. Measures of discrimination assume an autonomous taste for discrimination.

In this paper I shall review and comment on the mainstream economic analysis, very briefly discuss the colonial model, and examine the less well-developed class perspective.

While much excellent work has been done to measure inequality, the causal reasoning inherent in such work is often weak. People are said to be poor because they are elderly, less educated, and/or born female or black. If the goal is to reduce inequality, policy work must identify levers for change based on general equilibrium rather than on descriptive or partial equilibrium models.

THE MARKET MODEL

Most economists look at problems of resource allocation in terms of neo-classical price theory. The central focus is on the workings of the market in allocating goods and services and on imperfections which prevent these markets from operating efficiently. If markets worked perfectly, there would be far less racism. Discrimination involves denial of equal access to markets and paying persons less than the value of their marginal product simply because of their membership in some pariah group. In a perfectly competitive market this would not happen -- unless non-economic tastes for discrimination were so strong that individuals, to indulge their preference, would accept a lower standard of living; that is, satisfying racist passions would have real costs for the discriminator. Under a market system, if such autonomous tastes were not present, racism would be irrational and should disappear.

The economy of the United States is admittedly no longer laissez-faire capitalism, and even when it might be in their financial interest, many whites choose not to buy from or sell to black people. From the point of view of capitalist ideology, such behavior is anomalous; it is seen in the neo-classical context as a deviation from normal capitalist practice. Such discriminatory behavior, according to Bergmann,

> undoubtedly injures the Black people against whom it is directed. <u>But it also causes financial losses to the discriminator</u>. The reason is that the discriminator is trifling with the law of supply and demand, the most sacred law in the capitalist canon. When he refuses to hire Blacks, he artificially reduces the supply of labor to himself, raising the price he must pay to the white labor he does hire, and therefore hurting himself financially. When he refuses to sell his product or his house to Blacks he artificially reduces the demand for them, thus reducing the price he extracts from the white customers he does deal with (1970: 2-3).

These arguments--that discrimination hurts the discriminator as well as the victims, that race is not a relevant consideration to a rational capitalist qua capitalist, and that therefore racism is "a deviation from normal capitalist practice" and does not exist for economic reasons--are at the heart of the neo-classical model of race relations.

While much sophisticated statistical work has been done in recent years, the most important theoretical study to date is still Gary Becker's The Economics of Discrimination. In Becker's model, individuals are seen to have a "taste for discrimination" which can be indulged at a cost to the individual, a cost which can be measured monetarily. Thus, "if an individual has a taste for discrimination," he must act as if he were willing to pay something, either directly or in the form of reduced income, to be associated with some persons instead of others. When actual discrimination occurs, he must either pay or forfeit income for this privilege. This simple way of looking at the matter gets at the essence of prejudice and discrimination (Becker, 1957: 6).

The discriminator pays for the privilege of discriminating. He does not gain, but rather loses, monetarily speaking, from discrimination: satisfaction is gained for a price. Non-economists are often surprised that this postulate can be thought acceptable by economists. But the point is central. For market economists, those who discriminate pay a cost to indulge their dislikes. Becker does not deal with how such tastes arise--a non-economic question--but notes that a taste for discrimination may include a component of ignorance (lack of awareness of the true qualities of the people involved) and a component of true prejudice preference relatively independent of knowledge. Becker would include the amount of knowledge available as a determinant of taste.

Another proximate determinant is geographical and chronological location: discrimination may vary from country to country, from rural to urban areas within a region, and from one time period to another. Finally, tastes may differ simply because of differences in personality (1957:9).

In short, Becker has little to tell us about the cause or causes of discrimination. He does not know, and does not seem much interested in, the determinants of a taste for discrimination. His interest is in measuring it.

Central to Becker's analysis is that, assuming equal wage rates, not hiring a qualified black for a job, and accepting a less qualified white, costs the employer money. Potential monetary costs are incurred because the less qualified person will add less to total output. Thus, competitive industries cannot afford to discriminate against blacks but monopolists can. Monopolists pass on their costs to the customer, while competitive industries cannot.

The study of theories of discrimination is difficult because alternative explanations based on a priori assumptions are difficult to test statistically since available data often support contending hypotheses.

For Becker, the market discrimination coefficient

$$(MDC = (W_w - W_b) / W_b)$$

where W_w is the equilibrium wage rate for White workers and W_b for black workers, is a measure of the cost of compensating the psychic cost experienced by the discriminator. Alexis (1974) developed an envy-malice model of white preference for their own kind. But such models, whether based on aversion for those perceived as different or on a stronger yet still psychologically grounded theory, do not explain why those free of such feelings would not, in a competitive market, drive the discriminators out of business. Attempts by Freeman (1973) to show that there might not be many non-discriminating white employers nor too few qualified blacks does not explain why, over time and assuming competition, market forces would not undercut discrimination; or indeed why black capitalists, presumably lacking a taste for discrimination against their own, would not drive the white discriminating capitalists from a large share of the market--to the point where all black labor is absorbed.

Using race as a proxy for skill evaluation, training, and experience may be common, as Phelps (1972) and others have suggested. But if it were not a good proxy, competition between firms and better information should lead to its being abandoned.

43

Economists who hold strongly to this neo-classical premise seem to go to great lengths to deny it in the case of discrimination. Thus, Arrow takes refuge in such psychological rationale, saying "...if individuals act in a discriminatory manner, they will tend to acquire or develop beliefs which justify such actions" (cited by Marshall, 1974:855). But this hardly brings us closer to the origin of such beliefs.

MEASURING THE COSTS OF DISCRIMINATION

Becker's analysis has been challenged by another neo-classical economist, Lester Thurow, on the grounds that racial discrimination occurs in one society, not two. The dominant group does more than indulge some ethereal taste. It prevents the minority group from refusing intergroup interaction. As Thurow (1969) says, "Negroes live in a white supremacist society, not just a segregated society."

Thurow's alternative to the Becker model replaces individual tastes for discrimination with a desire on the part of whites, acting monopolistically as a group, to exploit blacks. In his model, whites may also wish to maximize social distance (rather than, as in Becker's model, to avoid any contact with blacks). One way to maximize white income at the expense of blacks is through enforced social distance.

Thurow enumerates several types of discrimination. One is employment: blacks work fewer hours, parttime and part year, and are more unemployed. Whites are thus protected from the costs of cyclical instability by a black buffer pool. Another is wage discrimination: blacks are paid less for the same work. Occupational discrimination prevents blacks from gaining qualifications and experience on an equal basis.

Thurow measures the effect of each of these types of discrimination by asking, statistically: What if whites and blacks were distributed in the work force in the same manner as in the population as a whole? Using 1960 data, he finds--from discrimination in employment, wage payment, human capital, and occupational and labor monopoly discrimination--the total gains for whites under such assumptions to be $15.5 billion, or $248 per member of the white labor force in 1960, and that the loss to non-whites from such discrimination was $2,100 for each member of the labor force. However, as Thurow himself states, "To the extent that there is a surplus of labor of all types and skills, eliminating discrimination and reshuffling the labor force would result in a reduction of (white) income but in no real gain in actual output."

Thurow's model shows whites monetarily gaining from discrimination and stresses the interdependence of different types of discrimination. Yet, in measuring its effect, Thurow lumps all members of a racial group into a single category and relies on the tools of marginal analysis and comparative statistics. These are major problems.

Thurow calculates that equalizing education levels between whites and non-whites would take an investment of almost 26 billion

44

dollars and would produce a high net return, 65 percent a year. But this is similar to the full employment example. If a few people are highly educated, they command high incomes. If "too many" are trained, they compete against one another, and returns on investment in education fall dramatically. In an economy which has as a norm substantial unemployment, this approach is misleading. Using neo-classical assumptions (an economy with perfect competition and in equilibrium), the distribution of marginal products is equal to the distribution of earned income. The cause of low income under such assumptions must be individual deficiencies. Once the causes of each person's low marginal productivity are identified, corrective steps can be taken. While race cannot be "corrected," other correlates of poverty are by neo-classical economists thought to be amenable to policy. In fact, it is possible (using regression analysis) to explain poverty by such factors as whether or not families live on farms, are in the labor force, and/or have a family head with less than eight years of schooling; the type of job held by the family head; and the overall unemployment rate. Statistically, these factors have significant effects on marginal productivities and "explain" poverty.

These associations merely demonstrate one point: When a social policy permits the existence of a reserve army of unemployed, certain groups are in a worse position to defend themselves economically than are others.

Within the neo-classical model the question is phrased (given the existing distribution of black and white skills and of course not questioning the form of economic control): "If discrimination were ended and workers were hired on the basis of their education and skill levels, which white workers would lose out?" The answer is, not surprisingly, that lower-skilled whites would have the most to fear from such a change.

The conclusion to be drawn is that racism benefits white workers, especially less-skilled white workers. Capitalists as well lose by discrimination. They must pay whites more than equally qualified blacks and they must not hire blacks for better jobs for fear of offending white workers. Is such a conclusion correct? We think not. It might better be argued that all workers, especially those most oppressed and underpaid, would gain from working class unity.

CRITICIZING THE NEO-CLASSICAL MODEL

The major shortcoming of the neo-classical model is that it takes institutional factors as given and does not inquire into how they developed and under what conditions they may be modified. At the extreme, Becker takes a "taste for discrimination" as given and thus "accents in a relatively static fashion the subjective aspects of discrimination and neglects the historical, institutional, and objective circumstances that operate in various types of market situations."

The interesting questions start after most micro theorists think the discussion is over. If employers pay blacks less, this does not

45

mean that they necessarily raise the wages of their white employees in absolute terms, but only relatively to those of blacks. They may in fact lower their total labor costs by having jobs for blacks only at the bottom of the occupational hierarchy; when blacks are not promoted out of such jobs, whites experience a sense of relative well-being. It is not at all clear that all employers, or even employers as a group, do not benefit from discrimination of this kind. The neo-classical model assumes workers are paid the value of their marginal product. This might be true if capitalist and worker had equal bargaining power, but such is not the nature of capitalism.

More fundamentally, if wages are set through a bargaining process under which what counts are relative power, militancy, and willingness by workers to undertake united action or by individual employers and industrial associations to endure strikes, then the present situation hardly resembles the neo-classical model. If the government is unable or unwilling to bring about full employment and if there are always surplus workers, mostly minorities, to bid down wages, does not such a situation keep down workers' ability to bargain for better earnings? Are not all workers, exploited because they do not control the means of production, also oppressed by racism?

As opposed to mainstream liberal economists' assumptions of "ignorance" on the part of white workers (ignorant of the "fact" that all men and women are created equal and that skin differences are superficial and unimportant), the conservative economists' "taste" explanation is somewhat more convincing. Since white workers in significant numbers do appear to hold racist attitudes and, in fact, those living in neighborhoods bordering black ones appear more antagonistic than those living at a great distance from black inner-city neighborhoods, the former's prejudice may be based on more information than the latter's well-schooled understanding. The radical who looks at the material interests involved would note that "middle-class" tolerance of "lower-class" blacks is coupled with antagonism toward "working-class" whites--the group just below them on the status hierarchy. This suggests that in a stratified class society (using "class" in the Marxist sense, not the general usage of lower-, middle-, and upper-class), divisions among those forced to sell their labor power are encouraged by the dominant class, those owning the means of production. Thus, prejudice results from perceived self-interest in a society of created scarcity, in which distinctions between social groupings based on color, religion, and national origin are real but represent a false consciousness of who is the real enemy. In this sense, within a system which imposes competition for jobs, urban services and so on, racism is not irrational. It is, however, irrational when opposed to achievements possible through class unity--a possibility not considered by mainstream economists who deny the importance of these features of capitalist social relations.

While the Marxian model has been largely ignored by economists, it is more typically discussed and rejected as simplistic by mainstream sociologists, who pose the concept of social strata as an alternative formulation. Mayer and Buckley suggest:

> Differences in income, property, and occupation divide the members of modern societies into statistically distinguishable strata, or classes. Classes are thus aggregates of individuals and families in similar economic positions (44-5).

Thus the term "class" is used interchangeably with strata to connote the richer and more variegated pattern of prestige-ranking. Mainstream sociologists observe tendencies toward a clustering of attitudes, residential and educational patterns, tastes and other cultural attributes among status groups, people who view each other as equals, interact, and intermarry.

Some sociologists who identify with the Marxist tradition accept the richness of this view. They assert that Marx had no theoretical interest in the sociological aspects of inequality. Marx, argue Stolzman and Gamberg (1973-74), was not interested in describing how societies are stratified because his purpose was to explain structural changes in societies: he had bigger fish to fry.

Such a position, I contend, concedes far too much to the critics. Some of the best theoretical writing on the subtleties of stratification is to be found in Marx's historical writings on France (1963, 1964, 1968). And far from underestimating the importance of racism, he viewed slavery in terms of its effect on dividing the working class.

In the section of Capital on the working day, Marx notes that "in the United States of North America, every independent movement of the workers was paralyzed so long as slavery disfigured a part of the Republic. Labour cannot emancipate itself in the white skin where in the black it is branded." Marx goes on to say, "But out of the death of slavery a new life at once arose. The first fruit of the Civil War was the eight hours' agitation. That ran with the seven league boots of the locomotive from the Atlantic to the Pacific." Marx goes on to quote the General Congress of Labor (held in Baltimore in August 1866) on the necessity of freeing labor in the U. S. from "capitalistic slavery" (1967:301).

The situation of an internal colony was discussed a hundred years ago in a letter written by Karl Marx about Ireland as a British colony. He writes:

> And most important of all'. Every industrial and commercial center in England now possesses a working class divided into two hostile camps, English proletarians and Irish proletarians. The ordinary English worker hates the Irish worker as a competitor who lowers his standard of life ... feels himself a member of the ruling nation, and so turns himself into a tool of the aristocrats and capitalists of his country against Ireland, thus strengthening their

47

domination over himself. He cherishes religious, social and national prejudices against the Irish worker. His attitude toward him is much the same as that of the "poor whites" to the "niggers" in the former slave states of the U. S. A. The Irishman pays him back with interest in his own money.... This antagonism is artificially kept alive and intensified by the press, the pulpit, the comic papers, in short, by all the means at the disposal of the ruling classes. This antagonism is the secret of the impotence of the English working class, despite its organization. It is the secret by which the capitalist class maintains its power. And that class is fully aware of it (Marx, 1970: 136).

It would be possible, through extensive quoting, to vindicate Marx of the accusations of his mainstream detractors, but that is not within the scope of this present assignment. Rather, the intent of the remaining portion of this paper will be to explore the model of stratification which emerges from the Marxian paradigm and offers an alternative to concepts of class which merely aggregate individuals having certain common cultural characteristics.

STRATIFICATION AND THE SOCIAL RELATIONS OF PRODUCTION

In this section, the job characteristics of the major strata groups in U. S. society are discussed, as is the relationship between job characteristics and personal attributes of workers at different segments of the labor market. The intent is to derive Marxian class concepts from such strata distinctions.

At the low end of the spectrum are workers who are most easily replaced and who have the least bargaining power. To this group, the assumptions of perfect competition hold. These workers cannot ask for and receive higher wages because many others stand ready to take their jobs at the going subsistence wage. More skilled workers have received training specific to the firm and are therefore more costly to replace. The employers' investment in their training would have to be duplicated with new workers. Similarly, a more skilled worker could (at least initially) expect lower wages in a new job because his training is not completely transferable to other jobs. Therefore, both the segmented labor theorists and the neo-classical human capital school come to similar conclusions, that turnover should be higher for low-wage, less-skilled workers who have little incentive to stay at one job.

Workers higher up the labor market hierarchy can be influenced by their past investment to keep an eye on future prospects for higher remuneration, promotion, and pension rights which would be jeopardized if their work attitude is not perceived as acceptable. Workers adjust to these carrots and sticks. The minority worker, typically found under close supervision and subject to more arbitrary punishment, more frequently reacts with rebellious outbursts and

48

holds a continuingly simmering hatred. The more economically secure may have a more stable situation and a more pleasant work routine because rewards to more skilled unionized workers are greater and working conditions, seniority, and other benefits are protected. At the other end of the spectrum, the professional staff has scope for greater creativity, flexibility, and initiative. Their job requires it.

The question can be posed: Which came first? Does the political economy create slots and "produce" people to fill them? Or do individual characteristics limit people, and does the market reward their marginal productivity? There is little question that individuals try to maximize their incomes, and that employers try to minimize the cost of obtaining labor inputs of a given quality. At the most vulgar level, the question is one of blame. Is the existence of low earnings a function of individual worker characteristics, or of the system? While middle positions are possible, neo-classical economists in general stress the former and radical economists the latter.

There is a great deal of room for what may be called cultural interaction. On-the-job training is a matter of socialization as well as of skills training, of attitude molding through a mostly unconscious process of emulation and adaptation. Just as James Bond knows the imposter because he orders the wrong wine, so any subculture has its rules and rituals which define outsiders, and the cost of adjustment may be high.

Piore offers the hope that "in the case of black workers from the ghetto gaining access to white jobs, one hopes that the initial group of blacks placed in those jobs will set off a process through which the ghetto environment becomes better suited to the development of productive traits prior to employment and, by the same token, that the work environment becomes better adapted to the traits of ghetto workers" (1975:39). Such reasoning leads to stressing school integration to increase exposure of black ghetto children to the middle-class education process. The hope is to stimulate social mobility by facilitating learning skills in order to enter at higher-level stations.

Segmentation theorists have used the notion of mobility chains to describe the lines of progression where a worker enters employment at a relatively lower skill level and progresses upward (Piore, 1975). Since jobs are structured sequentially-hierarchically, promotion on a step-by-step basis is the norm for most workers. However, workers rarely enter a large corporation at the bottom and work their way to the top. Those at the top almost always enter at a far higher level. Indeed, there are a number of entry points, and where a worker enters is highly correlated with the neighborhood he grew up in, family characteristics, and other class background correlates.

Thus, in discussing a cultural division of labor, one is confronted with basic issues: where do cultural characteristics come from? How are they reinforced? Why do they persist?

The radical position asserts the primacy of class interest over technology. That is to say, the development of hierarchy was a conscious policy to offset tendencies toward job mobility. Control over workers was the guiding principle, not blind response to technological imperatives. The idea is to diminish the power a worker's skills provide in the capital-labor bargain. By splitting mental and physical, creative and routine work, management gains control over the terms on which labor is carried out. Piece-work and job ladders are conscious policies which, now institutionalized and seemingly inevitable, were not inevitable.

Katherine Stone, in "The Origins of Job Structures in the Steel Industry," quotes one manufacturer who in 1928 explained that he adopted incentives for output in order to:

> break up the flat rate for the various classes of workers. That is the surest preventative of strikes and discontent. When all are paid one rate, it is the simplest and almost inevitable thing for all to unite in the support of a common demand. When each worker is paid according to his record, there is not the same community of interest (Stone, 1975:43).

Enough has been written about Taylorism and the origin of scientific management to understand what bosses do. Job ladders and regular promotion make all seem fair, a stable and more contented workforce results, "pyramided and ... held together by the ambition of the men lower down," as one student of the process noted in 1908 (Stone, 1975:48).

Such mobility, however, is limited. Many jobs require permanent tenure, without hope of advancement. One solution to the problem is to compensate workers in this predicament with higher remuneration; another is to keep a large reserve army of unemployed and underqualified workers who will fill the vacant slots. Even where capital-intensive technologies are available, a company may use one technique for its core output, paying workers relatively well and developing a permanent skilled work force for part of its operation, and using labor-intensive processes to take up the slack. As orders diminish, these secondary workers are laid off while the costly capital-intensive processes are not allowed to be idled. Often, the firm contracts out these peak-season orders. Younger workers, women, and minorities are most easily recruited for these secondary jobs.

Manpower programs in the late 1960s worked to the extent that the economy's fuller employment at that time created the need to upgrade significant numbers of poor folks to stable job classifications. As Bowles and Gintis (1976) show, the schools have historically adjusted to changed labor requirements. Cloevard and Piven have made a similar argument for the welfare system (1974). If this general line of reasoning is correct, then changing the structure of demand for labor is the only solution for fundamental alteration of poverty and inequality. Merely, or even primarily, working on the supply side can be only minimally effective.

As labor reserves are used up and as wage costs begin to rise, it becomes important to find increasingly complex ways of enlarging the labor force and to increase labor-market segmentation, to find ways to divide workers so that they do not unite to make class demands. Divisions based on sex, race, ethnic origin, age, and education are all used. There is a growing body of literature which suggests that jobs are designed for maximal control rather than to increase technical efficiency.

Migration--internal from farm to city, and immigration from abroad either on a permanent or guest-worker basis--has historically been the mechanism for profit maximization of low-wage industries. However, with the growth of the welfare state, there has been an increasing pressure to include the reserve army under the protective umbrella of social welfare benefits. Another alternative to profit maximization is to move the production facility to low-wage regions. Increased capital mobility and decreased transportation costs make the latter preferable for many manufacturing firms.

The reserve army concept is supported by the non-linear relation between white and non-white unemployment among males. As total unemployment declines, black male gains become larger and larger relative to whites. That is, when there are fewer jobs, whites are hired preferentially because employers can discriminate at little cost. As full employment is approached, there are less available white workers and more blacks are hired. During expansionary periods, black income gains exceed those of whites; in recessions, white incomes rise relative to black incomes.

During periods of labor shortage, blacks have made important gains, and then during economic downturns they have been systematically displaced. The jobs that blacks were recruited for in the periods of labor shortage in World War I and of prosperity in the 20s were taken away in the Great Depression.

Harold Baron (1971) has argued the essential continuity of racial segmentation from the slave era to the present. The difference in form (dependent peasantry to urban proletariat) is secondary to the subordination through time of the black subsector of the market, which typically places blacks in the lower-paid and more disagreeable jobs. The interface of dual labor market stratification and racial oppression is clear enough. Blacks are overwhelmingly in secondary markets. The position of blacks in the society is primarily a result of their position as a marginal working class. Under American capitalism, someone has always played this role. Traditionally, immigrant groups have served as the structural equivalent of the blacks as a white marginal working class. In England, until the arrival of great numbers of Pakistanis in recent years, the Irish were the major incumbents in this position. Indeed, in all developed nations of Western Europe, guest workers form a marginal working force of this type and are exported back to North Africa or Southern Europe when demand slackens (Castles and Kosack, 1973).

Inequality in a competitive society is a structural reality. A system of inequality is most secure when individuals either blame themselves for their relative standing (the meritocratic rationale) or group divisions can be used to justify inequality by ranked status attributed to the different groups.

At the risk of belaboring the obvious, it is clear enough that capitalism requires an unequal ownership of capital and the necessity of workers to sell their labor power to exist. Further, wages must be unequal for labor markets to operate; segmentation and job ladders follow. It is conceptually possible to envision an alternative based on job rotation and collective investment (Campen, 1974).

It seems logical to move from the structural analysis of the segmentation theorists to a consideration of intra-class competition, the obstacles to working class unity, and measures to overcome these divisions. If the concern is to seriously treat inequality, this avenue can hardly be left unexplored.

Because power is relayed through a series of intermediaries, the hierarchical control system of the large enterprise means that anger is focused on the immediate source of personal frustration. This combines with segmented workplace groupings to make for strata-consciousness on a fairly narrow basis. The continual gradations, the individualized goal structures which job ladders engender, make each worker the competitor of the others (Rosenberg, 1953). It is to a large degree the consequence of racial and strata separations which reinforces divisions and allows race to be used as a proxy for status. Most whites see blacks as a threat because they are clearly a group of lower status challenging white privilege.

While class unity is the inescapable necessity for a successful effort to challenge hierarchy and alienated work relations, two uncomfortable questions plague the Marxist analyst: the extent to which whites really do gain from racism, and more broadly the revolutionary potential of workers. Do they really want to change the system?

A number of analysts have questioned whether any powerful interests gain from black poverty (see Sowell, 1971, Lasch, 1969 for particularly cogent formulations of this view). Indeed, some have asked: "Who needs the Negro?" (Wilhelm, 1970). If the line of reasoning presented here is correct, then it is not the marginal productivity as measured by wage rates which determines the contribution of black-Americans, nor transfer payments and other social expenditures the costs thereof.

The positive function of a clearly identifiable underclass, from the viewpoint of capitalism as a system, is to serve as a pariah group "against which all others can compete victoriously" (Sackrey 1971:55). That relative income and occupational distributions among various ethnic groups has remained fairly stable over the last two generations has also been noted (Parenti, 1970; van den Berghe, 1970:22).

Marxists avoid a simplistic "false consciousness" response to situations when workers do not unite by examining the barriers created and the cost of uniting in the face of strong intergroup competitive pressures. When groups are stratified on the basis of relative privilege, almost all have something to lose in any change. Marx understood the phenomena, as his discussion of the Irish and slavery questions demonstrate. His purpose was to overcome such differences. He did not stress the possibilities of fragmentation in the division of labor. Subsequently, Marxist theorists engaged in struggle have stressed the need to develop multiple interactions of working people with institutions they themselves dominate and which serve their interests at the neighborhood, workplace, and voluntary association levels, and have pointed out their importance in developing a common culture and a sense of solidarity and power. The class struggle proceeds through capital's attempts to enlarge the sphere of alienation in social life and in working class efforts to narrow it.

The task of blacks and their allies is to design demands and strategies which shake the pyramid in ways which unite rather than divide. Programs viewed as instances of special pleading are, in the present historical moment, apt to fall on deaf ears. There is little play in the system. We have continuing high levels of unemployment and sustained inflation and unemployment, which have held the real income of the working class stagnant for over a decade. In such a context, the potential constituency for "shaking the pyramid" is a substantial one. If the analysis presented in this paper has validity, it suggests a research agenda for those scholars who would like to see their research serve a policy purpose of a sort not set by elite decision-makers.

REFERENCES

Alexis, Marcus (1974). "The Political Economy of Labor Market Discrimination: Synthesis and Exploration," in George M. von Furstenberg, Ann R. Horowitz and Bennett Harrison, eds. Patterns of Racial Discrimination. Lexington, Mass.: Lexington Books.

Aigneo, Dennis J. and Glen G. Cain (1977). "Statistical Theories of Discrimination in Labor Markets." Industrial and Labor Relations Review (January).

Arrow, Kenneth F. (1972a). "Models of Job Discrimination", in Anthony H. Pascal, ed., Racial Discrimination in Economic Life Lexington, Mass.: Lexington Books.

Arrow, Kenneth F. (1972b). "Some Models of Race in the Labor Market," in Pascal.

Arrow, Kenneth F. (1974). "The Theory of Discrimination", in Orley Ashenselter and Albert Rees, eds., Discrimination in Labor Markets. Princeton, New Jersey: Princeton University Press.

Baker, Ray Stannard, Following the Color Line. New York: Harper and Row, originally published by Doubleday Page and Co.

Baron, Harold M. (1971). "The Demand for Black Labor: Historial Notes on the Political Economy of Racism," Radical America (March-April).

Becker, Gary (1957). The Economics of Discrimination. Chicago: University of Chicago Press.

Bergmann, Barbara R. (1970). "Can Racial Discrimination be Ended Under Capitalism," a paper presented at American University, November 26, 1970, mimeo available from the Project on the Economics of Discrimination, University of Maryland.

Bergmann, Barbara R. (1971). "The Effect on White Incomes of Discrimination in Employment". Journal of Political Economy, (March/April).

Black Enterprise (1973). "The Top 100," (June).

Blalock, Jr., Hubert M. (1967). Toward a Theory of Minority-Group Relations. New York: John Wiley.

Blauner, Robert (1972). Racial Oppression in America. New York: Harper and Row.

Bowles, Samuel and Herbert Gintis (1976). Schooling in Capitalist America. New York: Basic Books.

Blumer, Herbert (1965). "Industrialism and Race Relations", in Guy Hunter, ed. Industrialization and Race Relations: A Symposium. London: Oxford University Press.

Cain, Glen G. (1976). "The Challenge of Segmented Labor Market Theories to Orthodox Theory," Journal of Economic Literature (December).

Campen, Jim (1974). Socialist Alternatives for America: A Bibliography. New York: Union for Radical Political Economics.

Castles, Stephen and Godula Kosack (1973). Immigrant Workers and Class Structure in Western Europe London: Oxford University Press.

Cloevard, Richard A. and Frances Fox Piven (1974). The Politics of Turmoil: Essays on Poverty, Race and Urban Crisis. New York: Vintage.

Downs, Anthony (1970). Urban Problems and Prospect. Chicago: Markham.

Freeman, Richard B. (1973). "Changes in the Labor Market for Black Americans, 1948-72," Brookings Papers on Economic Activity.

Friedman, Milton (1962). Capitalism and Freedom. Chicago: University of Chicago Press.

Gamson, William W. (1968). Power and Discontent. Homewood, Illinois: Dorsey Press.

Gintis, Herbert (1971). "Education, Technology, and the Characteristics of Worker Productivity," American Economic Review. (May).

Glenn, Norval D. (1970). "The Role of White Resistance and Facilitation in the Negro Struggle for Equality," Phylon, Summer, 1965, in Sethard Fisher, Power and the Black Community: A Reader on Racial Subordination in the United States. New York: Random House.

Gordon, David M. (1972). Theories of Poverty and Underemployment: Orthodox Radical and Dual Labor Market Perspectives. Lexington, Mass.: Lexington Books.

54

Lasch, Christopher (1969). "Black Power: Cultural Nationalism as Politics," in The Agony of the American Left. New York: Vintage.

Levitan, Sar A., William B. Johnston and Robert Taggart (1975). Still A Dream: The Changing Status of Blacks Since 1960. Cambridge, Mass.: Harvard University Press.

Marx, Karl (1963). The Eighteenth Brumaire of Louis Bonaparte. New York: International Publishers.

Marx, Karl (1964). Class Struggle in France. New York: International Publishers.

Marx, Karl (1967). Capital, Volume I. New York: International Publishers.

Marx, Karl (1968). Civil War in France: One Paris Commune. New York: International Publishers.

Marx, Karl (1970). Letter to Meyer and Vogt (1870); reprinted in Howard Selsam, David Goldway and Harry Martel, eds., Dynamics of Social Change, A Reader in Marxist Social Science. New York International Publishers.

Marshall, Ray (1974). "The Economics of Racial Discrimination: A Survey," Journal of Economic Literature. (September).

Masters, Stanley H. (1975). Black-White Income Differentials New York: Academic Press.

Mayer, Kurt B. and Walter Buckley (1970). Class and Society. New York: Random.

Metzger, L. Paul (1971). "American Sociology and Black Assimilation: Conflicting Perspectives," American Journal of Sociology. (January).

Mincer, Jacob (1970). "The Distribution of Labor Income, A Survey With Special Reference to the Human Capital Approach," Journal of Economic Literature. (March).

Parenti, Michael (1970). "Assimilation and Counter-Assimilation: From Civil Rights to Black Radicalism," in Philip Green and Sanford Levinson, eds., Power and Community. New York: Vintage Books.

Phelps, Edmond (1972). Inflation Policy and Unemployment. New York: Norton.

Piore, Michael J. (1975). "Toward a Theory of Labor Market Stratification," in Richard C. Edwards, Michael Reich and David M. Gordon, eds., Labor Market Segmentation. Lexington, Mass.: D. C. Heath.

Rosenberg, Morris (1953). "Perceptual Obstacles to Class Consciousness," Social Forces. (October).

Ross, Arthur M. (1967). "The Negro in the American Economy," in Arthur M. Ross and Herbert Hill, eds., Employment, Race, and Poverty. New York: Harcourt, Brace and World.

Sackrey, Jr., Charles M. (1971). "Economics and Black Poverty," Review of Black Political Economy. (Winter/Spring).

Schiller, Bradley R. (1973). The Economics of Poverty and Discrimination. Englewood Cliffs, New Jersey: Prentice-Hall.

Sowell, Thomas (1971). "Economics and Black People," Review of Black Political Economy. (Winter/Spring).

55

Stolzman, James, and Herbert Gamberg (1973-74). "Marxist Class Analysis Versus Stratification Analysis as General Approaches to Social Inequality," Berkeley Journal of Sociology, XVIII.

Stone, Katherine (1974). "The Origins of Job Structures in the Steel Industry," Review of Radical Political Economics. (Summer).

Terrell, Henry S. (1971). "The Wealth Accumulation of Black and White Families," Proceedings of the American Economics Association. (May).

Thurow, Lester C. (1969). Poverty and Discrimination (Washington, D. C.: Brookings Institution.

U. S. Bureau of the Census (1971). Minority-Owned Businesses: 1969, Series MB-1, Washington: Government Printing Office.

van den Berghe, Pierre L. (1970). Race and Ethnicity. New York: Basic Books.

Wilhelm, Sidney M. (1970). Who Needs the Negro? Cambridge, Mass.: Schenkman.

Part II
International Inequality

3. Estimating the Marginal Utility of Global Income Transfers
Bruce Russet

If the poor will be with us always, how poor must they be? Should we abandon hope of any significant improvement in living conditions for hundreds of millions of terribly poor people in this world? Should we instead, by some desperate notion of triage, concentrate our limited resources on trying to help those who, while still poor, nevertheless start from something a little better than the bare subsistence level of India, Bangladesh, or poorest Africa? Such questions raise innumerable further questions about morality, about sources of global poverty, and about the organizational capacity of poor countries ever to cope with their problems. They also raise serious empirical questions about what improvement in living standards we could hope for if a minority of people, however rich, gave up part of their income or wealth to help large numbers of poor people. Recall the old anti-socialist argument: if the richest five percent of Americans gave up half their income to the poor, it would only bring the poorest half of the population one-third of the way toward the average income level for the country. In short, why should so few give up so much to help so many so little?

The same argument is being made on a worldwide basis. Suppose, for example, $100 billion per year were transferred from the 700 million people who live in the world's richest developed countries--in North America, Western Europe, Australasia, and Japan. That amount (almost $150 per capita) is seven times the current level of foreign economic assistance already being contributed by these countries. Distribution to the poorest half of the world, to countries with a total population of about 2.4 billion, would represent a per capita income increment of only $42--far from enough to relieve their poverty. Is it much of an improvement to have $292 a year instead of $250?

While the statistics of this argument are correct, the implication is very misleading. It misses all the possibilities arising from investment in new productive capacities in the poor countries. It misses the welfare implications of such a transfer, very different from proportionate effects implied by simple money amounts. As economists have long recognized, the marginal utility of $42 to the average citizen of a poor country is likely to be much higher--in terms of education, health, or life expectancy--than would be the loss of $150 to the average rich country citizen. Intuitively this is plausible, and is supported by most of the empirical work by economists under conditions where, as in the modern world, there is a yawning gap between income levels for rich and poor. But we have no measurements of the likely effect of such income transfers internationally; by how much the real welfare gains to the poor might exceed the losses to the rich, or for which aspects of welfare the differences might be greatest.

Formidable difficulties stand in the way of such a quantitative assessment. One must begin by positing how the transfer is made, and whether it would disrupt the overall international economy. If such disruption did occur, would markedly lower incomes everywhere result? What would be the effect on incentives for further economic or political actions affecting the distribution or overall level of income and welfare? One must also make some assumptions about how income gains and losses would be distributed within countries, both those gaining and those losing. Each of us probably has a different set of preferred strategies for making the transfer. Some prefer government-to-government grants, the standard form of economic assistance; others would prefer to see the poor countries succeed by greater action of their own--by extracting trade concessions from the rich, by forming cartels to raise the price of raw materials, by expropriating foreign property, or by feats of self-reliance. Each would have very different--and not readily foreseeable--consequences.

Nevertheless, a beginning has to be made about our knowledge on economic transfers. Various assumptions about the origins and means of the transfer can be built into an analysis, and assumptions modified as the analysis continues. Without concentrating here on just how the transfer might be carried out, we shall outline a strategy for making some crude estimates about its consequences, estimates that can be modified for different assumptions about means. The estimates will be crude, but we now live in a situation of almost totally data-free speculation. Providing the limits of the estimation methods are properly acknowledged, we should be able to reduce our ignorance.

We start with some basic data on average income level, and on average level of various aspects of welfare that are highly valued, both within and between nations. We will illustrate our approach with data on life itself--that is, average life expectancy and infant mortality rates for citizens of various countries. In so doing we focus on the most basic need or dimension of well-being. The approach is nevertheless adaptable, with energy and ingenuity, to literacy and many other dimensions of welfare specific to one's favorite schema of values (Lasswell and Kaplan, 1970; Galtung et al., 1975; Maslow, 1968)[1]. At least three different specific procedures are possible within this approach. We shall employ each of them to discover the degree of convergence in the results.

SYNCHRONIC CROSS-NATIONAL COMPARISONS

1. For all nations, we begin with data on the average income level and the average welfare level in most nations of the world in the 1970s. For presentational purposes, the position of each country is plotted on a graph, Figure 1. The GNP per capita in 1973 is on the horizontal axis; the average life expectancy at birth (1970-75 avg., both sexes) is on the vertical axis.[2]

The resulting curve displays decreasing marginal benefits from successively higher levels of income. The slope of the curve (the regression coefficient) indicates the relationship between income and life expectancy at various average income levels. The ratio of the percentage change in life expectancy "purchased" by a percentage change in income may be interpreted as the "elasticity" of life expectancy. Although there is a fair amount of scatter around the curve, probably indicative of varying local conditions and of error in data reportage, it is apparent that at GNP levels under $600 per capita (1973 dollars), typical of most of Africa, Asia, and much of Latin America, life expectancy varies somewhere between thirty-five years and about sixty. Approximately one year of life is gained for every $28 per year increment in GNP per capita.[3] At the other end of the curve, from about $1,800 upwards, the scatter around the line is more noticeable than the slope itself. At that level, life expectancy varies between seventy and seventy-five years with little regard for income levels. Nevertheless, some slope to the line is still discernible. On the average, a year of life can be bought by $2,700 in annual per capita GNP.[4]

The major outliers to the right of the curve are six newly rich OPEC states and South Africa. In each of these states the internal distribution is notoriously unequal. While we have no precise income distribution data on the OPEC states, South Africa shows the lowest percentage of income accruing to the poorest forty percent of income earners of any of the sixty-six countries with data (Hansen et al., 1976: 148-49). If the same sort of concave curve applies internally to these countries, reflecting a decrease in marginal welfare utilities with increasing income, then a highly unequal distribution of income within a country would produce a lower average life expectancy than would a more equal distribution. Hence there is a lower average life expectancy in the United States (seventy-one) than in more egalitarian Sweden (seventy-three) despite a slightly lower average income level in the latter.[5] In the case of the oil-rich states, achievement of high average income levels is very recent. It is reasonable to expect that improvements in public health that have been or will be made possible by the new income levels have not yet had their full effect on mortality rates. (Though these 1973 data precede the most dramatic income rises in the oil-exporting states.) Nor should we forget the very heavy and economically productive expenditures on arms by many OPEC nations.

We have documented a similar relationship for infant mortality rates on a global scale. Figure 2 shows the curve (concave in this instance, since higher income produces lower infant mortality as well

61

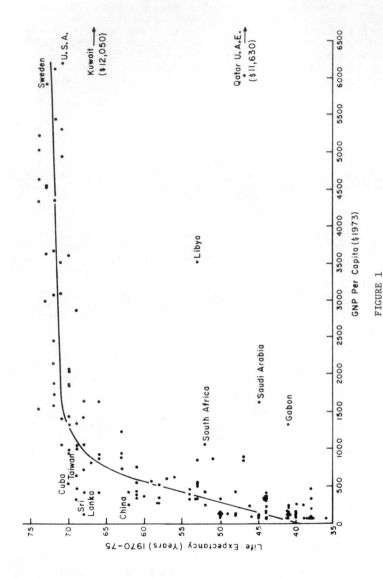

FIGURE 1

THE RELATION BETWEEN GNP PER CAPITA AND LIFE EXPECTANCY ACROSS NATIONS

SOURCES: GNP per Capita from United Nations, 1976b:xxii, xxiii. Life Expectancy from United Nations, 1976a:153–157.

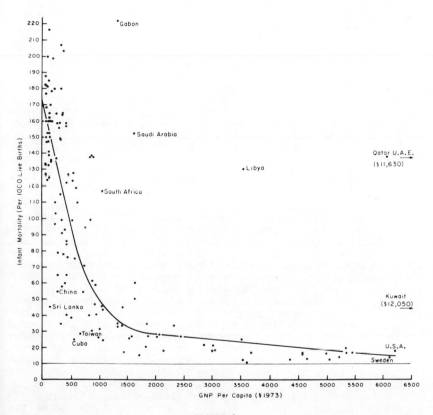

FIGURE 2

THE RELATION BETWEEN GNP PER CAPITA AND INFANT MORTALITY ACROSS NATIONS, 1974

SOURCE: Hansen et al., 1976:132-141.

as higher life expectancy) for roughly the same countries as in Figure 1. Less scatter perhaps reflects better data.[6] At the lower end of the income distribution, a point (per thousand) in infant mortality decline is associated with as little as $6.50 per capita income increment; at high income levels it takes nearly a $350 income increment to bring the infant mortality rate down one point.

By this crude estimating procedure, we project a very substantial increase in life expectancy and a reduction of infant mortality rates for the entire world if there were substantial income transfers from rich countries to poor ones. Using our initial example, taking $150 per capita from the 700 million people in the rich countries would correspond (ceteris paribus, and we shall discuss some of these assumptions below) to reducing average life expectancy by less than a month in those countries (1 year = $2,700). Spreading that total equally among the 2.4 billion people in the poorest countries of the world would represent an average income increment to them of about $42, "worth" a year and a half of additional life to each. A rather dramatic effect. But before we take this estimate too seriously, we must try other estimating procedures.

DIACHRONIC WITHIN-NATION COMPARISONS

2. Data on rich nations and poor ones can be examined for changes in income levels and welfare values, like life expectancy, that have been experienced within each nation over time. How much rise in life expectancy has been associated with income growth occurring over several decades? This kind of analysis looks at actual changes that have occurred over time, rather than inferring the probable effects of income transfer merely from a cross-sectional analysis. It has the disadvantage, of course, of being dependent upon particular improvements in medicine and public health already experienced, and upon patterns of their application in various countries, neither of which may be closely reproduced in the future. Diachronic analysis must therefore reflect both effect of rising income, and diffusion of technology independent of income rises.

Figure 3 shows the rise in life expectancy and the fall in infant mortality rates in the United States between 1950 and 1973. The vertical axis measures the change in welfare values; the horizontal axis shows per capita GNP in constant (1958) dollars. The first life expectancy reading (for 1950: 68.2 at $2,342) falls below the subsequent regression line, indicating the unusually great welfare increase associated with the rise in income to 1955 (69.6 at $2,650). After that we can compute a regression line that falls very close to the remaining points. The result is a slope of about one year added to life expectancy for every $750 of incremental income. Similarly, the regression line for infant mortality rates runs quite closely to virtually all points; its slope over the entire span indicates a decline in infant mortality of roughly one point for every $145. Note that each estimate offers a given welfare increment (one year of life expectancy, or one point on the infant mortality rate) at a cost of

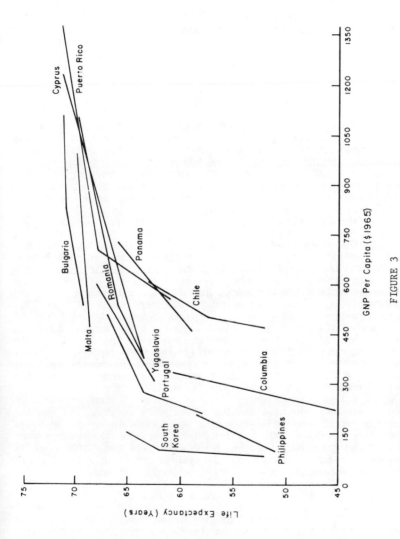

FIGURE 3

THE RELATION BETWEEN PER CAPITA INCOME AND LIFE EXPECTANCY AND INFANT MORTALITY IN THE UNITED STATES, 1950-73

SOURCE: United States Census Bureau, 1975:59, 63, 389.

about 30 percent of those estimates arrived at for rich countries from the synchronic comparison under point 1. above. That is, the slopes computed over time are more than three times as steep as are the slopes computed from comparing countries at the same time. This suggests that of the improvement in life expectancy and infant mortality actually experienced in the United States since 1950, a little less than one third may be attributed to the rise in the general income level, which made all citizens richer and thus able to afford better health care. The other two-thirds (or slightly more) should probably be attributed to scientific progress and the advance of medical and health technology, and possibly in some degree to public efforts to bring health care to previously neglected portions of the population. The latter, however, are not directly the result of rising consumer incomes.

We may continue this exercise with similar data on income in constant (1965) dollars and life expectancy increases in low and middle income countries. Figure 4 shows the situation for twelve countries of varying income levels where some reasonably reliable data are available. For each, the first (low) reading is from somewhere between 1948 and the middle or late 1950s, depending on data availability; the last (high) reading is from sometime in the early 1970s.

While the situation obviously varies between countries (as indeed was suggested by the scatter around the regression curve in Figure 1), there are nevertheless important similarities between what we can observe here and what emerged from the synchronic cross-country analysis of Figure 1. The slopes are clearly steepest for the poorest countries. They become flatter as we move to the right toward middle-income nations like Cyprus and Puerto Rico. At the poorest end of the scale (under $300 per capita GNP in 1965 dollars) a year of additional life expectancy was "bought" for as little as $10 per capita. At the middle level (around $600 per capita) it took $30 or more income increment to add a year to life expectancies, and at the high level ($1,000 per capita) the slope approximates one year per $150. Note that the slopes are not appreciably different for the three socialist countries (Yugoslavia, Romania, Bulgaria) than for the other (capitalist) ones.

Again these diachronic figures show a more dramatic welfare-per-dollar gain than did the synchronic analysis. At the low end of the world welfare and income scale, the diachronic analysis suggests one year for $10; the synchronic analysis showed one year for $28. The poor parts of the world also have benefitted more in achievement of basic needs from general progress in scientific and public health technology than from actual income increases.

SYNCHRONIC WITHIN-COUNTRY COMPARISONS

3. Finally, we examine data on the distribution of income and welfare values within countries at the same time. Unfortunately, adequate data for poor countries are rare, but good studies have been made of the relationship between welfare and income within the

66

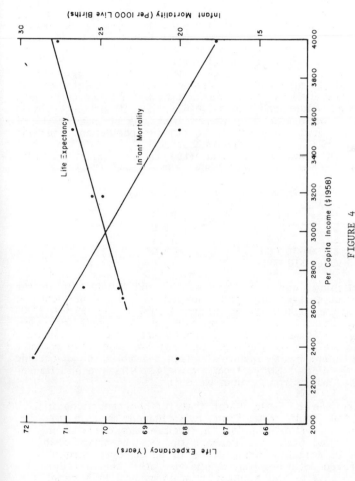

FIGURE 4

THE RELATION BETWEEN GNP PER CAPITA AND LIFE EXPECTANCY WITHIN SELECTED NATIONS OVER TIME

SOURCE: GNP per Capita for Latin American Countries from Wilkie, ed., 1976:231; others from United Nations, 1976b:252-270. 1965 comparative GNP per Capita Data from Taylor and Hudson, 1972:306-311. Life Expectancy from United Nations 1968:707ff., United Nations 1975:1004ff., and United Nations, 1976a:280-283.

United States. Kitagawa and Hauser (1973: 18) have computed "mortality ratios" (actual deaths for each income group of whites as a proportion of deaths "expected" for whites over the entire income range). Their data suggest a mortality ratio of 1.09 for those with family income under $2,000 in 1960, ranging down to a ratio of .90 for those with family income above $10,000. Using that slope, and converting the mortality ratios back into life expectancies, we can arrive at an estimate of about 1 year for each $700; if we compute the regression running only from the $2-4,000 income group to the over $10,000 income group (the poorest are again here modest outliers), the slope is a little less, more like one year for each $1,000. But both estimates are very close to the estimate of one year per $750 derived from the diachronic analysis of the United States in Figure 3. These estimates remain particularly approximate due to a number of methodological problems carefully pointed out by the authors; nevertheless, they conclude from a further comparison of mortality by educational levels (168) that if mortality levels associated with white men and women with one or more years of college education had prevailed throughout the population, one-fifth of all deaths in 1960 would not have occurred.

Similarly, Kitagawa and Hauser (28) compute infant mortality rates by family income group in 1964-66. These are:

Family Income	Infant Mortality Rate
Under $3,000	31.8
$3,000-5,000	24.6
$5,000-7,000	17.9
$7,000-10,000	19.6
Over $10,000	19.6

The flattening, and even reversal, of the relationship in the over-$5,000 groups is strange and unexplained. But if one looks at the lowest income groups (from under $3,000 to the $5,000-7,000 group) the relationship declines approximately one point for every $300 increment. These low income groups are, after all, the ones most likely to suffer from the high cost and low availability of basic maternal and infant health facilities. This resembles the diachronic estimate for the United States from Figure 4. Kitagawa and Hauser (180) conclude, more strongly than we did:

There can be little doubt that further reductions in national death rates can be achieved through the reduction of differentials in socio-economic status in the United States.... Perhaps the most important next gain in mortality reduction is to be achieved through improved socio-economic conditions rather than through increments to and application of biomedical knowledge.

68

SOME FURTHER ASSUMPTIONS AND IMPLICATIONS

If an international shift of income were to raise incomes throughout a poor country, what might then be the effect on life expectancies overall, and at different income levels? Similarly, what would be the effects of a transfer of income away from a rich country? Our three methods above produce different empirical results. Each in different ways taps different aspects of the situation prevailing in an actual shift. Nevertheless, the convergence among our preliminary analyses is substantial, especially if we separate income effects from technological effects.

The synchronic cross-national analysis (Figure 1) produced a difference between one year of life expectancy for $2,700 at the upper end of the range, and one year of life expectancy for $28 at the lower end-- a ratio of nearly 1:100 in benefits! The diachronic within-nation analyses (Figures 3 and 4) produced a figure of one year for $750 at the upper end and one year for $10 at the lower end--a ratio of 1:75. The synchronic comparison within the United States basically reconfirmed the one year for $750 estimate (or perhaps a little above $750). While there are problems with these estimates, the inescapable conclusion is that the marginal utility, in terms of life expectancy, of an incremental dollar at the lower end of the world income scale is at least seventy-five times greater than at the upper end, almost as great as the actual income spread (from Bhutan at $60 per capita GNP in 1973 to the U.S. at $6,200). In Figure 2 we obtained estimates of one point reduction in infant mortality rate for nearly $350 at the upper end of the global income scale and $6.50 per capita at the low end. Figure 3 and the subsequent synchronic analysis within the United States produced estimates of $145 and $300 respectively, but the former at least was compounded both of income and diachronic technological effects. Using the $300 estimate as something of a mid-point among the three estimates, and retaining the $6.50 figure as our only estimate for the low end of the scale, we again have a great gap in marginal utility, approaching 1:50.[7]

Of course these estimates are crude; they demand substantial micro-analysis of the mechanisms of nutrition, sanitation, and health care, the vehicles whereby income changes are translated into longevity. Of course the governments of many countries are corrupt and/or elitist, so that the effects of government-to-government income transfers from rich to poor nations might not be so dramatic as some of our estimates imply. Simple old-style foreign aid transfers, without specific attention to multi-dimensional patterns of development and the satisfaction of basic needs, might be no more successful in reducing misery than inflows of wealth to some OPEC countries. The point nevertheless is that the gap between well-being in rich and poor countries is so enormous, and the multi-method character of our estimating procedures indicates sufficient robustness in the results, that our basic conclusion appears sound. Even with a large margin for error in the estimates, income transfers from rich to poor countries would produce much greater gains in human welfare in the lower end of the spectrum than they would impose losses at the upper. We already know that citizens of rich countries are much more likely to consider themselves "happy" than are citizens of poor ones (Gallup, 1976). I am here reminded of John Rawls' (1971: 114) comments on the "duty of mutual aid," which requires us to "help another when he is in jeopardy, provided that one can do so without excessive risk or loss to oneself."

So far we have implicitly assumed the same proportionate income change for all people in a country. To do more, we should have more data on income and welfare within poor countries (like that discussed above on the United States) and we must make some important political assumptions--assumptions that probably would be more realistic than simple proportionate increments/decrements for all. One could assume an elitist government that gave most or all of the increase only to the richest (with results even more extreme than those we observed in some of the oil-rich countries in Figure 1). Or one might assume that the increase in income for the poor country was distributed so that all citizens had the same absolute increase in their income level. Or one could assume a highly egalitarian government that concentrated the income (and especially the welfare) increment on the poorest segments of the population. There are many ways to vary our assumptions to infuse more political and social reality into what has so far been primarily an economic and demographic exercise. Furthermore, there are likely to be some special complications, such as unfavorable climatic conditions or stubborn endemic diseases, that might limit the prospective improvement in health unless special efforts were made to raise educational levels.

Herrera et al. (1976) emphasize the need for income redistribution within as well as between countries. Note that while the left outliers (countries with better life expectancy and infant mortality rates than would be "predicted" by income) in both Figure 1 and Figure 2 include China and Cuba, they also include Taiwan and Sri Lanka. To quote Tinbergen et al:

> There is encouraging recent evidence from a number of Third World countries, operating under a wide range of systems, that the minimum needs of human well-being can be met for the great majority of the population even under very modest per capita income levels when specific attention is given in development strategies to addressing the needs of the poor majority (1976: 130).

Several social scientists (e.g., Tinbergen, et al., 1976: 130; Herrera, et al., 1976: 91-94) have proposed as a goal the achievement of a life expectancy of about sixty-five years in the poor countries by the year 2000. Let us suppose that goal were to be achieved more quickly, say within ten years. That means 2.4 billion people living fifteen years longer. Our synchronic analysis in Figure 1 generated a marginal utility, at the poor end of the income scale, of one year in life expectancy for every $28 increment. But over ten years in the future we can anticipate advantages in medical technology and public health independent of income effects: recall the one year for only $10 estimate generated by the diachronic analysis of Figure 4. A fairly conservative estimate for transfers occurring over the next 10 years is one year for $20. Thus, the arithmetic becomes 2.4 billion x 15 x $20 = roughly $720 billion. Over ten years that is markedly less than the $100 billion per year projected at the start of this article.

Furthermore, the marginal utilities we used assumed an identical proportionate increase in income for all citizens of the poor countries--a "wasteful" assumption not in accord with the experience of those countries where life expectancy is relatively high for the income level. Targeting the transfer more pointedly, either through direct distribution within poor countries or through explicit concentration on public health, sanitation, and nutritional mechanisms necessary to assure basic needs to the poor, would provide an increment in life expectancy for substantially less. An appropriate adjustment to our calculations could bring them into line with "two estimates resulting from different approaches and methodologies" which "suggest that absolute poverty could be virtually ended" in the world for approximately $375 billion (1973 prices; Sewell et al., 1977: 67). This is not grossly out of line with a 23 year annual continuation (from 1977 to 2000) of the $13.6 billion in official development assistance from OECD countries in 1975. (Over 23 years, $13.6 billion would amount to $313 billion.) But current official development assistance is predominately not targeted to the poorest countries nor to the poorest citizens.

It might be objected that massive inflows of resources to poor countries would be "squandered" in a resultant population explosion. Immediate gains might, in the mid-to-long run, produce greater pressure on resources, less satisfaction of basic needs, and more misery. In point of fact, however, dramatic improvements in life expectancy and infant mortality seem to be associated with decreases in birth rates and rates of growth in population. This is particularly the case in countries where medical and health assistance reaches deeply into rural and other poor parts of the populace. All major outliers to the left of the curves in Figures 1 and 2 (China, Cuba, Sri Lanka, Taiwan) show birth rates (below 30 per thousand) and population increase rates (20 or below) substantially lower than usual for countries at their rather low income levels. Thus, filling basic needs seems to precipitate the means and/or the incentive to control population. [8]

One further objection: any drastic or forceable transfer of income from one set of countries to another would surely disrupt the global economy; the worldwide recession following the 1973-74 increase in oil prices stands as an example. A large decline in total world income resulting from each disruption could wipe out net welfare gains anticipated from redistribution, leaving not only the rich, but the poor as well, worse off than before. Okun (1975), for example, expresses a general economic reservation about the effect

71

of income transfers on incentives: a redistribution of income reduces the size of the total product (and everyone's income) if higher-producing people earn markedly less than the value of their marginal product.

The effects of redistribution on incentives, or on the structure of the economic system, are extremely hard to calculate and subject to great, often essentially ideological, debate. Nevertheless, we can extend our mental exercise to offer some insight. Imagine the pessimistic scenario where $150 per capita (roughly three percent of their GNP) was transferred from the rich countries to the poor ones (distributed more widely, to the equivalent of $42 per capita) instantaneously, and that such a sudden move produced a drop in total world income of as much as 10 percent. For this we should use the marginal utilities generated in Figure 1 (synchronic). GNP per capita in the rich industrialized countries ran about $5,000 in 1973; a 10 percent drop would be $500, equivalent to perhaps two months of life expectancy for the average citizen. For roughly 700 million such citizens, the loss is a little over 100 million person-years. For the poorest 2.4 billion people in the world, who have an average income of perhaps $250, a 10 percent drop is $25 or slightly less than a year of life expectancy--roughly a total of 2.1 billion person-years. Assuming a slope of about a year of life expectancy for $100 lost to each of the 1.2 billion people in the "middle" income range (around $1,000 per capita) costs another 1,200 million person-years. The disruption of the world economy thus would cost 3.4 billion person-years. On the other hand, the net gain from the transfer effect is as follows: 1.5 years x 2.4 billion persons gained at the low end and two months x 700 million lost at the upper end. The arithmetic comes to an even trade: 3.6 billion minus 140 million gained from redistribution, set against 3.4 billion lost from disruption. But this is extreme because the transfer was postulated to occur all at once. The gradual transfer postulated three paragraphs above would produce less disruption and would "purchase" a greater increment in life expectancy per dollar because of technological improvements anticipated.

So what? On a prudential level, citizens of rich countries must be aware of these discrepancies in well-being, and of the fact that citizens of poor countries are becoming increasingly aware of them. Rightly or wrongly, poor people's awareness is coupled with growing anger against the rich. Such anger--interacting with perhaps sharp short-term jumps in mortality due to widespread famines we may anticipate, with the proliferation of nuclear and sophisticated conventional weapons, and with the potential for transnational terrorism--raises a "security" threat to the rich. How, if at all, global income redistribution might defuse this threat is highly unclear, but not a question that prudence can ignore.

On a moral-ethical level, questions of responsibility for the condition of the poor have been debated for millenia. On a personal level, though I have worked with data of this sort for 15 years, I find myself shocked by the magnitude of the gaps, a magnitude I had not anticipated in advance of this inquiry. One must separate diagnosis of responsibility (if any) for producing the gap from the responsibility (if any) for reducing it. With this distinction, to require action one need not blame the rich countries for the poverty of the poor; "from a Rawlsian perspective, one need only show that redistribution would improve the long-run conditions of the poor" (Amdur, 1977: 455). For most, our sense of moral responsibility for others recedes as their physical and social distance from us recedes. Our immediate families get highest priority, our fellow-nationals may occupy some sort of middle ground, and more distant inhabitants of the globe, about whom we know little, are farthest from our sense of responsibility. Explanations vary, from the sense of mutual indentification or "we-feeling" that Deutsch et al. (1957) pinpointed for its political relevance, to the sociobiological perspective of preserving one's genes in biologically related populations (Wilson, 1975). Whatever the reason for a diminished sense of responsibility, these global inequalities are far greater than what we would tolerate within our own families, and greater than what we tolerate within the United States. (The difference between per capita incomes in the richest and poorest state is less than 2:1; between the richest and poorest nations, as noted above, it approaches 100:1.) Perhaps awareness of this enormity will keep a sense of global responsibility above the null level.

ACKNOWLEDGEMENTS

I am grateful to the Concilium on International Studies of Yale University and the National Science Foundation for financial support, and to Steven Jackson, Marguerite Kramer, Miroslav Nincic, Duncan Snidal, and David Sylvan for comments. Of course all responsibility is my own.

NOTES

1. Note Herrera et al. (1976:53): "Life expectancy at birth is without doubt the indicator that best reflects general conditions of life regardless of country. Its value is a function of the extent to which the basic needs are satisfied..." For the development of a composite Physical Quality of Life Index including life expectancy at birth, infant mortality, and literacy rate, see Sewell et al., 1977: 147-54.
2. I discussed this procedure in Duvall and Russett (1976), and in Russett (1975). It is basically the same as I employed in Russett et al. (1964: 299-301). The same procedure has been used by Köhler and Alcock (1976) taking off from a suggestion by Galtung and Høivik (1971). Köhler and Alcock, however, are primarily concerned with the number of deaths occurring globally as a result of the deviation of the worldwide income distribution from perfect equality; here we attempt to measure the welfare effects of certain identifiable reductions in income inequality. Also see the careful work of Høivik (1977).

3.   This is similar to the coefficient that may be inferred from Köhler and Alcock (1976), allowing for the fact that they are using GNP per capita data for 1965.

4.   Here and in the following figure, separate regression coefficients were computed for countries with per capita GNP below $600 and for countries above $1800. At each of these levels a linear relationship (though different) provides a good fit. Between $600 and $1800 I have joined the two lines with a curve to estimate that portion of the relationship. The linear coefficients are referred to in the text. In computing the coefficients all OPEC countries were omitted; as explained in the text they are special cases.

5.   Hansen et al. (1976: 149) show Sweden as less egalitarian than the United States. This does not, however, agree with the opposite (and more generally accepted) conclusion of OECD studies (e.g., Sawyer, 1976), which show the United States as less egalitarian than all or nearly all of 12 major industrialized countries.

6.   For the two regression lines in Figure 1, respectively, .36 and .22; in Figure 2 they are .46 and .25.

7.   In a new analysis, Alcock and Köhler (1977) report that both synchronic and diachronic analyses show virtually the same relationship between wealth increments and life expectancy. The relationship is much stronger for poor countries than for rich ones, but very similar, within each subgroup, whether examined diachronically or synchronically. The reasons for the similarity (where we found a stronger diachronic relationship) are not clear, but may be an artifact of their use of GNP per capita in the synchronic analyses and energy consumption as the wealth measure in their diachronic analyses.

8.   Here, as elsewhere, we still cannot fully specify the mechanism by which our variables are related. It is clear, for example, that education is related (negatively) to rates of population increase as it is to life expectancy and low infant mortality. Some of the effects of these variables that we may seem to attribute to income are surely attributable more directly to education. Nevertheless, it is very difficult to sort out the separate effects, and the correlations of such variables as literacy with population growth, life expectancy, etc., are not systematically higher than are the correlations of GNP per capita with population growth, life expectancy, etc.

REFERENCES

Alcock, Norman, and Gernot Köhler (1977).   "Structural Violence at the World level: Diachronic Findings."   Oakville, Ontario: Canadian Peace Research Institute, mimeo.
Amdur, Robert (1977).   "Rawls' Theory of Justice: Domestic and International Perspectives," World Politics, 29, 3: 438-61.
Deutsch, Karl W., et al. (1957).   Political Community and the North Atlantic Area.   Princeton: Princeton University Press.

Duvall, Raymond, and Bruce Russett (1976). "Some Proposals to Guide Research on Contemporary Imperialism," Jerusalem Journal of International Relations, 2, 1: 1-27.

Gallup, George H. (1976). "Human Needs and Satisfactions: A Global Survey," Public Opinion Quarterly, 40, 4: 459-67.

Galtung, Johan, and Tord Høivik (1971). "Structural and Direct Violence: A Note on Operationalization," Journal of Peace Research, 8, 1: 73-76.

Galtung, Johan, et al. (1975). "Measuring World Development," Alternatives, 1, 1: 131-58.

Hansen, Roger D., et al. (1976). The United States and World Development: Agenda for Action 1976. New York: Praeger.

Herrera, Amilcar, et al. (1976). Catastrophe or New Society? A Latin American World Model. Ottawa: International Development Research Centre.

Høivik, Tord (1977). "The Demography of Structural Violence, "Journal of Peace Research, 14, 1: 59-74.

Kitagawa, Evelyn, and Philip Hauser (1973). Differential Mortality in the United States: A Study. Cambridge: Harvard University Press.

Köhler, Gernot, and Normal Alcock (1976). "An Empirical Table of Structural Violence," Journal of Peace Research, 13, 4: 343-56.

Lasswell, Harold, and Abraham Kaplan (1950). Power and Society: A Framework for Inquiry. New Haven: Yale University Press.

Maslow, Abraham (1968). Toward a Psychology of Being. Princeton: Van Nostrand, 2nd edition.

Okun, Arthur (1975). Equality and Efficiency: The Big Tradeoff. Washington, D.C.: Brookings Institution.

Rawls, John (1971). A Theory of Justice. Cambridge: Harvard University Press.

Russett, Bruce, et al. (1964). World Handbook of Political and Social Indicators. New Haven: Yale University Press.

Russett, Bruce M. (1975). "Hur fattiga måste de fattiga vara?" Rapport fran SIDA, 6, 7 (November) 3-5.

Sawyer, M. (1976). "Income Distribution to OECD Countries," OECD Economic Outlook, July: 3-36.

Sewell, John W., et al. (1977). The United States and World Development: Agenda 1977. New York: Praeger.

Taylor, Charles L., and Michael C. Hudson (1972). World Handbook of Political Indicators. New Haven: Yale University Press.

Tinbergen, Jan, et al. (1976). Reshaping the International Order: A Report to the Club of Rome. New York: E. P. Dutton.

United Nations (1968). Demographic Yearbook, 1967. New York: United Nations.

United Nations (1975). Demographic Yearbook, 1974. New York: United Nations.

United Nations (1976a). Demographic Yearbook, 1975. New York: United Nations.

United Nations (1976b). Yearbook of National Accounts Statistics, 1975, III. New York: United Nations.

United States Census Bureau (1976). <u>Statistical Abstract of the United States, 1975</u>. Washington: United States Government Printing Office.

Wilkie, James W., ed. (1976). <u>Statistical Abstract of Latin America, 1976</u>. Los Angeles: U.C.L.A. Center of Latin American Studies.

Wilson, Edward O. (1975). <u>Sociobiology</u>. Cambridge, Mass.: Belknap.

4. International Inequality and National Income Distribution

Satish Raichur

National and inter-country income distributions have received much attention in mainstream economics literature, but the linkages between the two have not been as extensively examined. The oft-cited Kuznet finding, for example--that income distribution within a developing country worsens during initial stages of industrial development and then improves after some level of modernization has been achieved--often serves as a justification for the growth-plus-trickle-down approach to economic development. More recently, the so-called "gap" between rich and poor nations has occupied the interest of researchers. The linkages between international and national distribution of income have been ignored in the mainstream literature and, for the most part, are only implicit in Marxist literature. A Marxist analysis of these linkages, however, would contribute to the literature which does explore them (see Sunkel, 1973; Rubinson, 1976) and would make their effects and implications more clear.[1] This paper reviews the linkages between international division of labor and national income distribution in Third World countries.

The theoretical framework of this study is derived from Marxist-Leninist writings on capitalism and imperialism, and from dependency theory. The essay may be seen as an initial step toward drawing together and making explicit the reasons why national income distributions worsen over time in the countries which form the "periphery" of the imperialist "core" nations in a capitalist international economic system. Two major propositions are black boxed in this examination:

1. The concentration and centralization of capital leads to the emergence of monopoly capitalism (Baran and Sweezy, 1966);

2. Imperialism is the highest stage of monopoly capitalism (Lenin, 1939; O'Connor, 1971).

As Lenin specified, under imperialism the division of the world among major capitalist countries has been completed. This is not a merely territorial division but is rather an international division of labor, a specialization of functions and commodities. Though nation-states exist, imperialism cuts across political boundaries--as political scientists focusing on "transnational" relations are beginning to observe. Sunkel (1973) points out that the assumption in mainstream economics that nations are self-contained economic units which exchange products in an international marketplace is meaningless in an economic system which is in fact a global network. This study is therefore organized around a basic framework (delineated in Figure 1) which explicitly recognizes the international division of labor. The national division of labor and the class structure--that is, the character of the ownership of the means of production--are functions of the international division of labor. These, in turn, largely determine the internal distribution of income. In Section I, this schema is briefly elaborated. In Section II, an attempt is made to analyze the changes in the international system to determine their implications for national income distribution.

International Division of Labor and the National Division of Labor

The international division of labor is determined by the needs of the imperializing country and the relative strength or weakness of the imperialized country (Frank, 1969; Wallerstein, 1974). At its simplest, the need for agricultural raw materials and minerals in the core nation dictates the production structure of the peripheral country. At its most complex, inter-imperialist rivalry and competition among global corporations dictate patterns of world production. In this context, a number of considerations are operative, including (1) resource needs, (2) markets for commodities produced in core nations, (3) inter-imperialist rivalry and corporate

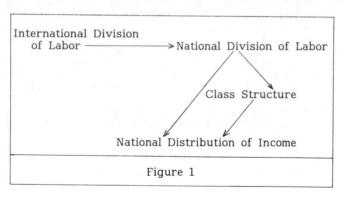

Figure 1

strategies, and (4) capital absorption needs. The first two are adequately covered in the literature (Magdoff, 1969; Jalée, 1968; Rodney, 1974), and only the aspects of these dimensions useful for the narrow purposes of this study are discussed here.

The rate of profit (r) in the Marxist theoretical framework is defined as r = s/c+v, where s is surplus value, c is constant capital, and v is variable capital (wage-bill). Alternatively, the rate of profit may be expressed in terms of the rate of exploitation and the organic composition of capital:

$$r = \frac{s/v}{\frac{c}{v}+1}$$

Resource needs of capitalist core countries are partly dictated by technological considerations, but in the context of imperialism, what is important is the ability to get raw materials at prices below their use-value or below the cost of alternative sources of supply. Lower-priced raw material, by decreasing the value of the organic composition of capital, translates into higher rates of profit. In effect, cheaper raw materials deny a certain proportion of their true value (in terms of either use-value or opportunity cost) to resource suppliers; that value is instead realized in the core nations. Flows of manufactured commodities from the center to the periphery form the other component of the dialectic of surplus creation and surplus realization. They help create the surplus value in the core countries by taking up the slack between the value of goods and services created there and the domestic demand for them. If the value of total output is expressed as TO = c + v + s and if c + v < TO, then s is fully realized by advertising, military spending, expansion of domestic investment, and export of commodities (Sweezy, 1942).

We may now turn to the discussion of inter-imperialist rivalry, corporate strategies, and capital absorption needs and their implications for the national division of labor in periphery countries. Economists primarily focus on the efficiency implications of the technical division of labor, as illustrated by Adam Smith's famed example of pin manufacturing. What has not been emphasized is the social division of labor, sometimes called "Babbage's principle" (Marshall, 1919). Harry Braverman (1974), in his discussion of this process, quotes from Commons' observation of the meat-packing industry:

It would be difficult to find another industry where division of labor has been so ingeniously and microscopically worked out. The animal has been surveyed and laid out like a map; and the men have been classified in over thirty specialties and twenty rates of pay, from 16 cents to 50 cents an hour . . . . In working the hide alone, there are nine different positions, at eight different rates of pay.

The point is that the subdivision of labor has a social as well as a technical significance. It permits some kinds of labor to be bought more cheaply than others, reducing the overall costs of production.

A technical division of a particular production process originates only within the country. The internationalization of the process, however, functions at the social level where the division of labor allows some kinds of labor to be bought more cheaply than others and permits a reduction in total labor costs by locating production activity in relatively low wage areas. The international division of labor, then, may be seen as an attempt to raise the rate of profit by moving from points of relatively low rates of exploitation and high organic composition of capital toward higher rates of exploitation and lower levels of organic composition of capital, or towards higher rates of exploitation and similar levels of organic composition of capital. While profitability increases in each case, the rate of profit is obviously higher in the first case.

The international division of labor is necessitated by cost considerations, and by conditions internal to advanced monopoly capitalism. If the upper limits of domestic rates of exploitation have been reached in the core countries, further increases in the organic composition of capital there are likely to yield minimal increases in the rates of profit. The implications for the national division of labor and the class formations in the periphery countries are straightforward. First, increasing the rate of profit requires technical and social divisions of labor in the periphery countries. A rapid destruction of crafts, artisans, and social groupings will take place, accompanied by rapid urbanization and the formulation of an industrial proletariat. Given the relatively high capital intensities of the production processes introduced, however, the ratio of the industrial proletariat to the labor force is small. A high-wage, elite labor force is created (Arrighi, 1970). The large wage differential between the rural-traditional sector and the urban-industrial one, with the resulting migratory pull factor, leads to the emergence of a large tertiary labor sector in urban areas--the lumpen-proletariat.

The Class Structure

A domestic bourgeoisie which emerges during colonialism and then fuctions as an aspect of neo-colonialism is likely to be weak, non-industrial, and, in brief, a comprador class (Fanon, 1963). In production, it is oriented more internationally than internally, and it exercises only a limited control over domestic economic activity. Where a domestic industrial bourgeoisie does exist, it is quickly integrated into the international division of labor. Wallerstein (1972) describes the decline of the Polish bourgeoisie in the sixteenth century along these lines. Typically, the domestic bourgeoisie controls, in conjunction with international capitalists, the export sector (usually a resource-intensive sector) and the import sector (including any import-substituting manufacturing activity). Its economic interests are virtually inseparable from those of the international capitalist class. This congruence of interests between the comprador bourgeoisie and international capitalism is by no means limited to production activity: it extends to consumption activity as well, as the international division of labor, in the process of imposing labor specialization, also imposes product specialization. The commodity specialization includes both import and import-substitution activity. Needless to say, the specialization of production (yielding high incomes) and the specialization of consumption (requiring high incomes) form a consistent pattern of economic inequality. Sunkel (1973) quotes from an advertisement in Time magazine:

> Time's 24 million readers are apt to have more in common with each other than with many of their countrymen: high incomes, good education, responsible positions in business, government, and the professions.[2]

These elements constitute the international capitalist class, composed of the dominant bourgeoisie in the core nations and the dependent ones in the periphery.

The dependent bourgeoisie of the periphery has a proletarian equivalent--the labor aristocracy. This high-wage, industrial, and typically urban elite develops simultaneously with the growth of a secondary labor force, the lumpen-proletariat, in the urban areas through induced rural-urban migratory flows. The lumpen-proletariat is that segment of the labor force whose alternative opportunities have been rendered less accessible and less rewarding, and, consequently, whose opportunity costs have been lowered. A resulting downward pressure on the wages of this sector means that rates of exploitation are higher and surplus values greater, despite the overall low productivity of the sector. The employment of this labor is characterized by low wages, low capital-intensity of production, and high turnover rates.

The development of the industrial proletariat and the lumpen-proletariat is also accompanied by the proletarianizing of the peasantry. The degree to which this takes place is a function of the penetration of the economy by foreign capital, the extent to which the agricultural sector is geared to the needs of the industrial sector, and the presence and nature of land reform. The higher the degree of external orientation imposed on the agricultural sector, the greater the likelihood of capitalist penetration, such as plantation-type economies, and the more complete the proletarianization. As capitalist penetration of the hinterland of the periphery proceeds, for either market or technological reasons, the development of an agricultural labor force is ensured.

Capitalist penetration fundamentally alters the relations of production in a peasant economy. First, land values increase in relation to labor, making it more profitable for landlords to retain direct control of the land by forcing peasants off their traditional land-holdings (Arrighi, 1973). Second, traditional, long-term ties between landlords and peasants are converted into short-term ties between landlords and hired labor. Third, the relationship is transformed into a purely contractual one, divorced from traditional networks of reciprocal obligations (Ahmad, 1971). These changes

81

are consistent with capital-intensive technological change accompanying capitalist penetration of the agricultural sector. The introduction of the "green revolution," for example, required not only the introduction of a new seed strain, but also a capital-intensive technological process. Its success in India, for example, was accompanied by an exacerbation of existing inequities in landholding, leading to capitalized farming, displacement of small tenants, and the polarization of the peasantry. Sharma (1973) quotes the former Union Home Minister for India, Y. B. Chavan, who declared in late 1969, "Unless the Green Revolution is based on social justice, I'm afraid the green revolution will not remain green." His comment may well have been promoted by the Venmani incident of December 1968. Venmani is a village in South India. The landless laborers' hamlet, Sharma recounts, was attacked at midnight by local landlords. Shooting into the air, they pushed as many people as possible into a single hut and set fire to it. Forty-four men, women, and children were burned alive while the jubilant landlords stood guard to prevent anyone from escaping. This is an extreme illustration of the typical disintegration of the agricultural sector under the impact of capitalist penetration.

All classes discussed are defined on the basis of their relationship to domestic and international means of production. What seems clear is that within this kind of class structure, the creation of a lumpen-proletariat and a comprador bourgeoisie and the polarization of the peasantry in an agricultural sector dominated by capitalist farming, class conflict is inevitably sharpened and the repression of the dispossessed increases.

Income Distribution

In this section the implications of the division of labor and class structures for income distribution are drawn together. Table 1 will be of assistance in organizing these patterns.

There are two basic sources of income: ownership of the means of production, and sale of labor power. (We may ignore income transfers, but it is likely that any such transfers would favor organized groups.) We may further limit the discussion by lumping economic activity into two broad types: that related to tradeable commodities (exported and imported, including import-substitution activity) and that related to non-tradeable commodities (housing, most services, and the like).

In the industrial/urban area, income distribution is skewed because of high unearned incomes accruing to the bourgeoisie and high wage rates accruing to labor engaged in the capital-intensive, high-productivity sector producing tradeable commodities, while low wage rates prevail in the tertiary labor sector. The income distribution pattern is even more unequal than those in developed capitalist countries because of the existence of the large tertiary labor market, the lumpen-proletariat. Income distribution in the traditional/rural area depends on the degree of capitalist penetration. The imposition of a capitalist mode of production leads

82

TABLE 1

Classes	Sources of Income		Kind of Productive Activity	
	Ownership	Labor Power	Tradeable	Non-Tradeable
Comprador Bourgeoisie	X		X	X
Domestic Bourgeoisie	X			X
Labor Aristocracy		X	X	
Lumpen Proletariat		X		X
Rural Proletariat		X	X	X
Rural Peasantry (rich, middle, poor)	X	X	X	X

to the proletarianization of the peasantry, and the adoption of a relatively capital-intensive technology in agricultural production generates increasing rural unemployment. Capitalist penetration and technology also result in the polarization of the peasantry into landlords, rich peasants, and landless rural workers, eliminating middle and poor peasants. If the agricultural sector is engaged in the production of tradeable commodities, access to international markets facilitates the spread of a capitalist mode of production and skews income distribution even more severely. A skewed income distribution in both rural and urban/industrial areas, combined with high levels of rural and urban unemployment, necessarily result in highly unequal national income distribution.

THE DYNAMICS OF INTERNATIONAL AND NATIONAL INCOME DISTRIBUTION

The principal actors in the international economic system, in addition to Third World governments, are multi-national corporations and core-dominated international institutions, such as the IMF and the World Bank. The development of imperialism is facilitated by these transnational actors. An examination of selected patterns of development and policies will allow us to observe their impact on national income distribution.

Monopoly capitalism's ideology of high growth-plus-trickle-down effects, leading over time to the betterment of most members of a society, has an obvious international analog in rapid global economic growth (through the transnational actors) coupled with international redistribution through growth. This conviction has no empirical referents, as bourgeois theorists are themselves beginning to acknowledge (Chenery et al., 1974). The discrepancy between conviction and reality stems from the failure to recognize one simple fact: the development of monopoly capitalism in one additional nation in an internationalized economy changes the nature of the international economic system, making capitalist development in underdeveloped countries that much more difficult. Individual states within a world economy seek to maximize their own national welfare within the constraints set by the global economy. Development of monopoly capitalism alters these constraints, making them more binding and more stringent. The constraints are most binding on the least developed (most underdeveloped) states. With increased monopolization of the world economy, then, nations not yet developed are likely to find their overall position deteriorating relative to that of developed countries. This argument may, of course, be viewed as a corollary to those made by Frank in his seminal work (1969). The central hypothesis put forward and supported by historical case materials drawn from Latin America are:

1. The development of periphery countries is limited by their satellite status;
2. The periphery experiences the greatest amount of development, especially industrial development, when its ties to the center are the weakest; and

3.   The regions which are most underdeveloped today are those which had the closest ties to the center countries in the past. Monopoly advantages are based on privileged positions. Privileges for the few mean exploitation of the many.

National Growth Strategies and Income Distribution

The nature of the class structure emerging in underdeveloped countries in the process of colonization and imperialism was spelled out earlier. The key groups are likely to be: a comprador and a domestic bourgeoisie, a labor aristocracy, and a land-owning elite. The kind of growth strategy developed in conjunction with such international institutions as the IMF and the World Bank is typically economic growth through intensive use of modern technology available from rich countries, principally through multi-national corporations. The familiar requirements of modern technology include (in addition to a labor aristocracy) high literacy rates, highly skilled personnel, and high capital-intensity. The fulfillment of these prerequisites means that earning capacity based either on ownership or on possession of required skills is skewed. An uneven earning capacity translates directly into uneven income distribution. At the same time, on the demand side, goods produced by modern technology are suitable for consumers with relatively high incomes. Uneven income distributions are both the necessary prerequisite to and the result of the growth strategy likely to be selected, given the national class structure and its relation to an international capitalist class. Practically all modern technology is created in the rich countries, and its commercial exploitation is organized by multi-national corporations (MNCs). Technology is a key variable in the development and preservation of monopoly advantages. From the point of view of periphery countries, MNCs are engaged in excessively sophisticated products and processes geared to advanced countries because of their privileged access to these markets and in order to maintain their monopoly advantage (Vernon, 1966). Because of inter-corporate competition, the kinds of products developed and the technology used lead to uneven distribution of resources. This, together with domestic class structures, suggests that inequality in underdeveloped countries will not be ameliorated by capitalist development, but, on the contrary, will be exacerbated. The role of the governments of underdeveloped states, when not directly supportive of international and comprador capitalists, is a passive acquiescence which will hardly mitigate the situation. Indeed, inequality begets policies leading to inequality (Stewart and Streeten, 1976).

Imperialism, Factor Prices, and Income Distribution

The international division of labor may be seen as an attempt to raise the rate of profit by moving from points of relatively low rates of exploitation and high organic composition of capital toward higher rates of exploitation and lower levels of organic composition of capital. The organic composition of capital reflects class struggle. Length of working day, intensity of work, and degree of worker organization affect the denominator of the organic composition of capital, while the degree of technical and social division of labor, as well as labor-saving innovation embodied in capital, affect the numerator of the ratio.

Capital-intensive technology may be introduced into underdeveloped countries with or without accompanying flows of capital. If the technology is introduced without capital flow, a shift in factor prices in favor of capital results. This would have implications for comprador bourgeoisie, domestic bourgeoisie, labor, and, of course, international capitalism. The comprador bourgeoisie would gain directly in terms of increased income because of the higher price of capital. The domestic bourgeoisie, to the extent that it is competing with MNCs for a limited amount of capital, would have to shift to a more labor-intensive method of production, but the shift is likely to be, at best, minimal, given the characteristic low productivity and high labor-intensity of non-tradeable domestic production. If factor substitutability is severely delimited in this sector, it could lead to lower levels of output and higher unemployment for the urban proletariat and a swelling in the ranks of the lumpen-proletariat. Whether or not the domestic bourgeoisie suffers an absolute drop in income in this case would be a function of demand elasticity in the non-tradeable item. A rise in the price of capital, however, also means that the valuation of a given mode of production is likely to be higher than it would have been in the absence of changes in factor prices. Such an investment would take place only if the increase in the rate of exploitation more than compensated for the increase in the organic composition of capital, yielding a higher rate of profit. In this situation, wage rates of the labor aristocracy increase as do their numbers. The increase, however, is less than the increase in the ranks of the lumpen-proletariat if labor is released from the low-productivity sectors.

Most typically, capital in underdeveloped countries is underpriced in real terms. The market price of capital is kept below its scarcity value (shadow price). The implications of this policy are to ensure higher profitability for capital-intensive undertakings; to prevent (or at least ameliorate) adverse effects on the domestic bourgeoisie; and to increase the numbers of the labor aristocracy. While the comprador bourgeoisie experiences an increase in income, there is a key difference when factor prices are allowed to change in favor of capital and when the market price of capital is artificially kept below its shadow price. In the first instance, the comprador bourgeoisie experiences a direct gain in income; in the second instance, the gain (probably smaller) results through a sharing of the higher return to capital with the international capitalist class. In any case, the policy of subsidizing capital has an inflationary bias, especially if it is maintained through open market operations and/or deficit spending.

Capital flows accompanying the introduction of capital-intensive technology would modify the changes discussed above, but would not alter the direction of the changes. In the limiting case, if capital inflows were of a magnitude sufficient to prevent any change in factor prices, the tradeable sector would expand, but with gains limited to the classes involved in it -- the international and comprador bourgeoisie and the labor artisocracy. In all cases, including the limiting one in which no change in factor prices occurs, this analysis suggests that income distribution will become more unequal as a result of capitalist penetration. The degree of inequality is a function of the conditions surrounding the introduction of modern technology.

Changes in inequality of income distribution lead to further inequality because of preference patterns. Given that factor ownership and taste preferences are not uniform across a population, changes in factor prices redistribute income among people with differing consumption preferences. Capitalist penetration of underdeveloped societies leads to a distribution favoring foreign, comprador, and domestic bourgeoisie, and an urban labor aristocracy. This, in turn, is likely to skew consumption patterns toward imported and importable commodities, typically capital-intensive. A sufficient shift sustained over a period of time could lead to trade deficits and, possibly, devaluation. Even if a devaluation occurred, however, the Samuelson-Stolper result would hold -- that is, if tradeable production is capital-intensive, devaluation leads to an increase in the real return to capital and a decline in the return to labor. While devaluation would result in an increase in the price of imports and hence in a decline in their demand, the increased return to capital would simultaneously effect an increase in income for high-income groups involved in capital-intensive priorities, allowing them to maintain consumption of costly imports. If exports are land/ resource-intensive and demand for them is price inelastic, the effect of devaluation would be to increase rentier incomes. If land is distributed unevenly, the increased benefits will also be distributed unevenly. If resources are organized by large expatriate or domestic firms, the gains from devaluation would occur as windfall profits for the resource-extracting corporations (Knight, 1976). In sum, if tradeable production is land/resource or capital-intensive, and given the long-term factors implicit in typical development processes, it is likely that income distribution will be more skewed over time, as a succession of devaluations, among other policies, tends to increase the return to capital and land. This result holds for domestic firms engaged in import-substitution activities as well. A devaluation would obviously increase excess profits by increasing the price of imports (world price of commodity plus import tariffs) and hence the price of the domestic commodity substituted for the imported item (Knight, 1976). The amount of labor used in this sector would decline (increase), if demand is elastic (inelastic).

CONCLUSION

This analysis has explored the relationship between the current organization of the international economic system and the resulting distributional inequities in the underdeveloped countries of the periphery. A highly unequal international system, based on the cooperation of periphery elites and core capitalism, suggests that inequity is built into the countries of the periphery as well as into those of the center. Further, the most common growth strategies pursued by peripheral countries have adverse distributional effects. An international division of labor, built around multi-national corporations and international economic institutions which, by definition, support capitalist penetration and the resulting inequities, can hardly alleviate distributional inequality and uneven development. So long as international corporations and institutions play a vital role in the economies of periphery countries, income distributions will remain unequal, if not, indeed, grow worse. Perhaps more importantly, though, so long as the surplus generated in the periphery must support a comprador bourgeoisie domestically and monopoly capitalism internationally, any "trickle down effects" of growth will be minimal if not wholly absent. If this condition is coupled with a positive population growth rate in periphery countries, it is reasonable to expect greater marginalization of larger segments of the populations of these countries. The marginalization will, of course, be manifested in the size of the lumpen-proletariat, the rural work force, and the urban and rural unemployed. The key polarization is therefore likely to be not between rich and poor countries, but within poor countries, between the marginal masses and the privileged few. This polarization forces periphery countries to seek concessions from the center countries while simultaneously combating domestic polarization with increased repression.[3]

ACKNOWLEDGEMENTS

I would like to thank Bill Tabb and John Grove for some helpful suggestions on an earlier version of this paper.

NOTES

1. At a more general level, the dependency school has contributed a great deal to the understanding of the linkages between rich and poor nations. In addition, there is Johan Galtung's work on the structure of imperialism, in which he examines the economic, political, military, and cultural forms of imperialism and their implications for growing inequalities between the center and the periphery. For a recent empirical test of global inequalities, see Addo (1976).

2. An observation I like to repeat, especially at foreign student orientations, is that to emphasize "culture shock" is to misunderstand "class shock." The Peace Corps volunteer of the 1960s went through "culture shock" not because he was rudely

injected into an "Indian" society, for example, but because he was injected into a peasant society. Intra-class movements internationally do not produce cultural shock; inter-class movements do.
3. The center countries, principally the United States, again have monopoly advantage in both the software and hardware of the technology of repression. See, for instance, Klare, Agee, and two pieces in Computer Decisions: Laurie Nadel and Hesh Wiener, "Would You Sell a Computer to Hitler?" (February 1977), and a follow-up article in the next issue (March 1977), "U.S. Churches Score Gestapo Computers."

REFERENCES

Addo, Herb (1976). "Trends in International Value-Inequality, 1960-1970: An Empirical Study," Journal Of Peace Research XIII:1.
Agee, Philip (1975). Inside the Company: CIA Diary. New York: Bantam Books.
Arrighi, Giovanni (1970). "International Corporations, Labor Aristocracy,and Economic Development in Tropical Africa," in Robert Rhodes (ed.), Imperialism and Underdevelopment. New York: Monthly Review Press.
Arrighi, Giovanni (1973). "Labor Supplies in Historical Perspective: A Study of the Proletarianization of the African Peasantry in Rhodesia," in Giovanni Arrighi and John S. Saul, Essays on the Political Economy of Africa. New York: Monthly Review Press.
Ahmad, Saghir (1971). "Peasant Classes in Pakistan," in Kathleen Gough and Hari P. Sharma (eds.), Imperialism and Revolution in South Asia. New York: Monthly Review Press.
Baran, Paul and Paul Sweezy (1966). Monopoly Capitalism. New York: Modern Reader.
Baran, Paul and Paul Sweezy (1966). "Notes on the Theory of Imperialism," Monthly Review (March 1966).
Braverman, Harry (1974). Labor and Monopoly Capitalism: The Degradation of Work in the Twentieth Century (1974). New York: Monthly Review Press.
Chenery, Hollis et al., (1974). Redistribution with Growth. London: Oxford University Press.
Fanon, Frantz (1963). The Wretched of the Earth. New York: Grove Press.
Frank, Andre Gunder (1969). Latin America: Underdevelopment or Revolution? New York: Monthly Review Press.
Galtung, Johan (1971). "A Structural Theory of Imperialism," Journal of Peace Research, 2.
Gough, Kathleen and Hari P. Sharma, eds. (1973). Imperialism and Revolution in South Asia. New York: Monthly Review Press.
Jalée, Pierre (1968). The Pillage of the Third World. New York: Monthly Review Press.
Klare, Michael T. (1972). War Without End: American Planning for the Next Vietnams. New York: Knopf.

89

Knight, J. B. (1976). "Devaluation and Income Distribution in Less Developed Economies," Oxford Economic Papers 28:2 (July).

Kuznets, Simon (1955). "Economic Growth and Income Inequality," American Economic Review.

Lenin, V. I. (1939). Imperialism: The Highest Stage of Capitalism New York: International.

Magdoff, Harry (1969). The Age of Imperialism. New York: Monthly Review Press.

Marshall, Alfred (1919). Industry and Trade. London: Macmillan.

Nadel, Laurie and Hersh Weiner (1977). "Would You Sell a Computer to Hitler?" Computer Decisions (February).

O'Connor, James (1971). "The Meaning of Economic Imperialism," in K. T. Fann and Donald C. Hodges eds., Readings in U.S. Imperialism. Boston: P. Sargent.

Rodney, Walter (1974). How Europe Underdeveloped Africa. Washington: Howard University Press.

Rubinson, Richard (1976). "The World Economy and the Distribution of Income Within States: A Cross-National Study," American Sociological Review, 41 (August).

Sharma, Hari P. (1973). "The Green Revolution in India: Prelude to A Red One?" in Gough and Sharma, op.cit.

Stewart, Frances and Paul Streeten (1976). "New Strategies for Development: Poverty, Income Distribution, and Growth, Oxford Economic Papers, 28:3 (November).

Sunkel, Osvaldo (1973). "Transnational Capitalism and National Disintegration in Latin America," Social and Economic Studies, 22 (March).

Sweezy, Paul (1942). The Theory of Capitalist Development. New York: Oxford University Press.

Vernon, Raymond (1966). "International Investments and International Trade in the Product Cycle," Quarterly Journal of Economics (May).

Wallerstein, Immanuel (1972). "Three Paths of National Development in the Sixteenth Century," Studies in Comparative International Development, 8.

Wallerstein, Immanuel (1974). "The Rise and Future Demise of the World Capitalist System: Concepts for Comparative Analysis," Comparative Studies in Society and History, 6.

Wright, Erik Olin (1977). "Alternative Perspectives in Marxist Theory of Accumulation and Crises," in Jesse Schwartz (ed.), The Subtle Analysis of Capitalism. New York: Monthly Review Press.

Part III
Cross-national Inequality

5. Age and Gender Differentiation and Social Inequality

Elise Boulding

Age and gender are unique sorting devices for human beings, as compared to race, class and ethnicity, because every human being receives an imputed gender at birth, every human being is or has once been a child, and every human being moves through a biosocial succession of age statuses until cut off by death. In the case of gender, only half of the human race (the female half) experiences "minority status" in the sense of social limitations on life chances not directly related to biological capacity. In the case of age, every human being who lives long enough experiences two minority statuses--the first of being a child, the second of being old. Each has its own socially assigned limitations of opportunity. Both gender and age-based social constraints may be mitigated by membership in a favored race, ethnic group or class, but they do not disappear. They may be much exacerbated by membership in non-favored social categories. If we visualize all socially targeted minorities as being additionally subject to these universal sorting devices of gender and age, we see that certain groups in a society carry a much heavier loading of minority-hood and its attendant lack of control over conditions of life than do others.

It is the purpose of this paper to explore these two primary sources of human inequality. The primary social group that both multiplies and mitigates this inequality, the family, will be introduced for purposes of the social model, but not explored in detail in this study. How do the human universals of age, gender, and family groupings operate to hinder the rhetorical aspiration to human equality? Figure 1 represents schematically the conceptual model on which this paper is based. The individual is viewed as subject to a series of sorting processes from before conception to death, which determine further life chances. The first of these sorting processes is set in motion by the level of industrialization, and population, GNP, and urbanization growth rates of the society into which an individual is born, which establish certain parameters for all other life chances. The SES (socio-economic status) of the household into which an individual is born, and its associated community linkage systems and child-rearing practices, act as a further sorting device for individuals from the moment of conception. At the moment of

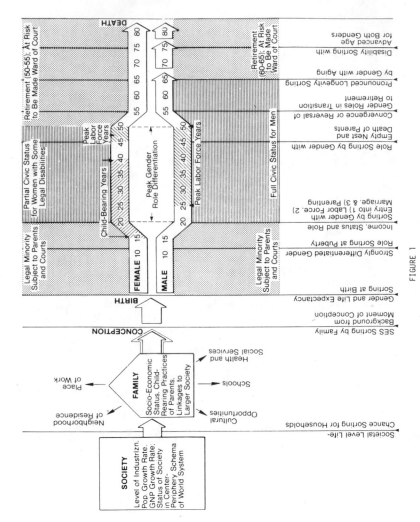

FIGURE 1

AGE AND GENDER SORTING OF HUMAN BEINGS OVER THE LIFE CYCLE, WITH PRIOR SOCIETAL AND FAMILY SORTING INDICATED

94

birth, there is further sorting by gender, and gender-related life expectancy. Birth also involves, for both males and females, being sorted into the minority status of childhood, which lasts, in terms of legal status, until age twenty-one in most countries.

Extent of gender role differentiation is relatively mild until puberty, when a sharp role differentiation takes place and lasts until about age 55, when gender roles either converge or reverse. The next major sorting after puberty comes with entry into the labor force, into marriage, and into parenting, events that usually come within a relatively short time period for most individuals. For most women, entry into the labor force involves a gender-determined income sorting; most women command lower wages than men throughout life. Entry into marriage involves status-resorting for most women, as they take on the SES of their husbands. The latter's SES remains relatively unchanged from childhood, allowing for small movements upward or downward in the status scale as a result of personal achievement or disachievement. If there are remarriages, for most women each marriage means a status resorting (if the new spouse's SES is different from the old); for most men, status stays the same throughout successive marriages.[1] Entry into parenting involves major role shifts for most women toward primary responsibility for child care, minor role shifts for most men toward increasing involvement in the household.

Apt to be lost in the complex of role sortings that take place with entry into the labor force, marriage, and parenting, is the sorting based on change in legal status that comes with reaching the twenty-first year of age. Full adulthood, involving contractual rights to dispose of one's person and property, comes for most young men after they have already entered into the adult responsibilities of work and marriage. Women never attain this sense of adulthood, although they begin childbearing, with or without spouse, at age 14 or 15. There are varying degrees of lifelong legal constraints on their contractual rights in every part of the world. They do, however, attain a significant increase in rights at age 21. The next major sorting for women comes at the close of the childbearing and rearing years, with the piling up of the phenomena of the empty nest, illness and death of the couple's own parents, and re-entry into the labor force, all of which occur within a short span of time. This is a period of release for most women from the care of the young and the old. This role sorting process has minimal implications for most men, whose labor force and household roles remain fairly stable from marriage to retirement.

The complex role sorting for women involved with the empty nest, death of parents, and heavier labor force participation, is followed, as retirement nears, by a gradual role convergence or actual role reversal for women and men. Noted in widely different cultural contexts, in societies with widely differing levels of industrialization, this convergence involves women taking on behavioral characteristics ordinarily conceived of as typically masculine, active, mastery-oriented. Men take on behavioral characteristics ordinarily conceived of as typically feminine, passive,

95

adaptive (Gutmann, n.d.). In nonindustrial societies, this stage is not accompanied by any formal retirement from the labor force, for either women or men, but by a gradual lessening of work load as declining strength dictates. In industrial societies, substantial sectors of the population, though not all, formally retire between the ages of 55 and 70. Entry into the earlier stages of advanced aging processes become evident during this period. There is a noticeable longevity sorting by gender. At each age throughout the life span more males have died than females, but the greater risk of death for males becomes more pronounced between the ages of 55 and 70. Numbers of women enter into widowhood roles as men die. Disability sorting is also noticeable by the seventies, but here the sorting applies to survivors of both sexes. By this age, women and men alike are at risk of being deprived of the rights they gained at age 21, and of once more being made into minors--this time as wards of the court, or wards of their own children. This rights deprivation may or may not be related to actual physical and mental incapacity.

Death brings the lifespan sequence, with its differential sorting stations for women and men as they move from age to age, to an end. At the close of life, as at its inception, gender differentiation is minimal. Aging, for the first and last third of the lifespan, seems to be the primary sorting device. Only in the middle third does gender differentiation predominate. Because the middle third of life has been treated, at least in the West, as the only significant part of the human lifespan, the gender differentiation of this period may have been receiving more attention than it deserves. A clearer recognition that the human lifespan moves from the androgyny of the young to the androgyny of the old may help to bring more objective considerations to bear on the utility of the violent gender differentiation in the middle third of life.

AGE AND GENDER SORTING: EQUALITY AND HISTORY

The significance of gender sorting and age sorting, in their separate and joint effects, lies in the powerful levers they provide to every type of society for unequal allocation of opportunities and resources. This leverage appears to be in direct contradiction to the currently voiced aspiration for equality for human beings, although it is not always clear what the aspiration to equality means. Does it represent a passion for honoring and empowering one's fellow humans in all their diversity, or does it represent a fierce desire to impose one's own limitations on everyone else? The political policies appropriate to equality-in-diversity concepts are very different from the policies appropriate to equality-in-likeness concepts. Rossi (1977) has written incisively about the dangers of the equality-in-likeness approach to sex equality, and the same considerations apply equally to age. The concept of social equality on which this paper is based is one of mutual honoring, particularly as related to age and sex. This diversity calls for a continuous process of complex balancing of human capacities, needs, and resources. Equality in this view is a heterostatic, not a homeostatic, concept.

Whether or not there is an evolutionary bias toward human equality cannot be settled here. Most twentieth century polities subscribe to equality as a suitable expression of a progressive social ideal, more honored in the breach than in the observance. The laws and edicts of major polities, from the Code of Hammurabi on down, are continually permeated with the notion of rights and opportunities, even when they are in fact cutting back rather than expanding rights for certain classes of human beings (such as women). The dialectic of successive expansions and contractions of human rights concepts--expansions through the teachings of the founders of the great universal religions, and contractions through the political necessities of the empires they nourished--has been the pattern observable throughout the historical record. One could argue that each expansion brings new insights, new dimensions, new inclusiveness to the concept of human rights. The United Nations Declaration of Human Rights, while a great advance over the French Declaration of the Rights of Man--which left to one side slaves, various ethnic and religious groups, the poor, women, children, prisoners, and the mentally ill--still bears the mark of western moral ethnocentrism. The Declaration of Human Rights of the year 3000 will read very differently. For the moment, we note that the United Nations Declaration does not recognize the classificatory principle of age as a basis of discrimination. This lack will create an increasingly serious problem in coming decades.

The interaction of physical and social technologies with environmental resources in the context of increasingly self-conscious social purposes in a gradually aging world population has brought human societies to yet another threshold comparable to past thresholds reached in the transition from hunting and gathering to agriculture, from agricultural village to urban life, from artisan urbanism to industrial urbanism. The labor-intensive, biochemically-oriented and electronically linked world society of the future may develop very different social and political technologies. In the past, poor adaptations of earlier social technologies to changing levels of complexity and scale meant that new devices for exploiting various classes of human beings from one's own and surrounding societies accompanied each major system change. Wallerstein's (1976) analysis of the mobilization of surplus economic value from the world's "peripheries" (most of the planet) for the use of the world's power center (Euro-North America) from the onset of the industrial revolution until the present is in my view simply a replication on a grander scale of a process that has accompanied each successive system break. I would date the system break that gave rise to the industrial revolution in the thirteen rather than the sixteen hundreds. New potentialities for human fulfillment that appeared at each threshold moment, particularly at the axial ages when new religious, social, and political insights accompanied technological breakthroughs (500 B.C.-100 A.D., 1200-1300 A.D., and possibly 1900-2000 A.D.), have so far evaporated unrealized, as recognition was succeeded by exploitation on the old mastery pattern.

It is not impossible that in the system break we now face, societies may avoid slipping into an Orwellian electronic nightmare of tight centralized control over individuals "for their own good." It depends on whether enough human energy can be mobilized to create new local solutions during the period of disorganization we probably face due to institutional slippage as old technologies are abandoned for lack of resources. Drawing on the full range of abilities and potentialities of persons of all ages and both sexes as well as of all racial and ethnic groups will be an important aspect of creating these new solutions, as will a new orientation of households to local communities. Certainly current planning technologies, which ensure that all target populations are assimilated into age and sex patterned inequality structures at a suitable level of economic dependence, will be inadequate at a time when individual human ingenuity will be at a premium. Whether human ingenuity will be up to the task of designing new kinds of decentralist structures within a heterostatic egalitarian federal framework that does not slip back into village ethnocentrism or forward into totalitarianism remains to be seen. At the least, the removal of age and gender-based status disabilities would make available for local mobilization that "minority"-majority of the human race consisting of women, children, and the elderly.

Since, as Figure 1 indicates, the structures of gender differentiation mediate the experiences of age differentiation throughout life, making aging a very different experience for women than for men, I will discuss gender differentiation before age differentiation.

GENDER DIFFERENTIATION

As primates go, human beings are only intermediately dimorphic. We slip into a class with the chimpanzees, only moderately sex differentiated by size and strength, as contrasted with the gibbons, who can hardly be distinguished by sex, and the baboons, whose males are twice as large and heavy as the females. The modest differences in physiological capacity between human males and females can be easily overcome for most tasks through a combination of training and technology. Newspaper reports of the performance of women cadets at the U. S. Air Force Academy in Colorado Springs in combat training, for example, suggest that women are performing creditably in relation to men, and that they have unsuspected reservoirs of physical endurance. Their problems appear to stem less from performance capabilities than from role definition.

The assymetry of the perceptions which hamper social classification, though not physical performance, of women, goes back to the uniqueness of the woman as breeder for the species. However, just as we question analogies with mammals for the analysis of other human behaviors and susceptibilities, so we might question the "sociobiology of mother's milk" approach to women's roles. Social and physical technologies available in the twentieth century, partnered to the human potentials concept, are logically leading to

98

the increased involvement of fathers with parturition, to minimized gender differences in parenting. The hormone-based entrainment of a woman's mothering behavior toward her newborn so graphically described by Rossi (1977) can probably be replicated to a substantial degree in the male through his total involvement in the childbirth process. I know of no studies of hormonal activities of fathers present and actively assisting with childbirth, but I have heard enough accounts by men of differing feelings of involvement with and capacity to respond to the needs of infants they have participated in birthing, as compared to infants from whose birth process they have been excluded, to conclude that there are probably hormonal changes involved for men assisting in parturition. This is of critical importance in breaking down inappropriate gender-differentiation, since the release of women into fuller participation in other socio-economic and political roles depends on shared parenting of the young, and corresponding limitation of other socio-economic and political roles of men. Childcare centers may supplement but not substitute for individualized parenting by men and women.

Historically, women and children have been part of every society's labor force. The withdrawal of both groups from that labor force with the industrial revolution might be seen as a historical anomaly. The return of women in the first world to a labor force they never left in the third world cannot be adequately discussed here in terms of the economic forces involved. If we look to the labor force requirements of the future, however, and if the systems break hypothesis is correct, those requirements will be heavier than in the past. These new requirements will face dwindling numbers of a nation's population available in "prime labor force age"--21 to 45--and dwindling numbers of migrant laborers available to the first world when its fossil fuel supplies have gone. This means an increase, not a decrease, in demand for women's labor in the future.

Contemporary labor force figures show on the one hand that women are indeed heavily involved in the world's labor force, in spite of enumeration slippage that leaves many women workers uncounted.[2] On the other hand, the same figures show that their participation is at lower rates, and at lower statuses, than their demonstrated capacities--and their training as revealed by the percent of women educated--warrant. Table 1 shows their participation in the world labor force by occupational category, and Table 2 the extent of their family responsibilities. Table 1 is misleading because it refers to percentage of women counted of all those counted, men and women. Many women are uncounted laborers. Table 2 shows that only 62 percent of the world's women have spouses to assist them. Many of the 38 percent single, widowed, and divorced have dependents to care for, and represent women-headed households. Whether they are working outside the home or not, whether they have spouses or not, the majority of these women have a household to care for and children to rear. The limited range of their work roles can be noted from the fact that they make up only 10 percent of the world's administrative and managerial personnel (Table 1). Table 3 shows how the total pool of

TABLE 1

RANK ORDERING OF WOMEN BY OCCUPATION IN THE LABOR FORCE:
WORLD FEMALENESS INDEX (WOMEN AS PERCENTAGE OF
ALL PERSONS IN THE OCCUPATIONAL CATEGORY)

Rank Order	Percentage Women	Occupation
1	50.1	Service
2	38.3	Professional, Technical
3	33.9	Sales
4	33.7	Clerical
5	21.7	Agriculture
6	15.3	Production
7	10.2	Administrative, Managerial
8	2.3	Armed Forces

SOURCE: Boulding (1977a:26).

TABLE 2

WORLD FAMILY AND HOUSEHOLD SITUATION OF WOMEN

Marital Status	
Percentage Never Married	23.0
Percentage Married	62.3
Percentage Widowed	11.5
Percentage Divorced, Separated	3.5
Household	
Average Size of Household	4.6
Child Woman Ratio	635.7
Child Woman Ratio, Urban	571.6
Child Woman Ratio, Rural	704.2

SOURCE: Boulding (1977a:22).

TABLE 3

RANK ORDERING OF WOMEN BY OCCUPATION IN THE LABOR
FORCE: WORLD DISTRIBUTION INDEX
(WOMEN AS PERCENTAGE OF ALL EMPLOYED WOMEN)

Rank Order	Percentage Women	Occupation
1	29.8	Agriculture
2	24.2	Service
3	18.7	Production
4	12.8	Professional, Technical
5	12.1	Clerical
6	10.4	Sales
7	7.1	Administrative, Managerial
8	0.1	Armed Forces

Percentage of Women in the Total Labor Force: 29.1

SOURCE: Boulding (1977a:28).

101

women workers is distributed among different occupations. We see that there are more women in farming than in any other occupation, with service and production workers ranking second and third in frequency, and professional (mostly teachers) a weak fourth. The discrepancy between women's labor force participation and their training is substantial. Sixty percent of the world's illiterates are women, and while three-fourths of young girls get elementary education, only one-fourth get an opportunity for any training beyond elementary school. Although more women are in agriculture than in any other occupation, only 10 percent of graduates from the world's agricultural training programs are women (Boulding, 1977a:24-25). Ester Boserup (1970) has documented how technological advance always widens the gap between the conditions of work of women and men, since the men get the new tools and women are left to work in the marginal areas of the occupation with the old tools. This "Boserup effect" is equally noticeable in the first and the third world. If we look at the participation of women in one subsystem in the world economy, such as food systems-related occupations, industries, and training, as in Table 4, we quickly see that education is the only area where women have anything like equal access for training and for jobs. The fact that only 10 percent of women ever get to be administrators, however, suggests that they are as tool-less in education as elsewhere. In fact, the ease with which women are admitted to the teaching field is probably related to the low status of the educational field.

In the third world there is a triple dualism effect at work loading extra handicaps on women. On top of the traditional gender-based dualism which leaves women working with fewer and poorer tools than men, there is the phenomenon to which dualism usually refers, the division of a society into a subsistence sector untouched by industrial development, and a small modernized sector where all the "advantages" of modernization are to be found in a privileged enclave.

In the third world the phenomenon of economic dualism puts an extra loading of disadvantage on women. First, unless they are part of a small privileged elite, they are part of the subsistence sector untouched by industrial development, barred with their families from the advantages of modernization. Second, within that subsistence sector, they have the poorest tools and the heaviest work load. Their long daily journeys hauling water and wood are now known to the world conscience, but this is only a small part of their total work day. When technical assistance experts come to improve agricultural practices, they work with the men and leave the women's work untouched, except for passing out nutrition and childcare information unusable by the women given their resources and work load. Documentation of women's actual work load, and publicity regarding their technical assistance needs, is growing as a result of International Women's Year projects, but technical assistance is still a very male-oriented field. The most helpful signal of changes to come is that agricultural schools in the United States and Europe are admitting increasing numbers of women. When technical assistance

TABLE 4

WORLD SUMMARY OF THE FEMALENESS OF FOOD SYSTEMS-RELATED
OCCUPATIONS, INDUSTRIES AND TRAINING*

Category	World Mean	World High	World Low
World Labor Force	29	54	04
Agriculture	23	59	00
Manufacturing	25	74	00
Transportation, Storage, and Communication Industry	08	24	00
Service Workers	50	88	06
Financing, Insurance, Real Estate and Business Services, and Community, Social, and Personal Services	41	75	04
Trade, Restaurant and Hotel Industries	31	88	01
Professional and Technical Work	38	64	06
Administrative and Managerial Work	10	47	01
Teachers: Elementary	51		
Secondary	37		
Women Graduates in:			
Education	49	90	07
Engineering	05	28	00
Agriculture	11	40	01

* Females as a proportion of the total population in that industry,
  occupation or training.

SOURCE: Boulding (1977a:154).

103

teams are 50 percent women, the Boserup effect may begin to fade in the third world. In the meantime, the ingenuity of women in maintaining complex barter and mutual aid systems outside the monetary economy, not only in Africa and Asia but in purdah-keeping parts of the Middle East, somewhat mitigates the hardships and even hints at a world of festivity and celebration rarely observed by outsiders (Boulding, 1977a: Chapter 4).

The Boserup effect still seems to hold in the first world, however. Strong public commitments to removing legal and occupational barriers to women's fuller participation in all sectors of society seems to have had little effect in terms of employment opportunities and income levels, as similar commitments have had little effect in improving the situation of other minorities. The income differentials between women and men with regard to that category of persons who have the most economic responsibility-- heads of households --is approximately 2:1. Partnerless women with dependent children are severely limited in what they can do for those children. Table 5 gives an idea of the extent of labor force participation of U.S. women with children, whether or not they are heads of household. Given the lack of norms for equal sharing of household and parenting tasks between women and men, it can be seen that increased numbers of women have a heavy double responsibility in home and work force in industrial societies. Table 6 summarizes gender-based labor force inequality for the world by rank ordering countries according to the amount of redistribution of women and men that would be required between occupational sectors in order to have equality of occupational participation. The figure that emerges from the appropriate calculations for each country we have labeled the Segregation Index. A high index of segregation means that there would have to be a great deal of reshuffling of women and men between occupations for equality of job opportunity to exist. It will be noted from Table 6 that substantial occupational segregation is found on all continents. The "top ten" for occupational segregation includes countries from Latin America, Asia, and Europe; only Africa is missing from the ten. Looking at the highs and lows by continent, we see that Africa has the least over-all segregation. When we realize that 68 countries, including North America and most of Europe, keep from 26 to 80 percent of their female work force relatively immobile in terms of job opportunity, we realize what a long road there is to travel to reach occupational equality.

The two most intractable aspects of exclusion of women from the types of societal participation they seek are on the one hand the continued exclusion of women from administrative and decision-making posts where they could effectuate significant social change, and on the other hand the continuing non-participation of fathers in substantial parenting activities in the home. Both are changing, though slowly. Some fathers participate in natural childbirth with their wives and take part-time rather than full-time jobs to spend more time with their children. The United Nations and many national governments and houses of parliament are now aware of how few

TABLE 5

LABOR FORCE PARTICIPATION RATES OF WOMEN: 1950-1972, BY
PRESENCE AND AGE OF CHILDREN (FOR EVER-MARRIED WOMEN)

Year[1]	Total	No children under 18 years	Children under 6 years	Children 6 to 17 years only
1950.	26.8	31.4	13.6	32.8
1955.	30.6	33.9	18.2	38.4
1960.	32.7	35.0	20.2	42.5
1965.	35.7	36.5	25.3	45.7
1966.	36.4	37.0	26.2	46.5
1967.	37.5	36.7	28.7	48.6
1968.	38.5	37.6	29.2	49.7
1969.	39.5	38.3	30.4	50.7
1970.	40.4	38.8	32.2	51.5
1971.	40.2	38.4	31.4	52.0
1972.	41.1	42.9	31.9	52.6

Note: Percent of civilian noninstitutional population. Includes women who are married, separated, widowed, or divorced.

[1]Data for 1950-1967 include women 14 years old and over; data for 1968-1972 include women 16 years old and over.

SOURCE: Social Indicators (1973:142).

TABLE 6

INDEX OF SEGREGATION OF ECONOMIC
ACTIVITY BY OCCUPATION

Rank	Country	Indicator	Rank	Country	Indicator
1	Nauru	0.7970	44	Austria	0.3634
2	Honduras	0.7487	45	Barbados	0.3622
3	Panama	0.6447	46	Switzerland	0.3593
4	Bahrain	0.6334	47	Singapore	0.3562
5	Dominican Rep.	0.6311	48	Malta	0.3541
6	El Salvador	0.6230	49	Cyprus	0.3538
7	Guatemala	0.6181	50	Tunisia	0.3517
8	Costa Rica	0.5894	51	Netherlands	0.3511
9	Norway	0.5486	52	France	0.3478
10	Kuwait	0.5408	53	Egypt	0.3468
11	Portugal	0.5188	54	Angola	0.3343
12	South Africa	0.5168	55	Spain	0.3327
13	Cuba	0.5128	56	Libya	0.3305
14	Luxembourg	0.5106	57	Czechoslovakia	0.3242
15	Chile	0.5105	58	Puerto Rico	0.3240
16	Nicaragua	0.5086	59	Poland	0.3236
17	Columbia	0.5069	60	Denmark	0.3203
18	Ecuador	0.4853	61	Namibia	0.3166
19	Ireland	0.4752	62	Ryukyu Islands	0.3095
20	Canada	0.4740	63	Hungary	0.2835
21	Venezuela	0.4724	64	Morocco	0.2704
22	Bahamas	0.4723	65	Belgium	0.2678
23	Paraguay	0.4718	66	Malaysia	0.2661
24	Australia	0.4675	67	Jordan	0.2577
25	Jamaica	0.4668	68	Japan	0.2475
26	New Zealand	0.4623	69	Yugoslavia	0.2413
27	Great Britain	0.4557	70	Greece	0.2387
28	Rhodesia	0.4463	71	Ghana	0.2368
29	Philippines	0.4444	72	Zambia	0.2348
30	Sweden	0.4425	73	Grenada	0.2329
31	United States	0.4416	74	Sri Lanka	0.2214
32	Uruguay	0.4308	75	Sierra Leone	0.2209
33	Algeria	0.4277	76	Liberia	0.2148
34	Surinam	0.4276	77	Germany, West	0.1812
35	Argentina	0.4270	78	Korea, South	0.1633
36	Nigeria	0.4212	79	India	0.1353
37	Peru	0.4133	80	Tanzania	0.1301
38	Guyana	0.3926	81	Khmer	0.1269
39	Trinidad/	0.3913	82	Pakistan	0.1255
40	Iran	0.3902	83	Hong Kong	0.0921
41	Swaziland	0.3794	84	Indonesia	0.0883
42	Mauritius	0.3746	85	Thailand	0.0872
43	Iceland	0.3718	86	Botswana	0.0452

TABLE 6 (CONTINUED)

```
        Africa
High            0.5168  South Africa
Low             0.0452  Botswana
Mean            0.2978  N = 13

        North Africa and
        the Middle East
High            0.6334  Bahrain
Low             0.2577  Jordan
Mean            0.3903  N = 9

        Asia
High            0.7970  Nauru
Low             0.0872  Thailand
Mean            0.2812  N = 17

        Latin America
High            0.7487  Honduras
Low             0.2329  Grenada
Mean            0.4860  N = 24


High            0.5486  Norway
Low             0.1812  Germany, West
Mean            0.3707  N = 23
```

SOURCE: Boulding, Nuss, Carson and Greenstein (1976:132-33).

women they have and of the tremendous "human rights" advantage socialist countries have with their 30 percent participation of women in state and national governing bodies, compared with a 2 percent participation in most of Western Europe and the United States. Token high-ranking appointments for women are the order of the day, and make the removal of gender differentiation even harder because of the abnormal social and occupational roles token women have to play. The development of new role performance patterns for both women and men who want to work in the public arenas of society less combatively will be slow in coming.

INTERACTION BETWEEN AGE AND GENDER: THE THREE AGES

Age, like gender, is a biologically-based status criterion. Yet unlike gender, one's age status changes from time to time. We have already discussed our conceptualization of the three different "gender ages" over a lifetime, from the androgyny of the young to the androgyny of the old. It is only from puberty to menopause (and its male equivalent) that each person is socially restricted to gender role behavior appropriate to that gender. While there are departures from the norm, during this period aggressive females and nurturant males are not as highly valued as nurturant females and aggressive males. Sometime in the fifties, or perhaps not until retirement (in societies that evoke that category), there is a role reversal (Gutmann, n.d.). Women move from passive to active mastery while the men move in the opposite direction. Often the wife and older son pair up to take control of the father and the rest of the family. Women's lifelong repertoire of adaptive skills, and especially their social bonding skills, put them at an advantage in any moves and in any new situations that must be met in the later years. Where older women, particularly widowed women, move to the city to seek new challenges and to find new members of old kin networks, older men return to the country to redevelop familiar parts of old kin networks. Where older men suffer from loss of former role and status, women are used to teasing as many dimensions as possible out of an initially thin role, and having to make do with inferior status. Reduction of domestic responsibilities with the empty nest and death of aged parents gives them new freedom to work at role creation. Addition of domestic responsibilities for older men give them new experiences of active nurturance roles. Older men "rule," to the extent that they do, by force of ascribed authority and knowledge of power systems; women "rule" by the force of an expanding social experience and knowledge of human nature. This force of older women is in fact sometimes feared in a society, and measures will be taken to control their power, such as labeling them witches.

Gender-role maturation for women then means moving from (1) androgyny with socialization for femininity to (2) full feminine role to (3) feminine role transformed with the aid of a strong masculine component. For men the same sequence involves (1) androgyny with socialization for masculinity, (2) full masculine role, and (3) masculine role transformed with the aid of a strong feminine component. One might characterize both sexes as moving, in the ideal sequence from an undifferentiated androgyny to a differentiated androgyny over a lifetime. A fuller awareness of this process may be the key to reducing inappropriate gender-based role assignments.

AGE DIFFERENTIATION

The Social Meaning of Age

Since aging has clearcut physiological concomitants, so that one has no difficulty in distinguishing the young from the middle-years person from the old, it is perhaps somewhat surprising that the more a society undergoes what is known as "modernization" the further that society departs from age categorizations based on physiological and developmental characteristics. Since it is the "modern" societies, primarily Western, that are supplying categories and methodologies for the application of equal rights concepts to human beings of various ages and conditions, the age-sorting to be described in this part of our study, even though it conforms neither to traditional usage nor to physiological reality, is increasingly being adopted as a national practice in all societies as part of the "modernization" process. The sorting process that divides human beings into under 25's,[3] 25 to 55-year-olds and over 55's, is a process that has been uniquely useful to one group of modernizing countries in Europe in the latter part of the last century, and in this century. Through mandatory schooling the sorting process upgraded the skill of the next generation's labor power while withholding it from the labor market as a competitive lower-cost source of labor. Through retirement it also excluded the competition of cheap elderly laborers. In each age group, as we shall see, women have been further differentially excluded (as have ethnic, racial, and class minorities). Other approaches to upgrading labor skills and spreading labor requirements over a larger share of the population have been considered anti-progressive in capitalist societies, although various socialist societies have experimented with alternative patterns. The three ages concept, however, with labor requirements being largely met by the middle-years population, has tended to operate as an ideal in socialist as well as in capitalist societies.
Persons under 21 (sometimes under 25) are legally minors in most countries. This means that they may not receive any economic or social services except through their parents, or, if parents are declared incompetent, through the courts. In no country, to my knowledge, is there a body of statutory law setting forth the rights of persons under 21. Neither is there any legal agreement on who is a child.

The age below which children are considered incapable of crime varies from country to country. In Scotland it is still eight years of age, though 10 or 12 is more commonly established as the age below which children are "incapable of guile." Ten to 14-year old offenders have special legal protection in most countries, and 14 to 18-year olds go before special juvenile courts. In some countries youth have some special treatment as young adult offenders from 18 to 25 or as old as 30, before they become "regular" adult offenders. In the United States a 13-year old can be tried for and convicted of murder, but an 18-year old needs parental consent to marry and under 21 (he or) she cannot sign contracts, sell property or do other business that will be upheld in a court of law, even if that person is married and supporting children. According to Foner (1973:29), "the adolescent is also denied service on juries, membership in the legislature and on government boards and agencies, control of his property and person, and a multitude of other rights and decision-making power." Children do not have the right to choose their own school, their own religion, or the parents they would like to live with if their parents divorce. They do not have the right of privacy over against parental censorship, nor the right to the money they earn, until they are 21 (Boulding, 1977b).

It is one thing for the young, who have never known any other condition, to experience the powerlessness of minority status. It is quite another thing for the old, who have once been powerful, to experience that minority status. Alexander (1975:268) writes about the entry of the elderly into a managed state after a life of freedom, with restricted rights to manage their own property, to determine their life style, and how "it is...because it is unaccustomed." Much of the power loss of the elderly relates to drastically reduced income and associated reduction of life style choices. Other power losses refer to loss of status with loss of job, particularly severe for men because their social identity and their job identity are one. The disinclination of the community to give important civic roles to retirees reinforces the sense of status loss. The most severe power loss of all, however, is to have the court appoint a guardian to manage one's affairs, an event that may occur to an elderly person with as much decision-making capacity as many middle-years persons whose right to manage their affairs is never contested. With age, the elderly person's judgment in business and personal affairs becomes subject to scrutiny in ways that would be considered an unwarranted invasion of privacy between the ages of 25 and 65.

Loss of power is of course relative to social class. In fact, the onset of aging is as much a matter of class definition as of biology. For the working classes, aging begins at 45; few are considered hireable after job loss at that age. For the middle class it is 55, and for the upper class it can be postponed for a long time--sometimes into the seventies. Income differentials increase sharply for the elderly. The rich get richer and the poor get much poorer. Women are the poorest of all, and live the longest in their poverty.

The characteristics of the old and young, and their untapped potentials for social participation, will be explored more fully in the next section. What will show up clearly is that the "powerful" suffer as much as the "powerless" from the exclusion of the young and old from the work force and from civic participation.

MATURATION PROCESS FROM YOUTH TO AGE

The three stages concept of the life cycle, in its emphasis on presence or absence of rights and status, masks the rich developmental processes that unfold from childhood to old age. In fact, the social attitutdes toward childhood and old age imply that persons in these age categories have nothing of importance to contribute to society. The sections that follow are intended to show how false those implications are, and how impoverishing for the societies that act on these attitudes.

Developmental Strengths of the Young

Basic intellecting capacities are present very young in children. Complex moral and political reasoning can take place at least by the ages of 12 to 14, if not younger (Piaget, 1932; see also Elkind, 1970, Susan Isaacs, 1930, Hess and Torney, 1967, Kohlberg, 1963, Erickson, 1964). The ages from 10 to 14 appear to be a period during which children's cognitive capacities and social institutions produce creative new social responses which remain cut off from the world of adults. (See for example the story of experimental children's communities from the 1920s on, in the Soviet Union, Europe, and England [Berg, 1971:9-50].) As discussed more fully elsewhere (Boulding, 1977b), in our own time...children from a very young age are required, as are women, to do heavy physical labor that in theory is not suited to their physical capacities. They serve and tend their own parents, and become parents themselves, all while still legally minors. They fight wars, mount relief operations, design international institutions--all between the ages of 12 and 21. It is only necessary for each of us to remember back to our own childhood, what we coped with, what insights we gained, to realize how much children endure, how much they have to give that adults never notice (Milgram and Sciarral, 1974; Boulding, 1963 and 1976). Least noticed of all, children enrich the lives of adults through play.

Elsewhere (Boulding, 1977c) I have analyzed the role of the child in the family as the provider of creative and playful activity which adults have lost the capacity to engage in alone. The low status of playful and creative activity in the community reinforces the low status of the child that engages in it, and renders increasingly inaccessible this recreative activity for persons of all ages.

111

<u>Developmental Strengths of the Elderly</u>

The loss-of-functioning findings based on cross-sectional studies of performance by age are now being questioned by longitudinal studies which do not show these decrements in functioning. Rather they show an increase with aging in what intelligence tests call "crystallized intelligence," measuring acculturational skills, and in visualization, the ability to organize and process visual materials, even in the period from age 70 to 77 (Barton, et al., 1975:224-236). The aged like everyone else vary in performance capacity according to genetic ability, educational level, life experience, health, and current circumstances, but the evidence seems to be increasingly clear that on the average the elderly keep growing in certain areas of mental functioning until death. Personality differentiation also continues until death. The much-noted withdrawal phenomenon associated with aging has to be seen in the context of need to protect the self from environmental and social stress, and also as a shift in value priorities according to new insights. The ancient wisdom of East and West about the withdrawal into the forest to ponder the nature of humanity and the social order after children have been reared appears to arise independently at the appropriate time in the life cycle, in widely differing types of societies. Generational analysis, linking the knowledge of the elderly with that of the middle-years shapers of society, has yet to be made. The elderly, knowing more of the past, may have more wide-ranging views of the future than those who have lived a shorter time. When the elderly are more optimistic than the young, as they sometimes are, it might be important to find out why.

The specific intellecting capacities of the young and the old, each at their own kind of biosocial peak, are important for society. The different capacities for social construction based on the most recent first-hand experience of social reality in the young, and the oldest accessible experience of that reality in the old, may be equally crucial in dealing with a time of systems break, when current modes of social operation and problem setting may be irrelevant.

THE EFFECTS OF INDUSTRIALIZATION ON AGE DIFFERENTIATION

Certain types of human experience appear to be very widespread if not universal, such as the experience of gender maturation for both sexes in most societies. Other types of experiences are markedly different, as between industrial and non-industrial societies. These differences are most clear in the extent to which the two types of societies involve the young and the old in major economic and social responsibilities. Figure 2 is a schematic representation of the participation of old and young in industrial and non-industrial societies. Figure 3 is a schematic representation of the status of the aged as societies modernize, based on the Palmore and Morton Equality Index (Gutmann,

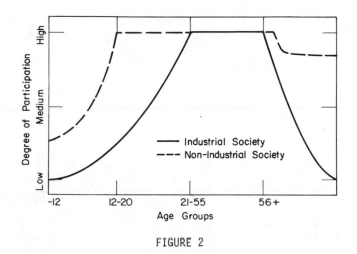

FIGURE 2

SCHEMATIC REPRESENTATION OF PARTICIPATION BY AGE IN LABOR
FORCE IN INDUSTRIALIZED AND NON-INDUSTRIALIZED SOCIETIES

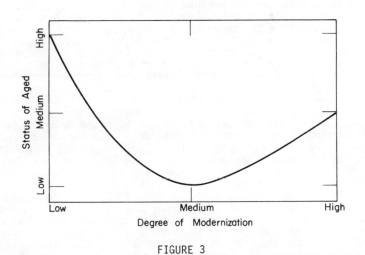

FIGURE 3

SCHEMATIC REPRESENTATION OF STATUS OF THE AGED
BY DEGREE OF MODERNIZATION

n.d.:51). The workload is spread more evenly across the total life span in non-industrial societies. With industrialization there is an increasing restriction of the social space of the elderly, and a heavy loading of economic and social responsibility on a narrow age range. Only among the well-to-do is there a status and participation curve similar to that of the non-industrial societies for the elderly. For the middle classes, aging is usually considered to begin at 55, an increasingly "popular" retirement age. For the working classes, aging begins at 45. Past that age an unemployed worker finds great difficulty in being rehired. Given that youth is generally not totally integrated into the labor force before 18 or 20, and not given major responsibility, either on the job or in civic roles, before 25, we have the phenomenon of much of society's work being done by persons between the ages of 25 and 55, a preponderance of them men. The rates at which all parts of the world's population are aging, and the greater longevity of women than men, suggest that this pattern, if followed by parts of the world now becoming industrialized, would place an increasingly heavy burden on middle-years folk. Table 7 shows the current and estimated distribution of first and third world populations among these age groups, and Table 8 gives United Nations estimates of the proportion of persons over 60 between now and 2000 for the first and third worlds. The industrialized world will increasingly feel the impact of human aging in the next twenty years.

Since problems of age and gender differentiation will be unequally felt by different parts of the world, the remainder of this study will present comparative data on participation of the young and the old for 15 countries representing major world regions. The countries are chosen mainly because of the adequacy of the data in the categories needed for this analysis. Table 9 gives some of the characteristics of the 15 countries, so their representativeness for our purposes can be seen. The three African countries, Egypt, Algeria and Tanzania, two of them from Moslem North Africa, range from 52 to 95 percent nonurban, and from $130 to $570 GNP. Only the richest, Algeria, has a GNP growth that outstrips population growth. Thus the African countries cover a fairly wide range of economic conditions, although they do not include the poorest countries, for which data are not available. The three Asian countries, Japan, Philippines, and Thailand, range from 24 to 91 percent nonurban, from $270 to $3,630 GNP, and two of the three countries have economic growth rates well exceeding population growth. In that sense they are not typical of Asia, but were chosen as the African countries were, because they have the most complete data on the young and the old. The six countries of Euro-North America (France, Hungary, Sweden, Spain, United Kingdom, United States) were chosen to include the richer and the less rich, socialist and non-socialist, and a variety of cultural traditions. All but the United Kingdom have more than 50 percent of their population living in centers of less than 20,000. All have economic growth rates substantially exceeding population growth rates, and are approaching zero population growth. Latin America (Colombia, Mexico, and Peru)

114

TABLE 7

COMPOSITION OF THE POPULATION OF THE WORLD AND MAJOR
AREAS BY AGE-GROUP, ESTIMATES FOR 1960

Age	World [a,b,c] Total	East [c] Asia	South [b] Asia	Europe	Soviet Union	Africa	North America	Latin America	Oceania [c]
% Population Age 0-25	53.5	53.8	59.3	40.3	46.9	62.4	45.0	60.2	46.4
% Population Age 25-55	35.2	35.9	32.9	39.4	39.1	30.6	37.4	31.8	37.9
% Population Age 55+	11.3	10.3	7.8	20.3	14.0	7.0	17.6	8.0	15.7

[a] Not including North Korea and the Ryukyu Islands.
[b] Not including Israel and Cyprus.
[c] Not including Polynesia and Micronesia.

SOURCE: United Nations (1964: Table II, Appendix B).

TABLE 8

ACTUAL AND ESTIMATED PROPORTIONS OF THE WORLD
POPULATION, AGE 60 YEARS AND OVER, FOR MORE
DEVELOPED AND LESS DEVELOPED COUNTRIES

Region	Year	Percent of Total Population
World	1950	7.6
	1970	8.0
	1985	8.2
	2000	9.0
More	1950	11.3
Developed	1970	14.1
Countries	1985	14.8
	2000	15.9
Less	1950	5.6
Developed	1970	5.4
Countries	1985	6.0
	2000	7.0

SOURCE: United Nations (1975:22, Table 7).

TABLE 9

ECONOMIC AND SOCIAL VARIABLES

	Africa			Asia			Euro-North America						Latin America		
	Egypt	Algeria	Tanzania	Japan	Philip-pines	Thailand	France	Hungary	Sweden	Spain	United Kingdom	United States	Colombia	Mexico	Peru
% Population under Age 24 [a]	59.0	63.7	60.2	39.5	62.9	63.7	39.9	37.5	34.0	43.2	38.6	43.9	64.7	65.1	62.8
% Population Age 25-54 [a]	26.5	26.9	30.6	44.6	29.6	26.5	35.7	39.0	38.9	37.9	36.2	36.3	38.2	27.2	28.9
% Population Age 55+ [a]	14.5	9.2	9.1	15.9	8.0	7.2	24.5	23.5	27.1	18.9	25.0	19.8	7.1	7.7	8.1
Population Growth Rate, 1965-1973 [b]	2.5	3.4	2.8	1.2	3.0	3.0	0.8	0.3	0.7	1.1	0.4	1.0	2.8	3.5	2.9
Population in Centers under 20,000 [c]	52.0	73.5	94.9	24.3	36.8	91.2	58.1	58.2	55.8	54.6	16.6	53.0	43.0	70.4	64.8
GNP Per Capita [b]	250	570	130	3,630	280	270	4,540	1,850	5,910	1,710	3,060	6,200	440	890	620
Economic Growth Rate, 1965-1973 [b]	0.8	4.3	2.6	9.6	2.6	4.5	5.0	2.7	2.4	5.3	2.3	2.5	3.1	2.8	1.8

[a] Yearbook of Labor Statistics (United Nations, 1976a:Table 1).
[b] Boulding Global Data Bank.
[c] Boulding, Carson, Nuss and Greenstein (1976).

has a wider range of nonurban, 43 to 65 percent. GNP per capita ranges from $440 to $890, and only one of the three, Colombia, has an economic growth rate that exceeds population growth. Taken all together, the countries represent the rich and the not rich of the first, second, and third worlds, but not the very poor.

AGE DIFFERENTIATION AND SOCIAL ROLES

Employment of the Young and the Old

One of the supposed blessings of modernization has been the removal of the necessity to work for the young and the old. Yet no welfare-oriented state, no matter how affluent, has been willing to provide adequately for the economic needs at the two ends of the age spectrum, nor has it been able to offer fully satisfying alternatives to economic production roles. The school drop-out rates in the United States, beginning in elementary school, suggest the inadequacy of schools as the main focus of life for the young. The bitterness of many on-the-shelf retirees suggests the inadequacy of workload removal as the focus of life for the old. At the same time, the assignment of minority status to the young and to the old, with legal restrictions on their activities and the attendant possibilities of employing the young and the old at substandard wages, has led to exploitation, poverty, and misery for both groups.

Comparative information about wage scales by age is not available, so in the analysis that follows only presence or absence from the labor force is documented. The fact that under 20s and over 65s are paid less than the middle-years work force is indirectly demonstrated by Figure 4 which shows the disproportionate number of under 22s and over 65s at the poverty level as determined by various federal agencies in the United States. The under 22s include children as well as the employed young, and the over 65s include both employed elders and pensioners.

There are enormous differences in patterning of employment by age and sex from country to country, even within the same region, and yet also certain similarities. The most striking similarity across culture regions and development zones is the disparity in employment of women as compared to men, although this disparity does not apply at all ages.[4] Looking first at the young, we see from Table 10 that countries from all regions report some employment of under 15s. One-half to two-thirds of 15 to 19-year-old males are in the work force in all regions, working at a time when they are still legally children and have no contractual rights. Teen-age women are employed at close to the same rate as men or higher in Tanzania, Japan, Thailand, and in Hungary, Sweden, and the United Kingdom. Elsewhere employment of teen-age women ranges from 4 percent in Moslem North Africa to nearly 50 percent in the United States. The large numbers of teen-age women not in the labor force are either unpaid family laborers or mothers rearing their own children.

If we compare the work load carried by the disfranchised young with the workload carried by the disfranchised old, the over-65s,

FIGURE 4

PERSONS BELOW THE LOW-INCOME LEVEL, BY AGE:
1959-1971, U.S.A.

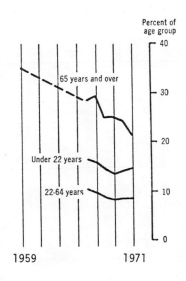

SOURCE: Social Indicators (1973:166).

TABLE 10

PARTICIPATION IN LABOR FORCE BY SEX AND AGE:
UNDER 15s, PEAK AGE EMPLOYMENT AND OVER 65s

Employment Age Group	Africa			Asia			Euro-North America						Latin America		
	Egypt	Algeria	Tanzania	Japan	Philippines	Thailand	France	Hungary	Sweden	Spain	United Kingdom	United States	Colombia	Mexico	Peru
% Men Under 15	9.6	2.0	6.5	--	5.7	10.1	--	0.3	--	2.2	--	--	7.2	2.2	1.6
% Women Under 15	1.1	0.6	6.6	--	3.6	11.7	--	0.9	--	1.1	--	--	4.0	0.9	1.3
% Men, 16-19	49.0	65.7	59.3	23.0	52.4	77.4	42.8	45.8	56.5	65.9	60.8	60.6	54.1	59.9	39.8
% Women, 16-19	4.2	3.7	65.5	22.6	31.5	77.2	31.3	49.1	52.2	36.7	55.7	49.0	25.1	20.9	17.7
% Men at Peak Employment Age															
15-19	--	--	--	--	--	--	--	--	--	--	--	--	--	--	--
20-24	--	--	--	--	--	--	--	--	--	--	--	--	--	--	--
25-29	--	96.2	--	--	--	--	--	98.5	--	--	--	--	--	--	--
30-44	98.4*	--	--	98.7	90.5	96.5	97.0	--	95.8	96.8	98.2	95.6	92.7	--	--
45-49	--	--	95.9	--	--	--	--	--	--	--	--	--	--	93.9	97.1
% Women at Peak Employment Age															
15-19	37.7	--	--	--	--	--	--	--	--	--	--	--	--	--	--
20-24	9.7	--	--	66.8	--	--	--	--	--	39.6	--	--	--	--	--
25-29	--	--	--	--	--	--	--	--	--	--	--	--	--	--	--
30-44	--	--	80.1	--	--	79.6	--	69.7	--	--	--	--	--	--	--
45-49	--	--	--	38.7	38.7	--	45.5	--	77.9	--	61.5	55.6	--	--	--
% Men Over 65	38.6	33.3	79.6	49.5	56.5	44.6	19.3	--#	12.6	21.4	19.3	20.8	61.8	70.4	61.5
% Women Over 64	0.7	1.4	42.0	15.5	17.7	21.2	8.2	--#	3.6	3.9	6.3	7.8	13.8	10.9	8.5

*Refers to age group 30-49.
#No over 65 reported; percentage men employed at 60-64 is 74.9; percentage women employed at 60-64 is 30.0.
SOURCE: Boulding Data Bank.

the differences between industrial and non-industrial societies are very great, including gender differences. In Euro-North America, only 12 to 20 percent of men over 65 are in the work force. In the rest of the world, from 33 percent to over 75 percent of men are still working. Only the women drop way back compared to earlier participation, though third world older women are much more in the labor force than first world women.

The middle section of Table 10 shows the percentage of men and women employed in the age period of peak employment for each sex in each country. There is some variation for the men. There are recorded peaks in the mid-forties for men in three non-industrial countries, but in most countries men between the ages of 30 and 44 are carrying the peak employment load in the enumerated labor force. For women, the peak load varies widely, with one clustering at ages 20 to 24, mainly in the third world, and another clustering at ages 45-50, for both Europe and the third world. The ages 25 to 45 are the prime childbearing and childrearing ages. The youthful women's labor force is a low-status group because of inexperience, and the older women's labor force is low-status because the mid-years' career of childbearing does not accumulate seniority in the job world. It would be interesting to know the reason for the greater rates of leaving the labor force for women after 65, considering that the entry to the labor force has already been so late, in the mid-forties. Whether the leaving is voluntary or involuntary is not clear.

The early leaving may have something to do with the character of the occupations available. Table 11 shows the six most frequent occupations for men and women in the United States, for over 65s. Household and service work which is the most common occupation for women after 65 may not seem very attractive. Early leaving also has something to do with the fact that norms about retirement in some countries mandate earlier retirement for women than men, as Table 12 shows. Given the different attitudes toward aging and retirement on the part of women and men mentioned earlier, women in comfortable circumstances might prefer the freedom to organize their own time outside the work force, and to rely on the kin network for social and economic support. However, available evidence indicates that poverty hits older women much harder than older men, particularly in industrial societies, where they also live much longer. Women may be more restricted than men from seeking employment by age rules or pension regulations, although both sexes are handicapped in employment by age. Women are also more likely to be in demand for home care and nursing of spouses or other relatives.

Family Role Transitions for the Young and the Old

While legal age of marriage for women varies from 12 in Spain, Colombia, and Peru to 18 in Sweden and the United States, the years between 15 and 19 see a significant role transition for many young women in all parts of the world as they enter marriage,

TABLE 11

RANK ORDERING OF SIX MOST FREQUENT OCCUPATIONS,
BY SEX, OF EMPLOYED PERSONS 65 AND OLDER

	Male Workers			Female Workers	
R A N K	Occupations	% Employed Persons of This Age Group in These Occupations	R A N K	Occupations	% Employed Persons of This Age Group in These Occupations
1	Farmers	15.9	1	Private and Household Workers	19.4
2	Craftsmen	14.3	2	Service Workers	15.5
3	Managers	13.8	3	Clerical	13.9
4	Professionals	8.4	4	Professional	12.9
5	Sales	8.2	5	Operatives	10.4
6	Clerical	6.2	6	Sales	8.8

SOURCE: Riley and Foner (1968:50).

TABLE 12

NORMAL RETIREMENT AGE FOR MEN AND WOMEN*

Country	Normal Retirement Age	
	Women	Men
France	65	65
Hungary	55	60
Sweden	55	67
Spain	65	65
United Kingdom	60	65
United States	65	65

* According to public policy.

SOURCE: United Nations (1975:33, Table 9).

122

consensual unions (not recorded), and motherhood in or out of wedlock. We see from Table 13 that for most of the third world, from one-third to one-half of teen-age women marry during this period. The same is true for some first world countries, including Hungary and the United States. In others, like Sweden, as few as 7 percent marry that young. The United States has one of the highest rates of birth for teen-age mothers in the world, Japan the lowest. The sorting that takes place with marriage and motherhood creates special roles for women, besides labor force roles, that they carry until menopause. The counterpart roles for men involve primarily labor force roles with some parenting.

If the teens are the years of family formation, the sixties and the seventies are the years of family dissolution as spouses die, separate, or divorce. Widowhood is the primary sorting experience at this age. In most countries during these decades divorce accounts for only 1 to 3 percent of marital dissolutions. (Tanzania is an exception. Divorce accounts for 28 percent of marital dissolutions.) The role convergence that develops as retirement nears helps both sexes deal with the special and demanding role of self-sufficient widowhood. This is a role that previous life experience prepares neither sex for. Both assertive and nurturant social capacities are required to create a new, live-alone life style (or new patterns of later-years remarriage). Legal and financial disabilities for elderly live-alones and remarrieds may be as severe as the legal and financial disabilities of teen-age parents. The elderly often avoid remarrying to avoid loss of testamentary rights to their property, or of pension rights.

Educational programs, which might serve as social balancers by offering educational opportunities at the interim, non-peak-load times in the life cycle for women and men, unfortunately do not work that way. Most young people struggle to finish their education by age 18 or 20, if not earlier, often loading parenthood and labor force participation on top of schooling activities. Only 8.3 percent of persons over 17 years of age participate in adult education programs in the United States, and the majority of these persons are concentrated in their late teens and early twenties. Only 1.5 percent of all participants in adult education programs are over 65. This is particularly sad since illiteracy rates are higher among the over 65s, who passed through school-age years at a time when availability and length of schooling were drastically limited compared to today (Social Indicators, 1973:110). Forced to compete with younger persons who have different rhythms of learning, and are often working under pressure, the elderly do not find adult education programs a source of pleasure, but rather one more source of insecurity. The many things the elderly could teach remain undiscovered by the young. There are signs that the tide is beginning to turn in some industrial countries, however, as agricultural and artisan skills now scarce among the young are being found among the elderly.

TABLE 13

YOUTH AND AGE: TEEN YEARS MARRIAGE AND BIRTH RATES, ELDERLY WIDOWHOOD RATES

	Africa			Asia			Euro-North America						Latin America		
	Egypt	Algeria	Tanzania	Japan	Philippines	Thailand	France	Hungary	Sweden	Spain	United Kingdom	United States	Colombia	Mexico	Peru
Women Under 20															
Legal Age of Marriage for Women[j]	16	--	--	16	14	--	15	14	18	12	16	18	12	14	12
Marriage Rates 15-19[g]	48.6	52.3	--	34.5	36.9	--	19.7	38.2	7.0	12.9	25.8	32.8	35.2	40.8	27.7
Births Per Woman 15-19[f]	.1921	.1276	--	.0122	.0772	.0831	.0635	.1487	.0486	.0278	.1021	.2536	.1115	--	.1187
Over 65, Both Sexes															
% Widowed 65-69[h]	--	45.5[abc]	14.6	32.9	--	32.7	24.1	27.5	18.5[a]	--	24.3[a]	24.2	26.7[ae]	21.9[e]	--
% Widowed 70-74[h]	--	--	23.9	45.0	--	49.3	36.0	40.0	27.9[a]	--	36.7[a]	33.9	33.4[ae]	26.7[e]	--
% Widowed 75+[h]	--	--	29.3	65.9	--	--	57.9	61.3	46.7[a]	--	56.5[a]	52.2	43.8[ae]	34.9[e]	--

[a]1971 Demographic Yearbook (United Nations, 1971:Table 12).
[b]Includes data for ages 65+.
[c]Divorced and separated are combined.
[d]Widowed and divorced are combined.

[e]Marriage rates do not include "consensually married."
[f]Boulding, Nuss, Carson, Greenstein (1976)
[g]1973 Demographic Yearbook (United Nations, 1974).
[h]1973 Demographic Yearbook (United Nations, 1974).

Inequality in Misery and Death

The greatest age and gender-related inequalities are found in illness, death from all causes, and suicide rates.[5] Not until age 65 (in some countries age 55) is an age cohort as susceptible again to fatal illness as it was in infancy. Tables 14a and 14b show what a heavy share of the burden of economic inequality and associated malnutrition and morbidity is borne by infants. The heaviest burden is borne by third world newborns, but a surprisingly heavy burden is also borne by newborns in countries like the United States, the United Kingdom, and Hungary. For the United States and the United Kingdom, these high infant death rates come from the internal third world of the poor. Survivors of that dangerous first year are given a brief respite from age 1 to 14, with the period from 5 to 14 being the safest age they will ever know in every country in the world. Death rates then climb slowly from 15 to 44 and then leap upwards from 45 until death. Death rates take longer to leap in the first world, since inequality in longevity is one of the major inequalities between first and third worlds.

The other most persistent inequality besides the heavy share of deaths among infants in every society, is the gender differential in death rates at every age in most countries. An inspection of the male and female death rates by age will show that more males than females die at every age from infancy on, in every country except Egypt, Colombia, Mexico, and Peru. Only in the more severe third world conditions is women's mortality higher, and then only at the two ends of the age spectrum. If there is genetic programming to protect the female of the species, it is a programming that lasts well into old age, long beyond the procreative years. What combination of genetic predisposition and differential social and physical stress produces this widespread effect is not understood.

Differential social stress would appear to be at work in generating the next major inequality, which is the differential suicide rate. Generally, suicide rates are much higher in the first than in the third world, and men's rates are much higher than women's, as we see from Tables 15a and 15b. A leap in suicide rates from the under 15s to the 15 to 24-year-olds in Euro-North America and Asia is notable. Lack of suicide figures for Africa leave us unable to guess whether they would be high as in Asia or as low as reported in Latin America. In Asia, women's suicide rates are much closer to men's than in Europe. They are actually higher for teen-age women than men in Thailand, where women and men participate in the labor force at the same rates (see Table 12). Nowhere do we see more clearly the generalized stress involved in entering marriage, childbearing, and labor force responsibilities in a concentrated brief period of time for teenagers than in the jump in suicide rates for this age group. What happens after the teen-age jump varies between first and third worlds? In Euro-North America there is a gradual climb from age 15 to death, with a second jump in rates after age 45. The same is true for Japan. In Thailand, the rates decline after age 24. The two suicide jumps associated with entry into and

TABLE 14a

DEATH RATES SPECIFIC FOR SEX AND AGE, PER 100,000 POPULATION (INFANT DEATHS PER 100,000 LIVE-BORN) (ASIA AND LATIN AMERICA)

Country	Sex	All Ages	0	1-4	5-14	15-24	25-34	35-44	45-54	55-64	65-74	75+
Egypt	T	1375.6	11156.6	2473.6	184.5	241.3	238.2	391.0	892.2	2006.4	6113.2	19889.2
	M	1381.0	10536.6	2135.3	202.2	284.2	304.5	498.6	1191.5	2727.4	7592.9	15820.0
	F	1370.1	11822.2	2831.2	165.4	195.7	179.2	280.4	593.8	1302.7	3790.8	23233.1
Japan	T	652.6	1132.1	98.5	35.4	82.2	105.1	213.5	443.2	1133.8	3196.2	10575.0
	M	719.3	1271.3	112.2	43.1	112.3	132.4	277.5	562.0	1496.0	4104.0	11999.8
	F	588.4	984.3	84.0	27.5	51.8	78.3	149.6	339.5	832.2	2432.3	9663.3
Philippines	T	704.8	7007.6	949.3	157.5	163.5	232.6	422.3	713.9	1260.4	5429.5	
	M	791.9	7777.2	984.9	172.5	206.2	281.4	493.3	903.7	1586.8	5670.7	
	F	618.5	6163.5	911.9	141.7	123.6	186.1	349.6	540.5	968.9	5200.3	
Thailand	T	534.7	2182.0	468.8	159.9	235.1	311.2	477.0	914.8	1671.7	3438.6	9389.5
	M	716.5	2469.6	485.7	172.1	290.0	380.3	555.1	1113.5	2074.7	4268.4	11014.7
	F	553.8	1875.9	451.5	147.3	182.6	245.1	399.0	720.0	1290.3	2746.5	8319.0
Colombia	T	713.1	5824.8	748.1	129.3	187.8	254.2	394.7	711.9	1663.4	4204.4	8965.3
	M	767.6	6343.1	728.2	141.1	235.8	312.0	425.8	785.4	1881.6	4690.6	9266.3
	F	660.2	5290.7	758.2	117.3	144.7	201.4	364.9	638.9	1451.6	3765.9	8737.9
Mexico	T	845.1	5185.3	723.7	125.6	213.4	345.3	543.2	904.6	1697.3	3721.6	10098.0
	M	917.3	5684.8	713.7	135.5	266.5	424.8	651.8	1080.3	1927.7	4010.0	10001.0
	F	773.1	4667.9	734.1	115.3	163.1	269.3	437.2	727.3	1473.1	3441.2	10178.5
Peru	T	640.3	7237.8	744.1	93.0	133.3	196.2	323.1	488.2	999.5	2363.5	9109.2
	M	656.2	7639.2	730.9	97.3	131.4	191.0	324.6	543.2	1147.3	2662.6	9080.3
	F	624.3	6816.3	757.8	88.6	135.1	201.6	321.6	433.7	859.6	2097.0	9132.1

SOURCE: United Nations (1976b:Table 7).

TABLE 14b

DEATH RATES SPECIFIC FOR SEX AND AGE, PER 100,000 POPULATION (INFANT DEATHS PER 100,000 LIVE-BORN) (EURO-NORTH AMERICA)

Country	Sex	All Ages	0	1-4	5-14	15-24	25-34	35-44	45-54	55-64	65-74	75+
France	T	1055.7	1262.5	74.5	36.3	106.9	115.8	253.2	577.7	1344.0	3069.2	9867.7
	M	1110.2	1409.4	83.1	43.1	151.7	156.8	338.6	801.2	1939.9	4351.8	11880.1
	F	1003.4	1107.6	65.6	29.3	60.0	71.1	163.8	360.4	820.0	2103.5	8932.7
Hungary	T	1182.6	3383.6	84.5	34.2	83.3	130.5	274.4	627.6	1602.9	4079.5	12074.7
	M	1267.0	3823.6	95.9	41.7	119.3	178.6	364.1	812.5	2083.8	5176.1	13898.7
	F	1103.0	2914.0	72.4	26.2	45.5	82.0	189.4	461.1	1196.2	3233.5	11025.0
Sweden	T	1057.6	950.2	43.9	27.9	68.6	90.5	181.5	451.2	1077.7	2879.9	9870.9
	M	1170.2	1049.7	49.0	32.2	95.2	124.0	231.8	585.2	1429.1	3760.8	11653.3
	F	946.0	844.5	38.5	23.4	40.9	54.7	129.8	317.6	736.7	2125.5	8653.6
Spain	T	856.8	1520.6	90.9	38.8	75.1	106.5	201.9	483.5	1214.1	3292.7	10888.3
	M	905.1	1724.8	97.1	46.6	104.4	139.4	260.3	638.4	1654.3	4271.3	12002.0
	F	810.7	1304.2	84.3	30.5	45.4	73.9	145.3	337.7	846.8	2546.0	10217.1
Great Britain	T	1194.7	1687.5	69.0	30.5	69.4	79.5	190.4	578.2	1506.6	3735.6	11208.9
	M	1240.0	1892.6	77.0	37.0	95.7	100.7	225.0	723.1	2042.2	5151.4	13635.7
	F	1151.8	1469.1	60.5	23.6	42.1	57.9	155.2	437.2	1022.2	2684.8	10098.3
United States	T	940.2	1771.8	79.5	41.0	128.2	153.6	295.9	697.4	1611.9	3440.0	9841.4
	M	1072.8	1988.8	88.8	50.0	189.8	214.5	380.4	916.6	2206.6	4731.5	11841.1
	F	814.1	1543.5	69.9	31.6	66.4	94.4	215.6	493.1	1079.8	2445.5	8635.9

SOURCE: United Nations (1976b:Table 7).

TABLE 15a

DEATH RATES SPECIFIC FOR SEX AND AGE, PER 100,000 POPULATION, FROM SUICIDE AND SELF-INFLICTED INJURY
(EURO-NORTH AMERICA)

Country	Sex	All Ages	0	1-4	5-14	15-24	25-34	35-44	45-54	55-64	65-74	75+
Japan	T	17.3	-----	-----	0.6	16.5	18.0	17.4	18.5	28.0	48.8	79.0
	M	20.1	-----	-----	0.8	19.9	22.4	22.9	21.7	33.6	53.5	87.4
	F	14.7	-----	-----	0.3	13.1	13.7	11.8	15.7	23.3	44.9	73.7
Philippines	T	1.4	-----	-----	0.1	3.3	2.0	1.4	1.7	1.7	2.1	
	M	1.6	-----	-----	0.1	3.6	2.4	1.9	2.7	3.0	3.4	
	F	1.1	-----	-----	0.2	3.1	1.6	1.0	0.9	0.6	0.8	
Thailand	T	4.4	-----	-----	0.5	10.5	6.3	5.6	5.6	5.1	5.3	6.4
	M	4.9	-----	-----	0.4	9.6	7.6	7.4	8.5	7.8	7.8	12.5
	F	3.9	-----	-----	0.7	11.5	5.0	3.9	2.7	2.5	3.2	2.4
Colombia	T	3.5	-----	-----	0.4	7.6	6.2	4.9	5.3	4.7	6.4	5.0
	M	4.9	-----	-----	0.4	8.6	10.7	8.0	8.4	8.7	13.1	9.7
	F	2.1	-----	-----	0.4	6.8	2.2	1.9	2.2	0.9	0.4	1.5
Mexico	T	0.7	-----	-----	-----	1.3	1.2	1.2	1.2	1.4	1.7	1.6
	M	1.1	-----	-----	-----	1.9	1.8	2.2	1.9	2.5	3.3	2.9
	F	0.3	-----	-----	-----	0.7	0.5	0.3	0.4	0.3	0.1	0.5
Peru	T	1.8	-----	-----	-----	3.5	2.7	2.5	3.2	2.5	4.1	7.4
	M	2.4	-----	-----	-----	3.5	3.7	4.1	5.8	4.5	8.1	8.4
	F	1.2	-----	-----	-----	3.6	1.7	0.9	0.6	0.7	0.6	6.6

SOURCE: United Nations (1976b:Table 7).

TABLE 15b

DEATH RATES SPECIFIC FOR SEX AND AGE, PER 100,000 POPULATION, FROM SUICIDE AND SELF-INFLICTED INJURY (ASIA AND LATIN AMERICA)

Country	Sex	All Ages	0	1-4	5-14	15-24	25-34	35-44	45-54	55-64	65-74	75+
France	T	15.5	---	---	0.3	7.7	12.1	16.6	23.8	30.5	35.1	39.4
	M	22.6	---	---	0.5	11.0	17.1	25.1	35.4	45.3	55.9	83.0
	F	8.7	---	---	0.1	4.3	6.7	7.7	12.5	17.6	19.4	19.1
Hungary	T	36.9	---	---	1.1	15.7	31.8	40.2	55.2	62.0	76.2	109.0
	M	53.2	---	---	1.9	24.8	48.7	64.4	82.7	92.5	106.0	177.4
	F	21.5	---	---	0.3	6.1	14.8	17.3	30.4	36.2	53.2	69.6
Sweden	T	20.1	---	---	0.3	12.5	21.1	26.4	32.9	31.5	31.8	24.2
	M	28.7	---	---	0.5	17.2	31.3	37.0	47.6	40.0	49.1	47.4
	F	11.5	---	---	---	7.5	10.3	15.4	18.3	23.2	17.0	8.3
Spain	T	4.2	---	---	0.2	1.4	2.7	4.2	6.8	9.3	13.6	14.1
	M	6.2	---	---	0.3	1.9	4.1	6.1	9.8	14.1	23.2	27.0
	F	2.3	---	---	0.0	0.8	1.3	2.3	4.0	5.2	6.3	6.4
Great Britain	T	7.8	---	---	0.1	4.4	7.2	10.2	12.0	13.3	14.6	14.2
	M	9.4	---	---	0.1	5.7	9.8	12.7	13.6	16.3	18.8	22.1
	F	6.2	---	---	0.1	3.0	4.6	7.7	10.5	10.7	11.5	10.6
United States	T	12.0	---	---	0.4	10.6	14.9	16.4	19.5	20.3	19.8	21.1
	M	17.7	---	---	0.6	17.0	21.9	21.8	26.9	30.5	34.5	44.7
	F	6.5	---	---	0.2	4.3	8.1	11.3	12.6	11.2	8.5	6.8

SOURCE: United Nations (1976:Table 7).

exit from the world of work and householding suggest how painful youth and age can be.
An added source of misery at the two ends of the age spectrum are the practices of child abuse and granny abuse. Poorly reported but receiving growing attention and concern in the industrial countries, these acts of deliberately inflicting injury on the young and the old are in a sense the answer of the proportionately shrinking population in the middle third of life to the concentration of responsibility thrust upon them. A recent eight-country study of child abuse and neglect (Kamerman, 1975: 34-37) indicates that few countries are prepared to define this as a serious social problem, and only two countries are attempting to develop a national reporting system for it (Boulding, 1977:53-61). Granny abuse is only beginning to be reported in the geriatric literature, and no statistics are available yet.

AGE AND GENDER-BASED INEQUALITY AND SOCIAL POLICY

We have examined how gender and age interact to limit the participation of women, and of the young and the old, in ways that do not relate to individual capabilities. We have noted that these limitations are varied in extent and effect according to degree of industrialization, and according to family-transmitted social class. The model presented at the beginning of the paper conceptualizes a series of sorting processes, beginning with the level of industrialization of a society and going on to the family SES, each of which in turn determine life chances of an individual before birth. At birth gender provides a further sorting process, ensuring greater longevity for females but a wider range of life chances for males. Pronounced gender sorting does not begin until puberty, and from puberty on women and men move through similar age-sorting but with far greater role shifts for women than for men. Age-sorting into adulthood does not occur until some years after entry into labor-force/marriage/childbearing status, causing great role strain in this period.

If age-sorting into adulthood is excessively postponed, age-sorting into retirement and the status of being elderly is excessively premature. The age-sorting process mismatches responsibility, status, and capacity from puberty on, particularly in industrial societies. This mismatch puts a heavy loading on the middle third of life as the only period in which persons participate fully in the work of maintaining and shaping society and their own lives. It also puts a special kind of loading on women who carry extra responsibilities without full civic status. As the world moves toward population equilibrium with declining resources, an aging society will need the fuller participation and wisdom of its elders, as well as the imagination and energy of its young. Removal of legal age barriers to full civic status will be required. This means the identification of age as a constitutionally suspect category in the laws of nation states, and the identification of age as an unlawful basis of discrimination in the United Nations Declaration of Human

Rights. For first and third worlds alike it means a careful examination of development policy in terms of education and employment infrastructures, and of the implicit or explicit age-grading policies associated with these infrastructures. The life cycle perspective offered in this study, buttressed with statistics about actual participation rates of human beings in various age categories and by gender, makes clear the absurdity of age-sorting. In terms of the ideal of a heterostatic society engaged in a continuous process of complex balancing of human capacities, needs, and resources, and discussed in the early part of this paper, the rigidities of age-sorting are clearly counter-productive. The same life cycle perspective, by demonstrating the gradual growth from undifferentiated to differentiated androgyny, suggests alternatives to ancient customs of gender-sorting in the years between puberty and menopause. Such alternatives might foster more differentiated personality development in both sexes, and produce a more peaceful and humanly fulfilling social order.

NOTES

1. Various kinds of "living together" arrangements without marriage are not considered in the model, for simplicity's sake, though they may affect status of both men and women.
2. Unless otherwise indicated, all figures used in this paper refer to the period 1968-1970, the period for which the most complete international comparative data is available.
3. 21 to 25 is an anomalous age status, with full legal rights for men, but not yet full recognition of civic adulthood.
4. In our conceptual model the age breaks are under 24, 25-55, and over 55. In order to emphasize the employment situation at the extremes of youth and age, however, the discussion that follows emphasizes the under 19s and the over 65s.
5. This analysis is based on World Health Organization causes of death statistics. While suicide statistics may be questioned, reporting is steadily improving. Differences within and between countries appear consistent with other data, though reported absolute levels may in some countries be unrealistically low.

REFERENCES

Alexander, J. (1975). Foreward to Symposium: Law and the Aged," Arizona Law Review, 17,2.
Alicia Patterson Fund (1971). Various Reports from The Alicia Patterson Fund, 535 Fifth Avenue, New York, New York, 10017.
Barton, Elizabeth M., et al. (1975). "Recent findings on adult and gerontological intelligence." American Behavioral Scientist, 19, 2 (November/December):224-236.
Bengston, Vern L. and Robert S. Laufer, eds. (1974). Youth, Generations and Social Change. Special Issue of the Journal of Social Issues, 30, 3.

Berg, Leila (1971). "Moving towards self-government. 9-50 in Paul Adams, et al. Children's Rights: Toward the Liberation of the Child. New York: Praeger.

Boserup, Ester (1970). Woman's Role in Economic Development. New York: St. Martin's Press.

Boulding, Elise (1977a). Women in the Twentieth Century World. New York: Halsted Press (A Sage Publications Book).

Boulding, Elise (1977b). "Children's rights and world order: a global survey of the role and status of children and youth in the 1970s." Boulder: University of Colorado, Institute of Behavioral Science (mimeo).

Boulding, Elise (1977c). "The human services component of nonmarket productivity in ten Colorado households." Boulder: University of Colorado, Institute of Behavioral Science (mimeo).

Boulding, Elise (1976). The Underside of History: A View of Women Through Time. Boulder, Colorado: Westview Press.

Boulding, Elise (1963). The Fruits of Solitude for Children. Wallingford, Pa.: Pendle Hill Pamphlet.

Boulding Global Data Bank (n.d.). Boulder, Colorado: Institute of Behavioral Science, University of Colorado.

Boulding, Elise, Shirley Nuss, Dorothy Carson, and Michael Greenstein (1976). Handbook of International Data on Women. New York: Halsted Press (A Sage Publications Book).

Clemente, Frank and Michael B. Kleiman (1976). "Fear of crime among the aged." The Gerontologist, 16, 3:207-210.

Cowgill, Donald O. (1968). "The social life of the aging in Thailand." The Gerontologist, 8, 3:159-163.

De Tocqueville, Alexis (1945). Democracy in America. Trans. Philips Bradley. New York: Alfred A. Knopf, Inc.

Erikson, Erik (1964). Insight and Responsibility. New York: W. W. Norton and Company.

Foner, Anne, ed. (1975). Age in Society. Special Issue of The American Behavioral Scientist, 19, 2 (November/December).

Gill, David G. (1976). The Challenge of Social Equality. Cambridge, Mass.: Schenkman Publishing Company.

Gutmann, David (n.d.). "The cross-cultural perspective: Notes towards a comparative psychology of aging." Ann Arbor: University of Michigan (mimeo).

Hess, Robert D. and Judith V. Torney (1967). The Development of Political Attitudes in Children. Chicago: Aldine.

Isaacs, Susan Sutherland (1930). Intellectual Growth in Young Children. London: Routledge and Kegan Paul.

Kaplan, Jerome and Gordon J. Aldridge, eds. (1962). Social Welfare of the Aging. New York: Columbia University Press.

Kohlberg, Lawrence (1963). "The development of children's orientation toward a moral order: I. Sequence in the development of thought." Vitz Humana, 6:11-33.

Lowe, John (1975). The Education of Adults: A World Perspective. Paris: UNESCO.

Margulec, I. (1965). "The care of the aged in Israel." The Gerontologist, 5 (June): 61-66.

Milgram, Joel I. and Dorothy June Sciarra, eds. (1974). Childhood Revisited. New York: Macmillan.

Miller, S. M. and Pamela Roby (1970). The Future of Inequality. New York: Basic Books, Inc.

Omachi, Chiyo (1962). "Gerontology practices in Japan." The Gerontologist, 2, 1 (March): 74-76.

Piaget, Jean (1932). Moral Judgment of the Child. New York: Free Press.

Riley, Matilda White and Anne Foner (1968). Aging and Society. Vol. I: An Inventory of Research Findings. New York: Russell Sage Foundation.

Rossi, Alice (1977). "A Bio-Social Perspective on Parenting," Daedalus (Spring): 1-23.

Shanas, Ethel (1963). "Some observations on cross-national surveys of aging." The Gerontologist, 3, 1 (March):7-9.

Shanas, Ethel, et al. (1968). Old People in Three Industrial Societies. New York: Atherton Press.

Social Indicators (1973). Written and compiled by the Statistical Policy Division, Office of Management and Budget, and prepared for publication by the Social and Economic Statistics Administration, U.S. Department of Commerce. Washington, D.C.

Tibbitts, Clark and Wilma Donahue, eds. (1962). Social and Psychological Aspects of Aging. New York: Columbia University Press.

United Nations (1977). The Aging in Slums and Uncontrolled Settlements. New York: United Nations.

United Nations (1976a). Yearbook of Labour Statistics. Geneva: International Labour Office.

United Nations (1976b). World Health Statistics Annual. New York: United Nations.

United Nations (1976c). Lifelong Education: The Curriculum and Basic Learning Needs. Final report of the Regional Seminar, Chiangmai, Thailand, 7-15 June. Bangkok: UNESCO.

United Nations (1975). The Aging: Trends and Policies. New York: United Nations.

United Nations (1974). 1973 Demographic Yearbook. New York: United Nations.

United Nations (1971). 1970 Demographic Yearbook. New York: United Nations.

United Nations (1969). 1967 Report on the World Social Situation. New York. United Nations.

United Nations (1966). Housing for the Elderly. 2 vols. Proceedings of the Colloquium, Belgium and The Netherlands, 4-15 October, 1965. New York: United Nations.

United Nations (1964). Provisional Report on World Population as Assessed in 1963. New York: United Nations.

United States Bureau of the Census (1973). Series P-60, No. 91, "Characteristics of the Low-Income Population": 1972. Washington, D.C.: U.S. Government Printing Office.

Wallerstein, Immanuel (1976). The Modern World-System: Capitalist
    Agriculture and the Origins of the European World-Economy in
    the Sixteenth Century. New York: Academic Press, Inc.
Weihl, Hannah (1970). "Jewish aged of different cultural origin in
    Israel." The Gerontologist, 1, 2 (Summer):146-150.
Yearbook of International Organizations (1974). Brussels, Belgium:
    Union of International Associations.

6. A Partial Test of the Ethnic Equalization Hypothesis: A Cross-national Study

D. John Grove

Despite the long-standing interest in notions of inequality throughout the history of mankind, we find no tradition of systematic work on ethnic or racial inequality. The crucial problem of this century is a greater redistribution of human wealth, not just from the rich to the poor, but among ethnic or racial groups. The field of ethnic and race relations has been dominated by Marxian or assimilation theories which assume either a natural progression toward ethnic or racial equalization, or a relative deterioration in class inequalities within ethnic groups--with very little empirical evidence to support either proposition. Marxism, which has considerably influenced the examination of inequality, has totally disregarded the importance of race and ethnicity; ethnic and racial ties become epiphenomena of class. For assimilation theorists there is an inevitable trend toward equalization as groups are incorporated into the dominant culture. Plural society theorists have begun to examine the relationship between ascribed cleavages and social inequality. Their theories, however, amount to little more than a classification scheme describing the hierarchical order. To simply describe "who gets what" is not enough; what we want to explain are the dynamics of ethnic redistribution in different parts of the world.

This lack of systematic work on ethnic or racial distribution patterns is especially surprising when one considers that ethnic or racial cleavages in many parts of the world are as important and as intractable as class cleavages. The growing number of political parties structured along ethnic lines, the number of separatist movements and the rising force of ethnic nationalism, and the fact that 90 percent of all nations in the world today are made up of heterogeneous populations point to the question: What do we know about the world's ethnic and racial distribution patterns? The answer is, very little.

This paper is, therefore, an examination and a test of the ethnic equalization hypothesis in nine societies that have governmental policies designed to redistribute ethnic socio-economic wealth. This study will assess the degree to which ethnic or racial groups have tended to converge in their level of inter- and intra-group socio-economic development, and to what extent the

135

redistribution is determined within specific policy contexts or political systems. We shall also examine the hypothesis that economic development has a leveling or equalizing effect on ethnic development. Economic development is believed to be an effective ethnic leveler; however, no systematic studies have tested this thesis in different societies over time.

Development economists have found in recent cross-national and time series studies that economic structure, not level of income or rate of growth, is the basic determinant of patterns of income distribution. Kuznets (1963) found that with economic growth, income inequality tends to increase, to become stable, and finally to decrease: the so-called inverted "u" hypothesis. Oshima (1962) expanded on this thesis arguing that countries pass through four stages -- undeveloped, underdeveloped, semi-developed, and fully developed -- and that income inequalities increase during the second and third stages but decline during the first and last stages. More recent studies support the curvilinear relationship between economic development and income distribution, showing the process of economic growth shifting the income distribution from the richest 5 percent to the top 20 percent of the population, but not filtering down to the poorest 60 percent in either developed or developing countries (Chenery et al., 1974; Paukert, 1972). Studies conducted by Adelman and Morris (1973), however, come to different conclusions concerning the importance of economic development. Six main determinants emerged as influencing the shape of income distribution, and economic development is not one of them; education and political participation, however, are. Other recent studies on dependency relations also question the developmental approach to income distribution (Amin, 1973; Galtung, 1971; Rubinson, 1976; Santos, 1970).

The number of studies conducted on ethnic and racial income distributions can be counted on one hand, and none are comparative. In the United States and Israel there are still widely divergent scholarly interpretations of changes in income distributions, but most of the recent empirical studies have found a moderate lessening of income inequality between Israel's oriental and western Jewish communities, and America's blacks and whites (Farley, 1977; Remba, 1972). Abeysekera's (1975) study of Sri Lanka concludes that racial income inequality has diminished over time, especially during the years 1963 to 1973. Likewise, regional studies of multi-ethnic societies show a slow trend toward income equalization (Williamson, 1965). Income distribution in West Malaysia, however, shows a trend toward increasing income inequality between the three major ethnic groups (Lean, 1974; Snodgrass, 1975).

Surprisingly, few empirical studies have been conducted on ethnic education and occupational mobility (see von der Mehden, 1977). The International Labor Organization has conducted a series of projects in India, Malaysia, Lebanon, and Brazil, but none of them have linked occupational mobility to income redistribution (Arles, 1966, 1971; Rosillion, 1968). Likewise, other studies of Israel, Yugoslavia, Australia, Canada, Ghana, Kenya, and South

Africa have not made any systematic attempt to examine ethnic socio-economic distribution trends (Australian Government, 1975; Jambrek, 1975; Horrell et al., 1975; Lissak, 1969; Smooha and Peres, 1975; Mckown, 1974; Rothchild, 1969). The only exceptions to this are studies conducted in the United States, Malaysia, and the Soviet Union. Silver's study (1974) on ethnicity in the Soviet Union corroborates the inverted "u" hypothesis between economic growth and social inequality. Silver found that economic development had an initial detrimental effect on the ethnic gap, eventually leveling off and moving toward ethnic equalization. Similarly, in Hirschman's study (1975) of Peninsular Malaysia, the occupational trends show that the ethnic differentials narrowed between 1931 and 1947, then widened between 1947 and 1957, and then began to decrease again between 1957 and 1967.

Governmental Policies Toward Ethnic Equalization

The nine countries included in this study are: Belgium, Canada, Israel, Malaysia, New Zealand, Pakistan, Sri Lanka, the United States, and Yugoslavia.[2] The policies implemented to achieve a greater ethnic equal distribution range from welfare state systems to quota systems and decentralization policies. For example, Malaysia and the United States have affirmative action programs designed primarily to equalize educational and job opportunities for certain racial groups. The Second Malaysia Plan, 1971-1975, is quite explicit about equalizing the ownership of the means of production. The plan favors the Malay group with special rights and quota systems in education and government jobs. The target set by the government states that within twenty years the Malays should manage and own at least 30 percent of the industrial and commercial sectors (Means, 1972; Stockwin, 1973). Affirmative action programs in the United States also require that educators and employers actively favor racial minorities in the areas of admissions, hiring, and promotions (Glaser, 1975).

In other countries official doctrines of ethnic equalization have taken the form of decentralization policies, especially in nations where ethnicity is regionalized. The planners of Yugoslavia's decentralization program envision the goal of regionalized ethnic equality. The principal feature of this program is to sharply increase the powers granted to the workers' councils and thereby to increase the power of the Communist Party over the allocative mechanism (Lang, 1975; Jambrek, 1972). In Pakistan the government's response to the regional economic disparities between East and West Pakistan has been to implement a twenty-year prospective plan (1965-1985) meant to remove the economic disparities. The measures adopted were a greater redistribution of resources between the two provinces, which included regional economic planning and rural economic development through public works programs (Jahan, 1972; Ziring, 1971). This program was, of course, interrupted by the formation of Bangladesh.

137

Belgium's process of decentralization was fairly gradual until 1971 when the constitution was revised to provide for more equal development for the two major ethnic groups--Flemish and Walloons. These revisions had two explicit goals: first, to give each ethnic group a greater control over the linguistic and cultural development, and secondly, to give minorities some protection under the workings of a majority principle (Dunn, 1974). In Canada, similarly, bi-lingual/bicultural policies are designed to give equal partnership to the two major ethnic groups--Francophone and Anglophone. The policy envisions two separate communities, each having a degree of self determination and each given official recognition (Canadian Royal Commission, 1967).

Welfare state policies have been the primary means to accelerate egalitarian trends in Sri Lanka, New Zealand and Israel. The redistribution impact of production policies in Sri Lanka has been largely reinforced by social policies. Roughly half of current government expenditure has been directed towards social welfare, primarily free education, health services, and subsidized food and transporation. World Bank studies show that income distribution over the last two decades has moved markedly toward a greater equality (Jayawardeña, 1974). In New Zealand and Israel the government policies have been to combine social welfare measures with overall policies of assimilation. Beginning with the Maori Social and Economic Advancement Act of 1945, New Zealand's official policy has been to encourage the urbanization of Maoris. By 1959, the Maori Affairs department saw as one of its specific tasks the setting up of job and educational opportunities for Maoris in urban areas in order to accelerate the urban flow (Collette and O'Malley, 1974; Hartley and Thompson, 1967). The Israeli policy of absorbing different ethnic immigrants into the dominant Ashkenazim culture has primarily focused on socio-economic mobility and educational opportunities for all Jews. There is, however, no concerted effort to assimilate the non-Jewish population of Arabs, Christians, and Druzes (Curtis and Chertoff, 1972; Lissak, 1969).

This cursory review of the nine countries shows considerable variety of policy strategies. The surprising thing is that we know so little about the effectiveness of these programs in redistributing ethnic wealth nor how skewed the wealth really is.

A representative government is often thought to favor the achievement of a more egalitarian distribution of economic and social power. That is, without the representation of all ethnic groups, government policies are likely to enrich elites and dominant ethnic groups. Cutright (1967) found that political representation was second only to the level of economic development in explaining the variance in inequality among nations. Therefore, before testing the equalization thesis, we shall examine to what extent each group is represented in the policy-making structure, given that each political system has policies designed to increase ethnic equality.

138

METHOD

The equalization hypothesis is a test of the degree to which ethnic development has been redistributed between and within groups. The study will focus on the relative changes in the socio-economic gap between groups within nine multi-ethnic societies. In three selected countries we will examine income distribution within each group as well.[3] The convergence of ethnic development should take place both between and within groups. There is, however, some evidence that ethnic distribution patterns are significantly different from class patterns (Kuper, 1974). To what extent the two levels exhibit similar trends is of considerable importance to the ongoing debate between class versus ethnicity.

Before operationalizing the socio-economic variables, we shall define ethnic political representation.

Ethnic Cabinet Representation

Cabinet representation is one indicator of power distribution since cabinet members exercise executive authority and in many countries constitute the leadership of the political parties in the legislature. Representativeness (PRI) is measured in terms of the correspondence between the ethnic breakdown in cabinet membership and in the population at large. The correspondence between the two will be computed by a coefficient of concordance, C, which measures the extent to which ethnic proportions in cabinet membership deviate from the proportions expected from the national ethnic population (see Morrision et al., 1972:89).[4]

Inter-group Socio-economic Distribution

The test of the inter-group equalization hypothesis will be conducted over time across three variables which are the target of the redistributive policies: income distribution, enrollment in higher education, and percentage in professional and technical occupations.

Groups. Thirty-five ethnic and racial groups were selected within each society; they represent the major ethnic or racial cleavages of the nine nations. Table 1 shows the population size of each of the thirty groups. In all nine countries the specified groups represent at least 80 percent of the societal population; most range in the 90 percent bracket. The selection and inclusion of the groups were based on the reliability of the ethnic income, occupational, and educational data. This reliability requirement has given us, to some extent, a biased sample of groups as most of them are the larger groups; some of the smaller ones had to be left out because of insufficient or unreliable data.[5] Therefore, the ethnic inequality indices are not country scores, but represent socio-economic differences between groups. In three countries--Belgium, Pakistan and Yugoslavia--ethnic aggregate socio-economic data is not available. We have, therefore, relied on regional data and have made inferences about the ethnic aggregate.

139

TABLE 1

Population of Groups

Belgium % of total population	Flemish 56.5	Walloon 32.1				
Canada % of total population	British 44.6	French 28.6	German 6.1	Italian 3.3	Ukranian 2.7	Jewish 1.0
Israel % of total population	Ashkenazim (European/ American) 23.2	Oriental (Afro/ Asian) 21.1	Israeli (born) 40.8	Non-Jews (Muslims, Christians, Druzes) 14.9		
New Zealand % of total population	White 90.4	Maori 7.9				
Malaysia % of total population	Chinese 34.1	Indian 9.0	Malay 46.8			
Pakistan % of total population	Punjabi 29.0	Bengali 54.2				
Sri Lanka % of total population	Low Country Sinhalese 42.8	Kandyan Sinhalese 29.1	Ceylon Tamils 11.1	Indian Tamils 9.4	Muslims 7.1	
United States % of total population	White 85.0	Black 11.1	Chinese 0.2	Japanese 0.3	Mexican-Am. 2.7	Indian 0.4
Yugoslavia % of total population	Serb 39.7	Montenegrin 2.5	Croat 22.1	Macedonian 5.8	Slovene 8.2	

In all of these cases there is a strong relationship between ethnicity and regionalism: the regions are at least 70 percent homogeneous.[6]

Ethnic Income Distribution. Since there is no consistency in the collection of aggregate income statistics cross-nationally, we have had to rely on household incomes, personal incomes, and per capita incomes of groups. It is true that the extent of income inequality will vary according to the income units used, but since we are only interested in measuring redistribution within countries, not assigning country scores, we have been careful to only use comparable income units across time for each country.

Ethnic Groups in Higher Education. Ethnic enrollment in universities and technical colleges is a reasonable indicator of the existing educational differences between ethnic groups. A problem arises when it is applied to the developing countries, since, to eradicate illiteracy, formal education (primary and secondary) is in greater demand than higher. However, higher education in the developing countries has become an important policy arena for equalizing educational opportunities, and a number of governments have now set quotas on the students entering universities. For these reasons ethnic enrollment in higher education will be used as the indicator of ethnic education dispersion. The ethnic percentage is computed from educational enrollment figures in higher education divided by the number of 20-24 year olds of that group.

Ethnic groups in professional occupations. The percentage of ethnic groups in professional jobs will be used as the indicator of occupational dispersion; the percentage figures are based on the economically active population. The definition of the professional category is considerably more consistent and comparable across nations than the other occupational categories; most college graduates would strive for professional jobs.

Intra-ethnic Income Distribution

Unfortunately, all nine countries cannot be used to examine intra-ethnic trends because of the lack of reliable and comparable ethnic income data. We have selected, however, three multi-ethnic countries which are representative of different levels of economic development and which have reliable income data over time: Israel, Malaysia, and Sri Lanka. Household income is the unit of analysis in Malaysia and Israel, while personal income has been used in Sri Lanka.

Measurement of Ethnic Equalization

Our basic measure of inter-ethnic distribution is the coefficient of variation (V), a sensitive measure of dispersion. It is the standard deviation over the mean (Sen, 1973:27; Blalock, 1972:88). We did not weight the size of the group(s) for fear of obscuring

141

TABLE 2

CABINET ETHNIC REPRESENTATIVENESS

Country	Groups		Time Period		
I. DEVELOPED NATIONS					
Belgium			1962-66	1967-70	1971-75
	Walloons		52.7	44.7	50.5
	Flemish		47.3	55.3	49.5
		N=	55	85	103
		PRI=	.94	.84	.92
		MC= 0.2			
Canada			1961-63	1964-67	1968-71
	British		80.0	58.4	62.4
	French		15.4	39.6	28.2
	Ukranian		4.6	----	----
	German		----	----	3.5
	Italian		----	----	----
	Jewish		----	----	2.3
		N=	65	101	85
		PRI=	.94	.88	.85
		MC= 0.9			
Israel			1965-67	1968-71	1972-75
	Ashkenazim		74.4	73.7	72.2
	Oriental		14.9	12.5	11.1
	Israel born		10.6	13.8	16.7
	Non-Jews		----	----	----
		N=	47	80	72
		PRI=	.99	.99	.98
		MC= 0.1			
New Zealand			1951-57	1958-64	1965-71
	Europeans		100.0	97.1	100.0
	Maoris		----	2.9	----
		N=	102	105	110
		PRI=	.92	.84	.92
		MC= 0.0			
United States			1950-56	1957-63	1964-70
	Whites		100.0	100.0	96.2
	Blacks		----	----	3.8
	Chinese		----	----	----
	Japanese		----	----	----
	Chicano		----	----	----
	Indian		----	----	----
		N=	66	70	79
		PRI=	.86	.86	.79
		MC=0.4			
II. SEMI-DEVELOPED					
Malaysia			1958-62	1963-68	1968-74
	Malays		65.5	61.5	68.4
	Chinese		25.9	27.5	21.1
	Indian		8.6	10.9	10.5
		N=	58	91	114
		PRI=	.87	.82	.91
		MC=0.4			

TABLE 2 (CONTINUED)

CABINET ETHNIC REPRESENTATIVENESS

Country	Groups		Time Period		
Yugoslavia			1961-64	1965-69	1970-74
	Croatian		18.0	18.6	14.8
	Macendonian		10.5	14.4	14.8
	Montenegrin		11.3	9.3	14.8
	Serbian		27.8	27.9	30.6
	Slovene		10.0	14.4	13.8
		N=	133	118	101
		PRI=	.95	.91	.98
		MC= 0.3			
III. DEVELOPING NATIONS					
Pakistan			1959-61	1962-65	1966-69
	West Pakistan		61.7	65.0	48.7
	Bengali		38.2	35.0	51.3
		N=	34	40	39
		PRI=	.91	.94	.41
		MC= 5.5			
Sri Lanka			1953-59	1960-66	1967-73
	Sinhalese		88.6	89.6	88.3
	Tamils		2.8	1.4	3.9
	Muslims		8.5	9.1	5.5
		N=	70	77	128
		PRI=	.94	.94	.92
		MC= 0.1			

overall trends, nor is there any theoretical reason why some groups should weight higher than others. The gini coefficient will be the measure used to examine intra-ethnic distribution patterns. The gini coefficient, still the most widely used indicator of income concentration, is defined as the arithmetic average of the absolute differences between all pairs of incomes. Since the data is over time we need to determine whether the between or within group differences are becoming more equal. To test for equalization, we will use a measure of convergence (MC) to examine the degree to which ethnic socio-economic development is becoming more similar or dissimilar.[7] This measure of convergence will show whether the indices of the coefficient of variation (V) are converging. It should be noted, however, that intra-group level convergence is not interchangeable with equalization. The gini scores for each group could well be on the increase, but could also be becoming more similar. The convergence measure will also be used to examine the ethnic cabinet representation (PRI) trends.

FINDINGS

Ethnic Cabinet Representation

First let us examine the ethnic political representation of the nine countries and see what changes have taken place. Table 2 shows the representation percentages and indices (PRI) for each of the thirty groups divided up into three categories: developing (GNP per capita income up to U.S. $440), semi-developed (income between U.S. $440-1310), and developed (income above U.S. $1310).[8]

In the developing countries, Pakistan's figures show that ethnic representation at the cabinet level is becoming more equal over time (MC=5.5). The "principle of parity" was established in the first Pakistan constitution, 1956, but was never really implemented until after 1966. From 1959 to 1965 the Bengali representation decreased from 36 percent to 27 percent despite Bengali numerical superiority, and it was not until Ajub Khan's fourth cabinet that the composition became more representative. Sri Lanka's cabinet composition, on the other hand, has really not changed at all in the last twenty years (MC=0.1). Despite Mrs. Bandaranaike's and other prime ministers' attempts to maintain proportional balance, the record shows a trend of Sinhalese dominance and no change in Tamil underrepresentation. The Muslims have maintained their one cabinet position throughout the twenty year period.

In the two semi-industrial societies we found a decrease in ethnic representation. Cabinet representation in Malaysia, traditionally determined by party politics, race, and geography, was moving in a general direction of greater ethnic representation from 1958-1968 (MC=0.4). But after the 1969 elections, the racial riots of the same month, the ensuing martial law, and the ascendency of Tim Abdul Razak bin Hussein, the headway that had been made by the Chinese evaporated -- while the Malay representation increased. Yugoslavia's appointments to the federal cabinet have also been

144

largely based on the quota system. Consequently, few changes have taken place (MC=0.3). By 1970-1974 each group within the Yugoslavian Cabinet had equal proportions except for the Slovenes who had double the number of any group. This equality of composition has helped the Montenegrins, who only comprise 2.5 percent of the population but have 14.8 percent cabinet representation. The quota system, defined by each succeeding constitution, sets quotas for each republic and autonomous province for the federal executive council. Quotas on nationalities are usually worked out within each republic. However, there are no reliable data on nationality representation (Denitch, 1976:108).

In the industrial societies there is also no trend toward greater ethnic representation for groups. In Belgium there was, until 1970, an unwritten quota described as the "rule of parity," but it was never really practiced. In the 1970 constitutional revision, however, there were specific quotas set down for the cabinet which was to be equally divided between the two groups. Table 2 shows a slow trend toward equal representation favoring the numerically inferior Walloons (MC=0.2).

Two features emerge in the analysis of the Canadian cabinet. The first is that French-Canadian participation in the cabinet has steadily increased over the last century, except for the Dietenbaker period (1961-1963) when French representation never rose above 17 percent. During the Pearson and Trudeau cabinets, representation increased significantly. The other feature is the extent of representation of all other ethnic groups in Canada. Until the Trudeau cabinet there had never been cabinet participation by German or Italian communities.

In the United States there has been only a slight change in the racial composition of the cabinet (MC=0.4). Only one black served in the cabinet (1950-1970), and there has never been any representation by the other racial groups.

Cabinet composition in Israel and New Zealand has not changed at all, surprisingly. In Israel, ethnic representation has not been given a high priority. Consequently, the Ashkenazim have dominated each successive cabinet shuffle. Oriental Jews have consistently had only two cabinet members, while the Israeli-born Jews have slightly increased their representation; non-Jews have never been in the cabinet.

The PRI scores in New Zealand remained stable from 1951-1971 except for a brief period from 1958-1960 when a Maori held office in the Labour government. Although the Maori representation act of 1867 provided for four Maori elected members to be included in the house of representatives, there has not been a tradition of including them except when the Labour Party is in power. Since 1971, the Labour Party in power has elected two Maori cabinet members.

This brief examination of ethnic representation seriously questions the level of governmental commitment to ethnic political representation in the nine countries. There is no clear trend toward greater ethnic participation at the cabinet level. It is true that in a number of countries there are specific quotas to guide

TABLE 3

ETHNIC INCOME AND THE PERCENTAGE OF ETHNIC GROUPS IN HIGHER EDUCATION AND PROFESSIONAL JOBS

I. Developed Nations (Income above U.S. $1310)

1. Belgium

	INCOME 1964	1970	1974	HIGHER EDUCATION 1963-4	1965-6	1970-1	1974-5	PROFESSIONAL JOBS 1961	1970
Flemish	25100	45100	73000	4.0	5.2	8.6	9.7	7.4	10.2
Walloons	26400	43900	70700	9.4	11.9	17.2	17.8	8.9	12.8
V =	.036	.019	.023	.569	.554	.471	.417	.130	.159
MC =	3.6			2.4				-2.5	

2. Canada

	INCOME 1961	1971	HIGHER EDUCATION 1961	1971	PROFESSIONAL JOBS 1951	1961	1971
British	4852	10152	12.5	20.9	7.5	10.6	17.7
French	3872	8762	6.3	11.9	4.4	6.7	13.3
German	4207	9335	9.2	19.2	3.7	6.8	13.5
Italian	3621	9446	3.0	14.0	2.8	3.4	6.6
Jewish	7426	15955	25.5	60.8	10.7	16.0	32.4
Ukranian	4128	8839	7.9	24.5	3.0	7.4	12.6
V =	.299	.265	.735	.715	.561	.511	.548
MC =	1.1		0.3		2.4		

3. Israel

	INCOME 1965	1968	1970	1974	HIGHER EDUCATION 1964-5	1969-70	PROFESSIONAL JOBS 1961	1971
Ashkenazim	8600	10900	13200	26200	13.1	20.4	14.4	20.9
Oriental	6200	7700	9700	20600	2.1	4.5	4.1	8.3
Israeli Born	9400	11400	13600	27800	9.0	14.0	22.5	24.5
Non-Jews	----	7000	8100	23200	0.7	1.6	4.7	6.9
V =		.206	.241	.133	.939	.855	.767	.585
MC =	3.9				1.5		-0.1	

4. New Zealand

	INCOME 1951	1961	1970	HIGHER EDUCATION 1966	PROFESSIONAL JOBS 1966	1971
European	953	1818	3156	4.9	10.6	13.0
Maori	744	1475	2728	1.1	3.5	3.8
V =	.174	.147	.103	.896	.712	.744
MC =	2.0				-0.9	

5. United States

	INCOME 1950	1960	1970	HIGHER EDUCATION 1960	1970	1975	PROFESSIONAL JOBS 1950	1960	1970
Black	952	1519	4158	11.1	24.5	42.9	3.3	4.7	8.0
Chinese	1799	3021	5223	46.7	84.9	----	6.7	13.6	18.9
Japanese	1839	3205	7574	50.1	111.1	----	7.1	17.9	26.3
Indian	725	1348	3509	7.7	21.8	----	2.9	5.1	9.2
Chicano	1253	2294	4735	6.7	19.2	26.7	2.7	3.8	5.6
White	2053	3024	7011	25.2	19.2	53.6	9.3	11.9	15.2
V =	.374	.339	.299	.799	.737		.515	.610	.564
MC =	1.0			0.8			-0.5		

TABLE 3 (CONTINUED)

II. Semi-Developed Nations (Income U.S. $440–$1310)

1. Yugoslavia

	INCOME			HIGHER EDUCATION			PROFESSIONAL JOBS	
	1961	1969	1974	1952-3	1968-9	1972-3	1967	1973
Montenegrins	178	892	2192	0.3	5.4	7.9	5.6	8.9
Croats	197	1046	2623	3.9	13.5	17.3	6.2	7.8
Macedonians	143	841	2120	2.7	14.7	21.7	5.8	7.3
Slovenes	239	1141	2816	4.8	11.8	15.7	4.5	8.6
Serbs	174	948	2377	4.3	11.3	19.5	7.1	7.5
V =	.187	.126	.121	.562	.316	.321	.162	.087
	MC=2.7			MC=2.1			MC=7.7	

2. Malaysia

	INCOME			HIGHER EDUCATION				PROFESSIONAL JOBS		
	1957/8	1967/8	1970	1961-2	1965-6	1970	1973	1947	1957	1967
Malays	139	163	177	0.1	0.1	1.7	3.6	1.7	2.7	5.1
Chinese	300	349	399	0.3	0.9	2.1	2.6	1.6	2.8	4.6
Indians	237	260	310	0.3	0.7	0.9	1.4	2.1	2.6	5.4
V =	.363	.361	.378	.559	.483	.389	.435	.147	.037	.080
	MC=-0.3			MC=1.8				MC=2.3		

III. Developing Nations
Income up to U.S. $440

1. Sri Lanka

	INCOME			HIGHER EDUCATION		
	1953	1963	1973	1953	1963	1973
Kandyan Sinhalese	134	146	376	0.7	0.7	0.5
Low Country Sinhalese	147	199	425	0.8	1.3	1.0
Ceylon Tamils	166	198	385	1.8	2.2	0.6
Indian Tamils	96	118	180	---	0.1	---
Muslims	175	259	470	1.3	0.4	0.4
V =	.216	.296	.302	.441	.885	.472
	MC=-2.0			MC=-0.4		

2. Pakistan

	INCOME			HIGHER EDUCATION			PROFESSIONAL JOBS		
	1950	1960	1970	1956	1962	1966	1963	1965	1968
Bengali	287	278	331	.08	.2	.26	2.2	1.9	1.6
Punjabi	338	366	537	.1	.3	.42	3.1	1.9	2.1
V =	.115	.193	.336	.155	.318	.332	.24	.00	.191
	MC=-9.6			MC=-1.4			MC=4.1		

NOTE: Income figures are in the particular currency of the country. The income units in each country are: Belgium: average revenue per inhabitant; Canada: mean incomes of males; Israel: average gross annual money income per urban employee's family; New Zealand: median incomes of males; United States: median personal income; Yugoslavia: average net personal receipts; Malaysia: mean household income; Sri Lanka: median incomes; Pakistan: per capita income. There is no professional data for Sri Lanka.

representation, and in those nations there have been changes; but in the remaining countries there is not a discernible movement toward power redistribution. To what extent these trends are also reflected in socio-economic distributions is a question we shall now turn to.

Ethnic Socio-economic Equalization

Table 3 shows income distribution, enrollment in higher education, and percentage in the professional ranks for all thirty-five groups in the nine countries over time. The equalization test will examine changes toward greater socio-economic equality at different levels of economic development. If the relationship is curvilinear--the inverted "u" hypothesis -- then we would expect that in developing countries the socio-economic inequities would be on the increase, that in semi-industrialized societies socio-economic inequity patterns would reach a peak and remain fairly stable, and that in highly developed societies patterns of socio-economic redistribution would emerge.

In the two developing countries -- Sri Lanka and Pakistan -- the income, educational, and occupational inequalities have increased substantially over a twenty year period, confirming the first stage of the curvilinear relationship. The trends toward greater ethnic income inequality in Sri Lanka (MC=2.0) are in marked contrast with the findings of the World Bank, which found a significant shift toward greater equality by income sectors (Chenery et al., 1974:273). Over the twenty year period, the rankings of the ethnic groups remained fairly stable, except that the Low Country Sinhalese rose from third to second place, pushing the Ceylon Tamils to third place. The rates of change in the median incomes vary from group to group and from one time period to the next. During the first period, 1953-1963, the rates of increase were more or less evenly distributed, although the Muslims and the Low Country Sinhalese had a slightly higher rate of improvement. However, in 1963-1973, the rate of increase of the two Sinhalese groups was substantially greater than that of the other groups. The net effect is that the Sinhalese are fast catching up with the economically advanced position of the Moors and Malays, while the Tamils' position is slipping. Also, Tamil representation in Sri Lanka's universities has decreased dramatically in the last twenty years (the percentage of Ceylon Tamils that have attended university slipped from 1.8 percent in 1953 to 0.6 percent in 1973), partly because of government restrictions on Tamil university admissions and also from the "Sinhalese only" language policy.

In Pakistan, similarly, the income gap between West Pakistanis and Bengalis increased slightly from 1950 to 1960. But in the years 1960 to 1970 the Bengalis' income slipped drastically from 76 percent of the per capita income in West Pakistan to 61 percent (MC=-9.6). Also, the Bengali enrollment in higher education is substantially less than the Punjabi in West Pakistan, where the gap seems to have widened during the years 1965-1970 (MC=-11.4); the Bengali student

148

enrollment in universities is moving at a much slower rate than in West Pakistan. The occupational situation also deteriorated for Bengalis during the period 1965-1970; in 1965 the Bengali proportional representation in the professional ranks was equal to that of West Pakistan (1.9 percent), but by 1969 the Bengali representation had slipped to 1.6 percent, while West Pakistan's percentage had increased to 2.1 percent.

In semi-industrialized societies the curvilinear hypothesis predicts that the ethnic income gaps will reach a plateau and stabilize. However, Yugoslavia portrays a pattern which has gone beyond the peak and is heading toward redistribution, while in Malaysia the ethnic trends are mixed. The Malays and Indians have consistently earned 46 percent and 78 percent of the Chinese income between 1957-1970, and consequently, there has been no improvement in inter-racial equality (MC=-0.3). In education there have been significant changes in the racial representation at the universities, partly due to an educational quota system favoring Malays. The system has in effect allowed the Malays to catch up to and to overtake the traditionally dominant positions of the Chinese and Indians (MC=1.8). Similarly, in occupations there is a significant shift toward greater equality of access to the professional ranks (MC=2.3).

The income figures in Yugoslavia from 1961-1974 show a slow trend toward ethnic parity (MC=2.7), where all nationalities have made substantial gains on the economically advanced Slovenes. Likewise, the educational and occupational trends in Yugoslavia portray movements toward greater equalization. The higher education figures show that between 1952-1969 there was a significant change in the dispersion of educational nationality percentages (MC=2.1) for all groups except the Montenegrins. This low level of enrollment has not, however, constrained their entering the professional ranks--their percentage there is the highest. The occupational differences between all nationalities has significantly diminished (MC=7.7).

In the highly developed societies all five countries fit into the educational and income redistribution category; there is however, no consistent trend at the occupational level. The case of Belgium is interesting because the scales have tipped in favor of the Flemish for the first time. The Flemish earned 95 percent of the Walloon income in 1964; but by 1968-1970, their income had edged up and overtaken that of the traditionally economically advanced French-speaking Walloons. Although the scales tip back once again to the Walloons in universities and professions, the convergent trends show greater educational similarity between the two groups (MC=2.4), but increasing occupational differences from 1961 (MC=-2.5). The welfare state systems of New Zealand and Israel show that Maoris, Oriental Jews, and non-Jews have all made significant gains on the Ashkenazim and Pakehas (whites). However, the economic gains by Oriental Jews and non-Jews in Israel only made headway after 1970; the Maoris have made steady progress since 1951. Inequalities in education (MC=1.1) and professional jobs

149

(MC=2.4) have diminished in Israel, but the oriental Jews and non-Jews have a long way to go before catching up with the Ashkenazim. The occupational trends in New Zealand point in the opposite direction. The occupational gap between the two races has widened (MC=-0.9).

In the two North American countries there are surprisingly similar trends towards ethnic and racial equalization. In Canada the French, Germans, Italians, and Ukranians have all made gains on the British, while the Jewish groups have maintained their leading position (MC=1.1). In the United States there has been some improvement in racial income equalization (MC=1.0); blacks, Indians, and Chicanos have narrowed the income gap with whites; surprisingly, the Chinese have lost ground. Over the twenty-year period, the white/Chinese income ratio decreased from 88 percent to 74 percent. The Japanese, however, overtook the white income in 1960 and have held on to their lead in 1970. In both countries the differences in ethnic enrollment figures have decreased. This is especially true in America where both blacks and Chicanos have made substantial gains on whites. Despite the increasing educational opportunity in both countries, there has been little change in the occupational structure. Canadian census figures show a general trend toward occupational equality from 1951-1961, but in 1971 the trend is reversed (overall change, MC=0.1). Similarly, in the United States the census occupational data from 1950 to 1970 show in fact a slight increase in the occupational index (MC=-0.5). In both Canada and the United States the outlying groups that have very much affected the between group occupational variance are the Jewish Canadians and the Oriental Americans. These successful groups have outstripped the British Canadians and the American whites in their professional representation.

These socio-economic trends can now be correlated with GNP per capita for each of the nine countries. The gamma correlations--the test of the curvilinear relationship--are non-significant for education, professional jobs, and income.[9] The reason for this is simply that in the highly industrialized societies there has been very little improvement in racial or ethnic equality. In the United States and Canada the progress has been small. The greatest improvement has taken place in Belgium, New Zealand, Israel, and Yugoslavia, all of which have strong governmental commitments to redistribute societal wealth through socialist policies, the welfare state, and/or decentralization programs. In third world countries, however, the picture is different: inter-ethnic inequalities are steadily increasing.

Intra-ethnic Income Distribution

Now let us turn to the income distribution within groups in three selected case studies: Malaysia, Sri Lanka, and Israel. Table 4 shows the measures of income dispersion within each group, plus the overall mean convergence ratio. The picture in Sri Lanka shows that the within group income patterns for the six groups has become

150

TABLE 4

INCOME DISTRIBUTION WITHIN GROUPS:
GINI COEFFICIENTS

Sri Lanka

	1963	1973	% change 1963-73
Kandyan Sinhalese	.477	.332	30.3
Low Country Sinhalese	.476	.390	18.1
Ceylon Tamils	.500	.375	25.0
Indian Tamils	.377	.333	11.7
Moors & Malays	.528	.421	20.3
V =	.121	.103	
MC = 1.5			

Malaysia

	1957/8	1967/8	1970	% change 1957-70
Malays	.342	.400	.466	36.3
Chinese	.374	.391	.455	21.6
Indians	.347	.403	.463	33.4
V =	.048	.015	.013	
MC = 5.6				

Israel

	Urban Jewish Families			Employees Families			% change 1963-74
	1963/4	1968/9	1971	1972	1973	1974	
Ashkenazim	.204	.212	.273	.266	.261	.229	12.2
Oriental	.281	.231	.293	.328	.330	.304	8.2
Israeli Born	.267	.152	.143	.161	.176	.143	46.4
V =	.163	.207	.343	.333	.301	.360	
MC = -12.1							

The income units for each country are: personal income – Sri Lanka; household income–Malaysia and Israel.

151

less skewed over a ten-year period. The gini scores portray a significant decrease in income inequality among all groups, as well as a convergence of the scores. Yet, the rate at which each group is progressing towards intra-group equality differs. Kandyan Sinhalese and Ceylon Tamils have shown the most change, with Moors and Malays next, and Indian Tamils last.

In Malaysia intra-group income distribution patterns have steadily become more unequal; over time the gini scores for each group have risen, but most particularly for the Malays. In 1957-1958 the Malays had the least amount of income inequality, followed by Indians and Chinese. By 1970, the tide had reversed; the Malay gini coefficient was the highest and the Chinese was the lowest. However, the overall dispersion of the gini coefficients shows a shift toward greater convergence (MC=5.2). This means that although income inequality is steadily increasing for each group, the difference between the gini scores is becoming more similar.

Israeli income data on within group patterns was split into two periods--1963-1969 and 1971-1974--because of the different criteria used to collect the data: the urban population is used in the former and paid employees in the latter. However, since both surveys used family incomes as the unit of analysis, some useful comparisons can be made.[10] From 1963-1969, the income patterns of both Israeli-born and Oriental Jews became significantly less unequal, but for the Ashkenazim, the income dispersion remained relatively stable. Within the second period, the Oriental and Israeli-born Jew income distribution pattern became more unequal, but the gini ratios for 1974 show a sharp incline toward greater equality. Ashkenazim income, on the other hand, shows a gradual decline in skewness of income distribution. In fact, all three groups show a substantial shift toward income equality during the period 1973-1974. The differences between the gini scores have significantly increased over the ten-year period (MC=-12.1), mainly due to the substantial shift toward greater income equality within the Sabras. This supports those who argue that inequality within Israel will decline with length of stay.

CONCLUSIONS

Despite the scarcity of historical data on ethnic and racial groups which would give us a more complete examination of ethnic redistribution, there are some unmistakable trends which only partially confirm the inverted "u" hypothesis. We found no curvilinear relationship between economic development and ethnic socio-economic inequality, although there was considerable support for the notion that the ethnic gap in developing countries is on the increase. In the developed societies there was a general movement toward greater educational and income equality with the greatest progress taking place in countries with socialist policies or decentralization programs. There is no evidence in this study that socio-economic distribution reaches a peak or plateau at the semi-industrial stage, nor is there any evidence that changes in

152

socio-economic distribution increase with development. At the occupational level, however, the trends show no general movement toward equalization; on the contrary, in most countries the ethnic differences in the professional ranks have either stabilized or increased.

In the two countries below per capita GNP U.S. $440, the educational, occupational, and income inequalities are on the increase. To what extent this growth in ethnic inequality in the third world countries is due to the stage of development or to the dependency relationships within the global international system will have to be determined in follow-up studies. One thing is certain: the increasing differences may exacerbate ethnic tensions and separatist tendencies.

At the intra-group level we found that the level of economic development did not define the parameters of ethnic change. Sri Lanka's policy of redistribution has not been hindered by its level of economic development; the distribution within each group has become more equal over time. Malaysia, on the other hand, with one of the highest growth rates in Asia, has experienced increasing income disparities for all three groups. Similarly, the economic development in Israel has not trickled down to all segments within the two major ethnic groups, although there has been considerable redistribution within the Sabras.

In an examination of ethnic representation we found no widespread power redistribution, which may be one of the reasons for the lack of significant variation between political systems. In a few countries, quota systems have guided the selection of cabinet ministers, but in the remaining nations there has either been slow change or no change.

These findings, therefore, do not support the contention that there is a certain degree of inevitability in the development process. Multi-ethnic societies do not necessarily traverse a growth path which determines the size and degree of convergence of ethnic development. The inverted "u" hypothesis denies the importance of the external linkages to the international structure, and it denies the role of governmental policies in channeling societal resources. In short, deterministic growth models, which argue that the problem of ethnic income distribution can be solved automatically in the process of development, are too simplistic and focus on the wrong determinants. Ethnic redistribution is not the exclusive domain of the developed world.

In conclusion, built into the research agenda should be two important areas likely to have an impact on our understanding of ethnic and racial inequality. First, we must determine to what extent the shape and size of ethnic inequality is dependent on the global dynamics of inter-state inequalities. The slow trends found in this study would suggest that domestic factors within nations are only part of the story in changing income distribution. Secondly, we must determine whether a radical restructuring of society significantly changes the socio-economic gap between ethnic or racial groups. China and Cuba come to mind as obvious laboratories to answer this question. Unfortunately, very little systematic data comes out of China and Cuba on ethnic and racial groups. They have decided, like so many other countries, to suppress the level of information on communal groups. However, the lack of governmental statistics in this area should not distract the researcher from learning more about ethnic and racial distribution patterns which may bring us closer to the question of why race and ethnicity have become so important in recent years. This study is a start in that direction.

NOTES

1. This project is being conducted at the Center on International Race Relations, University of Denver. For a listing of the variables, groups, and countries, see Grove (1976). The project focus on redistribution includes trends towards greater socio-economic equality (equalization), as well as movements towards increasing socio-economic inequality. I would like to thank Pat West for helping to collect some of the data. Portions of this paper have been published in Ethnic and Racial Studies (April, 1978).

2. The other countries in the larger project are: USSR, Lebanon, Nigeria, Ghana, Kenya, India, Brazil, Trinidad, Guyana, and Australia. These countries were not included because of unreliable income data. Many multi-ethnic countries refuse to collect ethnic data because of the fear that it will be used for political purposes. Therefore, it should be stressed that although the sample in this study is not necessarily representative of all multi-ethnic societies, it is representative of nations that collect ethnic socio-economic data on a regular basis.

3. Data on intra-group income distribution for the other nine multi-ethnic societies were examined, but their comparability over time was judged to be unreliable. We therefore chose only countries where the income data within groups had been checked by independent sources.

4. There are numerous conceptual and empirical problems with measuring political representation, especially in using cabinet members as a proxy. However, since this is not part of the equalization test, this proxy test measure will give us some indication of the changes in ethnic representation. The formula for the political representation index (PRI) is as follows:

$$PRI = \sqrt{\frac{x^2}{n+x^2}} \; ; \quad x^2 = \sum_{i=1}^{N} \frac{(o_i - E_i)^2}{Ei}$$

where N = the number of ethnic groups within each country

o_i = the proportion of the cabinet membership belonging to the ith group

154

E_i = the proportion of the national population belonging to the ith ethnic group.

It should be noted that cabinet figures do not included prime ministers, presidents, etc. The time period for cabinet representation matches the income period for each country.

5. Some of the more obvious groups that had to be excluded were: Israeli Arabs and Christians, ethnic minorities in Yugoslavia, Belgium, and Pakistan, and the indigenous Malays. In countries where multiple cleavages divide the society, the selection is based on income equivalence across groups. For example, in the United States racial groups were included, not ethnic categories. Likewise in Canada, ethnic categories were used rather than racial groups. In Israel, the Israeli-born category (which includes both Ashkenazi and Oriental Jews) had to be used because the government census material does not break the Jews born in Israel down by ethnicity.

6. In making judgments about ethnic inferences, the degree of regional homogeneity is difficult to assess, but 70 percent and above is a reasonable cut-off point. The degree of regionalized ethnicity in the four countries is as follows:

A. Belgium
   Flanders region - 94% Dutch speaking
   Wallonia region - 91% French speaking
   Bruxelles region - excluded

B. Pakistan
   East Pakistan - 98% Bengali
   West Pakistan - 70% Punjabi

C. Switzerland
   German region (19 cantons) - 96% German speaking
   French region (5 cantons) - 92% French speaking
   Italian region (1 canton) - 79% Italian speaking

D. Yugoslavia
   Slovian region - 97% Slovenes
   Montenegrin region - 71% Montenegrins
   Croatian region - 78% Croats
   Macedonian region - 70% Macedonians
   Serbian region - 75% Serbs

7. The measurement of convergence per year is expressed as follows:

$$MC = \left[\frac{V_{t1}-V_{t2}}{V_{t1}} \times 100 \right] \div (t_2-t_1)$$

where:

$$MC = \text{Mean convergence per year}$$

$$V_{t1} = \text{Coefficient of variation at earlier date}$$

$$V_{t2} = \text{Coefficient of variation at later date}$$

For a similar use of the statistic at the nation-state level, see Williamson and Fleming (1977). At the inter-group level, greater similarity will mean greater equality. At the intra-group level, however, the mean convergence scores will simply show a greater degree of ethnic similarity/dissimilarity in income distribution trends.

8. There is no single variable which reliably represents all dimensions of economic development. However, GNP per capita has been shown as the most reliable indicator correlating highly with all other developmental variables (Finsterbusch, 1975). The criteria for the three levels is based on Chenery's (1974) income level classification. The per capita gross national product data is taken from the World Bank Atlas (1973).

9. The gamma correlations between GNP per capita and inter-ethnic income distribution (0.24), ethnic enrollment in higher education (0.18), and ethnic professional occupations (0.27) are all non-significant at the 0.1 level.

10. For a discussion of the problems of comparing ethnic income over time in Israel, see Remba (1973).

REFERENCES

Abeysekera, G. (1975). The Distribution of Income in Sri Lanka, 1953-1973: Its Structure, Trends and Interpretation. Ph.D. Dissertation, Madison: University of Wisconsin.

Adelman, I. and C.T. Morris (1973). Economic Growth and Social Equity in Developing Countries. Stanford, California: Stanford University Press.

Amin, S. (1974). Accumulation on a World Scale. New York Monthly Review Press.

Arles, J.P. (1966). "The Economic and Social Promotion of the Scheduled Castes and Tribes in India." International Labor Review, 93 (May): 477-508.

Arles, J.P. (1971). "Ethnic and Socio-economic Patterns in Malaysia." International Labor Review, 103 (December): 527-553.

Australian Government (1975). Commission of Inquiry into Poverty. Canberra: Australian Government Press.

Blalock, Jr., H.M. (1972) Social Statistics, 2nd Edition. New York: McGraw-Hill.

Canadian Royal Commission (1967). Bilingualism and Biculturalism, Book I. Ottawa: Canadian Government Press.

Chenery, H., M.S. Ahluwalia, C.L.G. Bell, J.H. Duloy, and R. Jolly (1974). Redistribution with Growth. London: Oxford University Press.

Collette, J. and P. O'Malley (1974). "Urban Migration and Selective Acculturation: The Case of the Maori." Human Organization, 33 (Summer): 147-153.

Curtis, M. and M.S. Chertoff (1972). Israel: Social Structure and Change. New Jersey: Transaction Books.

Cutright, P. (1967) "Inequality: A Cross-national Analysis." American Sociological Review. (August): 562-578.

Denitch, B. (1976). The Legitimation of a Revolution: The Yugoslav Case. New Haven: Yale University Press.

Dunn, J. (1974). "The Revision of the Constitution in Belgium." Western Political Quarterly, 27 (March): 143-163.

Farley, R. (1977) "Trends in Racial Inequalities: Have the Gains of the 1960s Disappeared in the 1970s?" American Sociological Review, 42 (April): 189-208.

Finsterbusch, K. (1975). "Recent Rank Ordering of Nations in Terms of Level and Rate of Development." Studies in Comparative International Development, 8 (June): 52-70.

Galtung, T. (1971). "A Structural Theory of Imperialism." Journal of Peace Research, 8, 81-117.

Glazer, N. (1975). Affirmative Discrimination: Ethnic Inequality and Public Policy. New York: Basic Books.

Grove, D. J. (1976). "Current and Future Research at the Center on International Race Relations." Studies in Race and Nations, 7, Center on International Race Relations, University of Denver.

Hartley, E.L. and R. Thompson (1967). "Racial Integration and Role Differentiation." The Journal of the Polynesian Society, (December): 428-446.

Hirschman, C. (1975). Ethnic and Social Stratification in Peninsular Malaysia. Washington: American Sociological Association.

Horrell, M., D. Horner, and J. Hudson (1975). A Survey of Race Relations is South Africa. Johannesburg: Institute of Race Relations.

Jahan, R. (1972). Pakistan: Failure in National Integration. New York: Columbia University Press

Jambrek, P. (1975). Development and Social Change in Yugoslavia: Crisis and Perspectives of Building a Nation. Lexington: Lexington Books.

Jayawardena, L. (1974). "Sri Lanka" in Chenery et al.

Kuper, L. (1974). Race, Class and Power. Chicago: Aldine.

Kuznets, S. (1963). "Quantitative Aspects of the Economic Growth of Nations: Distribution by Income by Size." Economic Development and Cultural Change, 11 (January): 1-79.

Lang, N.R. (1975). "The Dialectics of Decentralization: Economic Reform and Regional Inequality in Yugoslavia." World Politics, 27 (April): 309-335.

Lean, L.L. (1974). "The Pattern of Income Distribution in West Malaysia 1957-1970." World Employment working paper, 2-23. Geneva: International Labour Office.

157

Lissak, M. (1969). Social Mobility in Israeli Society. Jerusalem: Israel University Press.

Mckown, R.E. (1974). "The Impact of Education on Ethnic Groups in Ghana and Kenya," in W. Bell and W.E. Freeman eds. Ethnicity and Nation-Building, Beverly Hills: Sage.

Means, G.P. (1972). "Special Rights as a Strategy for Development: The Case of Malaysia." Comparative Politics, 5 (October): 29-61.

Morrison, D.G., R.C. Mitchell, J.N. Paden and H.M. Stevenson (1972). Black Africa: A Comparative Handbook. New York: Free Press.

Oshima, H.T. (1962). "The International Comparison of Size and Distribution of Family Incomes with Special Reference to Asia." Review of Economics and Statistics. 44 (November): 439-445.

Paukert, F. (1972). "Income Distribution at Different Levels of Development: A Survey of Evidence." International Labor Review, 105 (September): 97-125.

Pryor, F. (1968). Public Expenditures in Communist and Capitalist Nations. Homewood, Illinois: Irwin.

Remba, O. (1973). "Income Inequality in Israel: Ethnic Aspects," in M. Curtis and M.S. Chertoff, eds. Israel: Social Structure and Change. New Brunswick: Transaction Books.

Rosillion, C. (1968). "Cultural Pluralism, Equality of treatment and Equality of Opportunity in Lebanon." International Labor Review 98 (September): 225-244.

Rothchild, D. (1969). "Ethnic Inequalities in Kenya." The Journal of Modern African Studies, 7 (September): 689-711.

Rubinson, R., (1976), "The World Economy and the Distribution of Income with States: A Cross-national Study", American Sociological Review, 41 (Aug.): 638-665.

Santos, R.D. (1970). "The Structure of Dependence," The American Economic Review, 42 (May): 231-236.

Sen, A. (1973). On Economic Inequality. New York: Nortin & Co.

Silver, B. (1974). "Levels of Sociocultural Development among Soviet Nationalities: A Partial Test of the Equalization Hypotheses," American Political Science Review, 67 (December); 1618-1637.

Smooha, S. and Y. Peres (1975). "The Dynamics of Ethnic Inequality," Social Dynamics, 1 (June): 63-69.

Snodgrass, D.R. (1975). "Trends and Patterns in Malaysian Income Distribution, 1957-1970," in D. Lim Readings on Malaysian Economic Development. Kuala Lumpur: Oxford University Press.

Stockwin, H. (1973). "A Racial Balance Sheet." Far Eastern Economic Review, 82 (December): 40-43.

von der Mehden, F. (1977). "Communalism, Wealth and Income in Afro-Asia." Program of Development Studies, Rice University, Houston.

Wilensky, H. (1975). The Welfare State and Equality. Berkeley: University of California Press.

Williamson, J.G. (1965). "Regional Inequality and the Process of National Development: A Description of Patterns." Economic Development and Cultural Change, 13 (July): 3-82.

Williamson, J.B. and J.J. Fleming (1977). "Convergence Theory and the Social Welfare Sector." International Journal of Comparative Sociology, 18 (September-December): 242-253.

World Bank, (1975) World Bank Atlas. Washington: World Bank.

Ziring, L. (1971). The Ayub Khan Era: The Politics of Pakistan, 1958-1969. Syracuse: Syracuse University Press.

APPENDIX

Sources

Belgium

Higher Education:	Institute National de Statistique, (1975), Annuaire Statistique de la Belgique, Tome 95, Bruxelles: T. 130.
Professional:	Institute National de Statistique, (1975), 1970 Reccnscment de la Population Active, A Royamme, Provinces, Arrandisements et Regions Linguistic, Bruxelles: T. 100.
Income:	Institute National de Statistique, (1976), Bulletin de Statistique, No. 7-8, Juillet-Aout: T. 655.
Cabinet:	The Europa Yearbook, London, 1962-1975.

Canada

Higher Education:	Census of Canada (1974), The School Population, Vol. 1, Part. 5, Ottawa: T. 3.
Professional:	Census of Canada (1971), Population of Ethnic Groups, Vol. 1, Part. 3, Bulletin 1.3-2, Ottawa: T. 4; C. Porter (1963), The Vertical Mosaic: Analysis of Social Class and Power in Canada, Toronto: 564.
Income:	Canadian Report of the Royal Commission on Bilingualism 1969: The Work World, Book III, Ottawa: 19; Census of Canada (1977), Income of Ethnic Groups, Ottawa: T. 2B.
Cabinet:	W.H. Mallory ed., (1961-1967), Political Handbook of the World: Parliaments, Parties and Press, New York; Europa

Yearbook, 1963, 1967; P.G. Normandin, The Canadian Parliamentary Guide, Ottawa, 1969, 1970-1971.

Israel
Higher Education:

Central Bureau of Statistics (1971), Students in Academic Institutions, Special Series No. 354, Jerusalem: T. 52-53; Students in Academic Institutions, Special Series, No. 249: T. 4.

Professional:

Central Bureau of Statistics, (1964) Labor Force Surveys, 1955-1961, Special Series, No. 162, Jerusalem: T. 49; Labor Force Surveys, 1974: T. 373.

Income:

Central Bureau of Statistics (1975), Statistical Yearbook of Israel, No. 26, Jerusalem: T. 263.

Cabinet:

Mallory, 1965: 136-137; Europa Yearbook, 1966-1975.

Malaysia
Higher Education:

Malaysian Statistical Office (1973), Mid-Term Review of the Second Malaysia Plan, 1971-1975, Kuala Lumpur: T. 4; J.P. Arles, (1971), "Ethnic and Socio-Economic Patterns in Malaysia", International Labor Review, 104 (December): 534.

Professional:

N.S. Choudry, (1970), Malaysian Socio-economic Sample Survey of Households, 1967-1968, Kuala Lumpur: T.100; Population Census of the Federation of Malaya, 1957, No. 14, Kuala Lumpur: T. 16.

Income:

T.H. Silcock and E.K. Fisk (1963), The Political Economy of Independent Malaya: A Case Study of Development, Berkeley: 279; Mid-Term Review of the Second Malaysian Plan: T. 4.

Cabinet:

Europa Yearbook, 1960, 1962, 1966-1975; The Statesman's Yearbook, 1958-1959, London, 1970-1971; Mallory, 1961, 1963-1966; The International Yearbook and Statesman's Who's Who, 1971, London: 34.

New Zealand
Higher Education: Department of Statistics (1970), Census of
Population and Dwellings, 1966 Industry and
Occupations, Vol. 8, Wellington: T. 124.

Professional: Census of Population and Dwellings,   1966:
T. 164; Maori Population and Dwellings,
1966 Vol. 8, Wellington (1970), T.52; Maori
Population and Dwellings, Wellington (1970),
T. 2.

Income: C. Collette and P. O'Malley (1974), "Urban
Migration and Selective Acculturation: The
Case of the Maori, Human Organization,
33(September):   150; M. Lee, (no date),
Nga Kaimaki, Polynesians in Industry,
Wellington: 8; Census of Population and
Dwellings, (1971), Wellington: T. 3.

Cabinet: Mallory, 1959-1967; G.H. Scholefield (1951).
Who's Who in New Zealand.   Wellington:
11-12; Europa Yearbook, 1960, 1968,
1970-71.

Pakistan
Higher Education: Pakistan Yearbook 1970.   38 Karachi:T.5

Professional: Government of Pakistan (1972).
Twenty-five Years of Pakistan in Statistics
1947-72. Karachi: T.33.

Income: K.U. Ahmad (1972).   Breakup of Pakistan:
Background and Prospects of Bangladesh.
London: 30.

Cabinet: Mallory, 1959-67; Europa Yearbook, 1962,
1967;   Chiefs of State and Cabinet Members
of Foreign Governments 1968. Karachi: 52.

Sri Lanka
Higher Education: Central Bank of Ceylon (1974), Survey
of Sri Lanka's Consumer Finances,   1973,
Columbo: T. 16.

Income: Central   Bank   of   Ceylon,   (1976).
Survey of Sri Lanka's Consumer Finances,
1973.   Columbo: 83-84; part 11: 140-159;
and Survey of Ceylon's Consumer Finances,
1963. Columbo: 121-131.

Cabinet:	A. J. Wilson (1970). "Ceylonese Cabinet Ministers 1959-67: Their Political, Economic and Social Background, "The Ceylon Economist; Europa Yearbook, 1960, 1962-64, 1966-68, 1970-73; Mallory, 1961, 1965; P. Stebbins and A. Amoia (1970). Political Handbook and Atlas of the World 1970: Parliaments, Parties and Press. New York: 53.

United States
Higher Education:	Compiled from the Bureau of Census,
Professional:	Special Reports for 1950, 1960 & 1970
Cabinet:	R.J. Vexler, (1975), The Vice-President and Cabinet Members, Vol. II, New York: 834-836; Europa Yearbook, 1962-1964, 1966-1970.

Yugoslavia
Higher Education:	World Bank Country Economic Report, (1975), Yugoslavia: Development with Decentralization, Baltimore: 468; Statistical Yearbook of the Socialist Federal Republic of Yugoslavia, 1973, Belgrade: T. 224.
Professional:	Statistical Yearbook of Yugoslavia, 1967: T 202; Statistical Yearbook of Yugoslavia, 1975: 352.
Income:	Statistical Yearbook of Yugoslavia, 1975: 506.
Cabinet:	Mallory, 1962-1964; Stebins and Amoia: 429; Europa Yearbook, 1970-1974.

NOTE: Population data are taken from the cross-national data files at the Center for International Race Relations, University of Denver.

7. Measuring Cross-national Ethnic and Racial Inequality: Alternative Perspectives

Baldave Singh

Poverty, like beauty, lies in the eye of the beholder. Poverty is a value judgment; it is not something one can verify or demonstrate, except by inference and suggestion, even with a measure of error. To say who is poor is to use all sorts of value judgments. The concept has to be limited by the purpose which is to be served by the definition.... A concept which can help influence public thinking must be socially and politically credible (Orshansky 1969:37).

The above statement on poverty (frequently a euphemism for inequality) can be equally well applied to inequality. While many authors write as if what they and others mean by inequality is self evident and has the same meaning to most persons, inequality is in fact a complex and often confusing concept. Depending on which definitions and measures one wishes to apply to the term, its estimation can have different and contrasting results. The selection of measures may heavily influence the results obtained and, while paying attention to the need for objective or "factual" methods, normative considerations ultimately do (or should) dictate the selection of specific measures. While inequality is a phenomenon of universal importance, this paper will be confined to an examination of socio-economic inequality among ethnic and racial groups.

In this paper we will demonstrate that various measures of inequality estimate quite particular formulations of the concept, and we will identify and briefly examine the effect that some normative considerations may have on the estimation of socio-economic inequalities among ethnic and racial groups cross-nationally.

We will examine socio-economic inequality on two levels. First, at the cross-cultural level we investigate the relative positions of fifty-five groups in seventeen different societies. Secondly, at the cross-national level we examine the effect of group size on ethnic inequalities between nations. Among the empirical considerations under examination are the following: (i) a comparison of all groups with the mean for the total society, (ii) a comparison of all subordinate groups in a society with the top group,[1] and (iii) the effect of group size on measuring inequality among nations. Our data are confined to three variables--income, professional occupations, and higher education--selected because they directly relate to most conceptions of socio-economic inequality.

METHOD

Measuring Inequality

As stated earlier, we will analyze inequality on two levels: the cross-cultural and the cross-national.

At the group level, the basic normative issues under consideration are the effect of (i) estimating inequality in relation to the societal mean (M), and (ii) estimating inequality in relation to the highest scoring group (T). These two considerations reflect two quite different views of inequality.

The first view is that equality is a state where all groups have the same property status, and will always be equal to the societal mean. The focus is on the societal mean as the point of parity; inequality is measured as a function of the deviation from that point.

The second view reflects the contention that groups, rather than viewing themselves in relation to a societal mean (which may not portray any group's position whatsoever), focus instead on their position relative to the superordinate group in each respective society. In this instance, inequality is a measure of the distance between each subordinate group and the highest scoring group in each country.

In reaction to proponents of the top group-based (T) view of inequality, advocates of the mean-based definition may argue that the aforementioned criticism is a non sequitur since equality, as it is used here, is still essentially a theoretical construct, and since measures of inequality have utility if they show the extent to which there is a deviation from the point of perfect equality (the Mean).

Both arguments have merit and it is difficult to choose one as categorically preferable to the other. It becomes important, then, to know the extent of deviation or similarity in results the two measures present.

When examining inequality between groups, we do not differentiate between groups of unequal size. Thus, all ethnic and racial groups--whether collections of a few thousand individuals or several millions, or whether a small fraction or a large majority of their societal populations--are accorded the same statistical treatment.

Since our data are confined to societal and group means, the relative mean deviation (M) is thought to be the most appropriate measure. It takes the entire societal distribution into account and therefore can be used where more than two groups need comparing. It (M) simply compares the mean values of each group with the mean value for all differences, and then evaluates these as a proportion of the total score.

Borrowing from Sen (1973:25) we may note the relative mean deviation (M) to be:

164

$$M = \sum_{i=1}^{n} (u - yi)/nu$$

where we have a distribution of a property over n persons, i = 1, ...n, yi is the property of person i, and the average property is u. The second inequality measure at the cross-cultural level of analysis compares all subordinate groups in relation to the top (superordinate) group within each respective society. This top group-based measure (T) may be noted as T = (t-s)/u where: t = top-group score, s = subordinate group score, and u = mean score for the total society. When necessary, the scores have been standardized so that the ethnic or racial groups in the most adverse positions always have a zero score while the most privileged groups have the highest scores.

At the country level we examine the effect of relative group sizes on the estimation of ethnic and racial inequalities amongst nations. This is computed by summing the scores of the respective ethnic and racial groups within each country and then dividing by the number of groups. Thus

$$M = \sum_{i=1}^{n} (u - i)/u$$

At the country level we propose to examine two formulations of group inequality. The first ignores the relative size of groups while the second accounts for the relative size of groups by multiplying each group's inequality score by its percentage to the total country population.

To estimate cross-national inequality when group sizes are ignored, we sum the group inequalities within each country and then divide by the number of groups. When accounting for group sizes, the country inequality scores are derived by multiplying each group's inequality scores by the percentage of the respective group to the total population. The results are then summed to obtain the country inequality scores, which are divided by the percent of the total country population with which we are dealing. Division of country scores by the percentage of total population is necessary since in some instances we deal with less than one hundred percent of a country's population. By division, the national inequality scores are standardized, and although between-country comparison is still problematical, such difficulties are substantially reduced.

Operationalization of the Socio-Economic Variables[2]

1. Mean per capita income for Ethnic and Racial Group.
Definition: This variable is usually the mean per capita income for each ethnic or racial group before taxes listed in domestic currencies. Occasionally average earnings per employed worker or

average household income either before or after taxation are used where the former forms of data are unavailable.

2. Percent of ethnic/racial group employed in Professional and Technical Occupations as a proportion of economically active group population.

Definition: Most frequently, the percentage of economically active population occupied in professional and technical positions follows the nomenclature of the International Standard Industrial Classification of all Economic Activities and the International Standard Industrial Classification of Occupations. The economically active population comprises the total number of employed persons which includes employers, salaried employees, wage earners and own account workers. Not included are students, retired persons, persons living on their own means, and those entirely dependent on others (see Taylor and Hudson 1972: 292-93).

3. Percent of Ethnic/Racial group enrolled in Higher Education.

Definition: Wherever possible, we have used data on the numbers of individuals in ethnic and racial groups enrolled in institutes of higher education. When such data were unavailable, we resorted to using numbers that have graduated from such institutes. In order to standardize the data for group size, we have divided each raw score by the twenty to twenty-four year old populations of the respective groups. In cases where this denominator was unavailable, an alternative denominator (e.g., numbers of group adult population) was applied. At all times, efforts were made to maximize comparability. Most if not all countries in our sample, conform to the UNESCO definition of higher education "which requires, as a minimum condition of admission, the successful completion of education at the second level (secondary or high school level), or evidence of the attainment of an equivalent level of knowledge" (UNESCO 1968: 30). The data includes students at public and private institutions such as universities, teachers' training colleges, and higher professional schools.

The Sample

The sample consists of fifty-five ethnic and racial groups in seventeen countries. Table 1 lists the sample of groups and countries with their respective population sizes and the years to which our socio-economic data refer.

The sample was selected with careful regard to maximizing geographic representation and data reliability. Among the primary considerations in the choosing of groups were the comparability and reliability of data, the importance of the groups, a limit of six groups per country, and the inclusion of at least seventy-five percent of each country's population.

We have tried to approximate the total population of each country. In some cases, it was unavoidable that less than one hundred percent of country populations be represented. Yugoslavia and Israel are the only two cases where less than eighty percent of

166

the total country's population are used (75.8 percent and 78.0 percent respectively).

In five of the countries, data on ethnic and racial categories were unavailable, but there is a high correlation between regionalism and ethnic or racial homogeneity. In Belgium, Pakistan, Switzerland, the U.S.S.R., and Yugoslavia, regional data are used as surrogates for ethnic data since the regions are at least seventy-five percent homogeneous.[3] The use of regional data to represent the status of ethnic and/or racial groups is especially problematical when measuring income inequalities since it is necessary to assume that production benefits and incomes of different regions are consumed, if not exclusively, then in large part, within the regions themselves. The problem is most acute where the federal or central government via taxation and income transfers alters the regional income distributions. Thus, it is most likely that the income inequalities within the Soviet Union and Yugoslavia are overestimated since these governments make substantial regional transfers of income. Income inequalities in Pakistan, on the other hand, may be underestimated if the present Bangladesh government is correct in charging the latter of "exploiting" East Pakistan to subsidize the Western region.

FINDINGS

Cross-Cultural

Tables 2, 3, and 4 show the relative status of groups in higher education, professional occupations, and income on the M index. Table 2 depicts group inequalities in higher education. The most disadvantaged groups (with M scores clustering around zero) are Australian Aborigines, Rhodesian Africans, Ghanaian Mole-Dagbani, and South African Africans; the most privileged groups are Canadian Jews, South African whites, and Rhodesian Europeans. The four lowest scoring groups cluster at one tail-end of the distribution followed by a sharp rise which includes New Zealand Maoris, South African Coloreds, and Israeli Oriental Jews. The next group shows no sharp increases with the group clustering around 0.96, which approximates the societal mean. As the group scores increase, we notice another sharp rise at 1.43, where Belgium Walloons, Pakistani non-Bengalis, Canadian Ukrainians, and Israeli European/American Jews concentrate. This is followed by another distinct cluster between 2.01 and 2.16, which includes American Orientals, U.S.S.R. Armenians, and Ghanaian Ga-Adangbe. Canadian Jews and South African whites form clear outliers with scores of 4.28 and 4.87 respectively. Finally, the privileged positions of these groups is outdone by Rhodesian Europeans which, as the most extreme outlier with a score of 11.39, exhibit the greatest distance (6.52) from all other groups.

Table 3 shows the M index distribution of groups in professional occupations. Here again Australian Aborigines are the lowest scoring group, followed by a cluster which includes Ghanaian

167

TABLE 1

THE SAMPLE

Country	Groups	Group as percent of total population
Australia (1966)	Aborigines	.7
	Whites	99.3
		100.0
Belgium (1970)	Flemish	56.5
	Walloons	32.1
		88.6
Canada (1961 & 1971)	British	44.6
	French	28.6
	Germans	6.1
	Italians	3.3
	Jews	1.0
	Ukrainians	2.7
		86.7
Cyprus (1960)	Greeks	77.1
	Turks	18.2
		95.3
Ghana (1960)	Akan	44.1
	Ewe	13.0
	Ga-Adangbe	8.3
	Guan	3.7
	Mole-Dagbani	16.0
		85.1
Israel (1971)	African/Oriental Jews	40.8
	European/American Jews	37.2
		78.1
Malaysia (1970)	Chinese	34.1
	Indians	9.0
	Malays	46.8
		89.9
New Zealand (1966 & 1971)	Europeans	90.4
	Maoris	7.9
		98.3
Pakistan (1961 & 1968)	Bengalis	54.2
	non-Bengalis	45.8
		100.0

TABLE 1 (Continued)

Country	Groups	Group as percent of total population
Rhodesia	Blacks	95.1
(1974)	Europeans	4.8
		100.0
Sri Lanka	Sinhalese	71.0
(1973)	Tamils	21.7
		92.7
South Africa	Asians	2.8
(1973/1974)	Blacks	71.2
	Coloreds	9.3
	Whites	16.7
		100.0
Switzerland	French	22.7
(1970)	Germans	72.7
	Italians	4.1
		99.5
Trinidad and Tobago (1960)	Africans	43.3
	East Indians	36.5
	Whites	1.9
		81.7
United States	Blacks	11.1
(1970)	Indians	0.4
	Mexican Origin	2.7
	Orientals	0.6
	Whites	85.0
		99.8
U.S.S.R.	Armenians	1.5
(1970)	Azerbaidzhani	1.8
	Belorussians	3.7
	Russians	53.4
	Ukrainians	16.9
	Uzbeks	3.8
		81.1
Yugoslavia	Croats	22.1
(1973)	Macedonians	5.8
	Serbs	39.7
	Slovenes	8.2
		75.8
(N = 17)	(N = 55)	

TABLE 2

GROUP HIGHER EDUCATION SCORES USING
MEAN-BASED MEASURE ·

Group	M Score*	Group	M Score
Australian Aborigines	0	Switzerland Italians	.93
Rhodesian Africans	.01	Ghana Akan	.95
Ghana Mole-Dagbani	.05	Australia Whites	.96
South African Africans	.06	Yugoslavia Croats	.99
New Zealand Maoris	.20	New Zealand Europeans	1.00
South Africa Coloreds	.26	U.S.S.R. Russians	1.03
Israel Oriental Jews	.27	U.S.A. Whites	1.04
U.S.A. Mexican Origin	.37	Canada Germans	1.05
U.S.A. Indians	.43	Canada British	1.08
Malaysia Indians	.44	Yugoslavia Mecedonians	1.09
Sri Lanka Tamils	.45	Sri Lanka Sinhalese	1.10
U.S.A. Blacks	.46	Malaysia Chinese	1.11
Ghana Ewe	.47	Yugoslavia Serbs	1.12
Ghana Guan	.53	U.S.S.R. Azerbaidzhani	1.13
Pakistan Bengalis	.56	Switzerland French	1.20
Canada French	.59	South Africa Indians	1.28
U.S.S.R. Ukrainians	.60	Belgium Walloons	1.43
Belgium Flemish	.69	Pakistan Non-Bengalis	1.45
U.S.S.R. Belorussians	.71	Canada Ukrainians	1.55
Cyprus Greeks	.77	Israel European Jews	1.58
Cyprus Turks	.80	U.S.A. Orientals	2.01
Yugoslavia Slovenes	.86	U.S.S.R. Armenians	2.08
Canada Italians	.87	Ghana Ga-Adangbe	2.16
U.S.S.R. Uzbeks	.88	Canada Jews	4.28
Switzerland Germans	.89	South Africa Whites	4.87
Malaysia Malays	.91	Rhodesia Europeans	11.39

(N = 52)

Missing data: Trinidad Africans, Asians, and Whites.

*   Groups with higher education scores below .96 are under-represented relative to their societal mean while groups with scores above .96 fare better than the societal mean.

170

TABLE 3

GROUP PROFESSIONAL OCCUPATION SCORES USING
MEAN-BASED MEASURE

Group	M Score*	Group	M Score
Australia Aborigines	0	Yugoslavia Serbs	.84
Ghana Mole-Dagbani	.14	Switzerland Germans	.85
New Zealand Maoris	.16	Ghana Ewe	.86
U.S.S.R. Uzbeks	.20	Australia Whites	.87
Canada Italians	.22	Malaysia Chinese	.88
South Africa Africans	.25	U.S.S.R. Russians	.89
U.S.A. Mexican Origin	.26	Yugoslavia Croats	.90
Israel Oriental Jews	.42	Switzerland French	.91
U.S.A. Blacks	.43	New Zealand Whites	.92
U.S.A. Indians	.50	U.S.A. Whites	.93
Canada Ukrainians	.61	Yugoslavia Slovenes	.99
Canada French	.63	Malaysia Indians	1.00
Canada Germans	.65	Belgium Walloons	1.01
U.S.S.R. Azerbaidzhani	.66	Pakistan non-Bengals	1.03
Switzerland Italians	.69	Canada British	1.07
South African Coloreds	.70	Ghana Akan	1.08
Trinidad Indians	.71	South African Asians	1.15
U.S.S.R. Ukrainians	.72	Ghana Guan	1.19
Pakistan Bengalis	.73	Israel European Jews	1.39
U.S.S.R. Belorussians	.74	U.S.A. Orientals	1.40
Belgium Flemish	.77	Canada Jews	1.65
Malaysia Malays	.80	U.S.S.R. Armenians	1.73
Yugoslavia Mecedonians	.83	South Africa Whites	3.15
		Trinidad & Tobago Whites	6.39

(N = 49)

Missing data: Cyprus Greeks and Turks; Rhodesia Africans and
Whites and Sri Lanka Sinhalese and Tamils.

*   Groups scoring below .86 are under-represented in professional occupations relative to their societal mean while
higher scores indicate above average representation in these
occupations.

171

TABLE 4

INCOME INEQUALITY SCORES USING MEAN-BASED MEASURE

Group	M Score*	Group	M Score
South Africa Africans	0	U.S.S.R. Ukrainians	.58
U.S.A. Indians	.22	South Africa Colored	.59
U.S.A. Blacks	.23	U.S.A. Orientals	.61
U.S.S.R. Azerbaidzhani	.24	Switzerland Germans	.62
Israel Oriental Jews	.27	Belgium Flemish	.63
Rhodesia Africans	.28	New Zealand Europeans	.64
Malaysia Malays	.29	Trinidad Africans	.65
Cyprus Turks	.31	Cyprus Greeks	.66
U.S.A. Mexican Origin	.35	Sri Lanka Sinhalese	.67
Sri Lanka Tamils	.37	Yugoslavia Croats	.67
U.S.S.R. Armenians	.38	U.S.A. Whites	.68
Trinidad & Tobago Asians	.39	Switzerland French	.71
Pakistan Bengalis	.40	Canada British	.72
Canada Italians	.44	U.S.S.R. Russians	.74
New Zealand Maoris	.46	Yugoslavia Slovenes	.77
Yugoslavia Macedonians	.47	Malaysia Indians	.78
Switzerland Italians	.48	Pakistan non-Bengalis	.89
Canada French	.50	South Africa Asians	.97
U.S.S.R. Belorussians	.53	Israel European Jews	1.01
Canada Ukrainians	.55	Malaysia Chinese	1.06
Yugoslavia Serbs	.56	Canada Jews	1.30
Canada Germans	.57	South Africa Whites	3.44
Belgium Walloons	.59	Trinidad & Tobago Whites	4.54
		Rhodesia Europeans	6.90

(N = 47)

Missing data: Australian Aborigines and Whites: Ghana Akan,
Ga-Adangbe, Ewe, Guan and Mole-Dagbani and U.S.S.R. Uzbeks.

*   Scores below .60 indicate groups which have incomes below
their respective country mean while groups with scores above
.60 have incomes above their country mean.

172

Mole-Dagbani, New Zealand Maoris, U.S.S.R. Uzbeks, Canadian Italians, South African Africans, and Americans of Mexican origin. The following group concentration, which includes Israeli Oriental/African Jews, American blacks, and American Indians, also demonstrates significant positions of underprivilege. The groups scoring close to .87 show approximate parity with their respective societal means. These are then followed by the distinctly privileged groups which include Israeli European/American Jews, Oriental Americans, Canadian Jews, U.S.S.R. Armenians, South African whites, and Trinidadian whites. The final two groups are privileged outliers.

In Table 4, we portray group income inequalities, again based on the M index. South African Africans on the most disadvantaged end of the distribution are a distinct outlier with a substantial .22 points between them and the American Indians. The next cluster rises gradually; the groups score about .60, approximating parity with their societal means. The remainder of the distribution shows clearly privileged groups with South African whites (3.44), Trinidadian whites (4.54), and Rhodesian Europeans (6.90) as distinct from all others.

Tables 5, 6, and 7 are concerned with the top group-based index (T). When the latter is adopted, all top groups in each society have the same score (before transformation, this equals zero) and they are therefore listed together at the beginning of each respective table. It should be noted that the top scoring group within individual countries sometimes varies from one variable to another. Since these superordinate groups have equal scores, it follows that we cannot make relative comparisons between them.

Table 5 (higher education) shows Rhodesian Africans as the only distinct outlier, with a zero score and over five points below the next most underprivileged groups--South African non-white groups. The spread between the remaining subordinate groups is relatively small with just over two points difference between all of them.

In Table 6 (professional occupations), Trinidadian Africans (0) and Trinidadian Indians (.02) are the clear underprivileged outliers, followed by Australian Aborigines (.86) and a cluster of South African Africans, Coloreds, and Asians. The remainder of the distribution again does not rise sharply; Malaysian Chinese, Yugoslavian Serbs, Ghana's Ga-Adangbe and Akan, Yugoslavian Croats, and Swiss Germans are among the least underprivileged of the subordinate group.

Table 7 (income) again shows Rhodesian Africans (0) as the underprivileged outlier followed by a cluster of Trinidadian Indians (2.46), Trinidadian Africans (2.17), and South African Africans (3.17). The rest of the distribution rises evenly with Swiss Germans, Oriental Americans, Yugoslavian Croats, and Belgian Walloons, while still subordinate groups, nevertheless approximating the mean.

When the cross-cultural rankings between the two measures (T and M) were compared for higher education, professional

TABLE 5

GROUP HIGHER EDUCATION SCORES USING
TOP GROUP-BASED MEASURE

Superordinate Groups

Australia Whites
Belgium Walloons
Canada Jews
Cyprus Turks
Ghana Ga-Adangbe
Israel European/American Jews
Malaysia Chinese
New Zealand Europeans
Pakistan non-Bengalis
Rhodesia Europeans
Sri Lanka Sinhalese
South Africa Whites
Switzerland French
U.S.A. Orientals
U.S.S.R. Armenians
Yugoslavia Serbs
(N = 16)

Subordinate Groups	T Score	Subordinate Groups	T Score
Rhodesia Africans	0	Ghana Akan	8.79
South Africa Africans	5.19	U.S.S.R. Uzbeks	8.80
South Africa Coloreds	5.39	U.S.S.R. Russians	8.95
South African Asians	6.51	U.S.A. Whites	9.03
Canada French	7.38	Australia Aborigines	9.04
Canada Italians	7.65	U.S.S.R. Azerbaidzhani	9.06
Canada Germans	7.84	Pakistan Bengalis	9.11
Canada British	7.87	New Zealand Maoris	9.20
Ghana Mole-Dagbani	7.99	Belgium Flemish	9.27
Ghana Ewe	8.31	Malaysia Indians	9.32
Canada Ukrainians	8.33	Sri Lanka Tamils	9.36
U.S.A. Mexican Origin	8.36	Switzerland Germans	9.69
Ghana Guan	8.37	Switzerland Italians	9.73
U.S.A. Indians	8.42	Yugoslavia Slovenes	9.75
U.S.A. Blacks	8.45	Malaysia Malays	9.80
U.S.S.R. Ukrainians	8.52	Yugoslavia Croats	9.88
U.S.S.R. Belorussians	8.64	Cyprus Greeks	9.96
Israel African/Oriental Jews	8.69	Yugoslavia Macedonians	9.97
(N = 36)			

Missing data: Trinidad and Tobago

TABLE 6

GROUP PROFESSIONAL OCCUPATION SCORES USING
TOP GROUP-BASED MEASURE

Superordinate Groups

Australia Whites
Belgium Walloons
Canada Jews
Ghana Guan
Israel European/American Jews
Malaysia Indians
New Zealand Europeans
Pakistan non-Bengalis
South Africa Whites
Switzerland French
Trinidad & Tobago Whites
U.S.A. Orientals
U.S.S.R. Armenians
Yugoslavia Slovenes
(N = 14)

Subordinate Groups	T Score	Subordinate Groups	T Score
Trinidad Africans	0	U.S.S.R. Russians	4.84
Trinidad Indians	0.02	New Zealand Maoris	4.96
Australian Aborigines	0.86	Canada British	5.13
South African Africans	2.84	U.S.A. Whites	5.24
South Africa Coloreds	3.29	Ghana Ewe	5.37
South Africa Asians	3.74	Pakistan Bengalis	5.44
U.S.S.R. Uzbeks	4.18	Belgium Flemish	5.48
Canada Italians	4.28	Malaysia Malays	5.50
U.S.A. Mexican Origin	4.56	Switzerland Italians	5.51
U.S.S.R. Azerbaidzhani	4.64	Yugoslavia Macedonians	5.54
Ghana Mole-Dagbani	4.66	Malaysia Chinese	5.56
Canada French	4.68	Yugoslavia Serbs	5.57
U.S.S.R. Ukrainians	4.69	Ghana Ga-Adangbe	5.58
Canada Germans	4.71	Ghana Akan	5.59
U.S.S.R. Belorussians	4.72	Yugoslavia Croats	5.61
U.S.A. Blacks	4.73	Switzerland Germans	5.67
Israel African/Oriental Jews	4.74		
U.S.A. Indians	4.81		
(N = 34)			

Missing data: Cyprus, Rhodesia and Sri Lanka

175

TABLE 7

GROUP INCOME INEQUALITY SCORES USING
TOP GROUP-BASED MEASURE

Superordinate Groups

Belgium Flemish
Canada Jews
Cyprus Greeks
Israel European Jews
Malaysian Chinese
New Zealand Europeans
Pakistan non-Bengalis
Rhodesia Europeans
Sri Lanka Sinhalese
South Africa Whites
Switzerland French
Trinidad Whites
U.S.A. Whites
U.S.S.R. Russians
Yugoslavia Slovenes
(N = 15)

Subordinate Groups	T Score	Subordinate Groups	T Score
Rhodesia Africans	0	Cyprus Turks	6.26
Trinidad Indians	2.46	U.S.S.R. Armenians	6.27
Trinidad Africans	2.71	U.S.A. Mexican Origin	6.28
South Africa Africans	3.17	Yugoslavia Macedonians	6.30
South Africa Coloreds	3.78	Sri Lanka Tamils	6.31
South Africa Asians	5.75	Malaysia Indians	6.32
Canada Italians	5.80	Switzerland Italians	6.38
Canada French	5.83	Yugoslavia Serbs	6.39
Malaysia Malays	5.86	U.S.S.R. Belorussians	6.41
Canada Ukrainians	5.87	New Zealand Maoris	6.45
Israel African/Oriental Jews	5.88	U.S.S.R. Ukrainians	6.46
Canada British	6.03	Switzerland Germans	6.51
U.S.S.R. Azerbaidzhani	6.11	U.S.A. Orientals	6.52
Pakistan Bengalis	6.12	Yugoslavia Croats	6.53
U.S.A. Indians	6.14	Belgium Walloons	6.58
U.S.A. Blacks	6.17		
(N = 32)			

Missing data: Australia and Ghana

occupations, and income, we obtained Spearman Rank order correlations of .29, .51, and .30 respectively (significant at the.01 level). These weak to moderate correlations corroborate the argument that the two formulations of inequality, though related, are still substantially different. The groups whose positions change most drastically according to which measures we apply are those of exceptionally small proportionate size (e.g., Australian Aborigines, Ghanaian Mole-Dagbani, and Canadian Ukrainians) or those which are relatively large (e.g., Australian whites and British Canadians). Since white Australians are 99 percent of the total Australian population, they essentially determine the mean, while Aborigines with only .6 percent of the population have no effect whatsoever. It follows that the impact of size is significant where the superordinate group is relatively small (Canada Jews, Trinidad whites, Rhodesia Europeans, South Africa whites, and Ghana Guan and Ga-Adangbe). Another substantial effect of these measures is on groups which, while approximating the mean score, still score significantly below the top group. The relative positions of such groups may undergo large changes as the base of comparison changes from M to T (examples are South African Asians and Coloreds; French, Italian, German, British, and Ukrainian Canadians; and Yugoslavian Macedonians). Although these groups approximate the societal mean, their relative position is still a subordinate one. Thus, South African Asians, who score higher than the mean, are nevertheless shown in an underprivileged position when compared to South African whites.

Cross-National

In Tables 8 and 9, scores on ethnic and racial inequalities for each country in our sample are depicted. Table 8 shows the country scores relative to the mean without taking into account group sizes; Table 9 does the same, but accounts for group sizes.

An examination of Table 8 (ignoring the group sizes) shows Trinidad and Tobago, Rhodesia, and South Africa as outliers exhibiting the greatest amounts of inequality on all three variables while Switzerland, Yugoslavia, Cyprus, and Belgium are among the most equal.

When we focus on Table 9 (accounting for group sizes), Trinidad and Tobago, rather than being among the most unequal outliers, become one of the most equal societies. Rhodesia and South Africa, although still the two most unequal countries, show less distance from each other than when group sizes are included. Australia, and to a lesser degree, Ghana, in contrast to their positions in Table 8, fall among the most egalitarian countries.

Rank order correlations between country inequality scores in Tables 8 and 9 are: .45 (higher education), .64 (professional occupations), and .91 (income). These findings suggest that group size has a marginal impact only on country inequality ranks for higher education and professional occupations. The impact of size on income inequalities appears to be negligible. A closer examination

177

TABLE 8

COUNTRY INEQUALITY SCORES - GROUP SIZES IGNORED

Country	Higher Education	Professional Occupations	Income
Australia	.48	.43	no data
Belgium	.39	.12	.01
Canada	.77	.37	.20
Cyprus	.18	no data	.18
Ghana	.61	.30	no data
Israel	.65	.49	.37
Malaysia	.26	.06	.31
New Zealand	.40	.38	.09
Pakistan	.45	.14	.25
Rhodesia	5.69	no data	3.31
Sri Lanka	.32	no data	.15
South Africa	1.45	.83	.80
Switzerland	.11	.07	.08
Trinidad & Tobago	no data	1.95	1.39
United States	.55	.40	.22
U.S.S.R.	.34	.33	.17
Yugoslavia	.10	.05	.11
	(N = 16)	(N = 14)	(N = 15)

TABLE 🔲

COUNTRY INEQUALITY SCORES - ATTENTION TO GROUP SIZES

Country	Higher Education	Professional Occupations	Income
Australia	.0066	.0059	no data
Belgium	.3503	.1054	.0136
Canada	.2524	.2416	.1119
Cyprus	.1843	no data	.0916
Ghana	.0117	.2827	no data
Israel	.6566	.4824	.3691
Malaysia	.1356	.0448	.2392
New Zealand	.0979	.1106	.0221
Pakistan	.4411	.3370	.2429
Rhodesia	1.4088	no data	1.3231
Sri Lanka	.2165	no data	.1020
South Africa	1.3678	.8286	.9231
Switzerland	.1071	.0157	.0263
Trinidad & Tobago	no data	.2859	.2045
United States	.1575	.1356	.0967
U.S.S.R.	.1604	.0981	.1071
Yugoslavia	.1073	.0294	.0806
	(N = 16)	(N = 14)	(N = 15)

of country ranks reveals that the largest changes in rankings are for Ghana and Australia. Unfortunately, it is for these countries that we do not have racial and ethnic income data. The high correlation for income inequality between the two measures (size and no size) is likely to be a result of this.

The results of this study suggest that "inequality" is a relative term. That is, the basis of comparison largely determines the inferences made about inequality between ethnic or racial groups. This applies not only to whether groups are compared with the societal mean or with top groups, but also to group size. Most statistical measures often have biases with different baselines for comparison. It is, therefore, important to spell out the normative assumptions underlying the selection of certain types of measures.

With respect to the measurements of group inequality, two indices (mean and top-group based) were presented. Generally, it was found that South African Africans, American Indians and blacks, Soviet Azerbaidzhani, Israeli African/Oriental Jews, Australian Aborigines, and Rhodesian Africans were among the most disadvantaged groups. While Rhodesian Europeans, Trinidadian whites, South African whites, Canadian Jews, Malaysian Chinese and Israeli European/American Jews were among those groups, which, relative to other communities within their respective societies, were in a privileged socio-economic position.

In measuring and comparing the extent of ethnic and racial socio-economic group inequalities between countries, two mean-based inequality indicators were adopted. The first of these measures inequalities without regard to the relative sizes of groups, while the second index accounts for relative group sizes. When group sizes are ignored, South Africa, Rhodesia, Trinidad and Tobago, Australia and Israel are among the most unequal countries. With the application of group sizes, the positions of Australia and Trinidad change dramatically from among the most unequal countries to among the most equal. Overall, it can be concluded that Belgium, Yugoslavia, Switzerland, the U.S.S.R., and Canada exhibited the smallest socio-economic inequalities in our sample while Rhodesia and South Africa, the two extreme outliers, are by far the most unequal countries. Although Trinidad, Israel, and Malaysia are other cases of substantial inequalities, they appear to be much more equal than Rhodesia and South Africa.

NOTES

1.   Top or superordinate groups should not be confused with dominant groups. Although the top group may be the dominant group in certain societies (e.g., South African whites), this is not always the case. An illustrative example of the differences is Canada where the British Canadians are the dominant group while Canadian Jews are the top scoring group in the variables examined here.

2.   These three variables were obtained from the Ethnic and Racial Cross-National Data Archive, Center on International Race

Relations, University of Denver. The data are part of an ongoing data-gathering project on the status of ethnic and racial groups cross-nationally. The raw data which are used in the computations are not presented here.

3. For a description of the relationship between ethnicity and regionalism in Belgium, Pakistan, and Yugoslavia, see the chapter by D. John Grove, fn. 6. Regionalized ethnicity in Switzerland and U.S.S.R. are as follows:

Switzerland
German Region (19 cantons) - 96 percent German speaking
French Region (5 cantons) - 92 percent French speaking
Italian Region (1 canton) - 79 percent Italian speaking

U.S.S.R.
RSFSR Region - 82.8 percent Russian speaking
Ukrainian SSR Region - 74.9 percent Ukrainian speaking
Belorussian SSR Region - 81 percent Belorussian speaking
Armenian SSR Region - 88.6 percent Armenian speaking
Azerbaidzhan SSR Region - 75.0 percent Azerbaidzhani speaking
Uzbek SSR Region - 75.6 percent Uzbek speaking

REFERENCES

Orshanky, Mollie (1969). "How Poverty is Measured." Monthly Labor Review (February).
Sen, Amartya (1973). On Economic Inequality. Oxford: Clarendon Press.
Taylor, Charles Lewis and Michael C. Hudson (1972). World Handbook of Political and Social Indicators. New Haven: Yale University Press.
UNESCO (1968). Statistical Yearbook (1966), Paris.

8. Spatial Distortion in Education and Income Differentials Among Communal Groups

Fred R. von der Mehden

This paper is an outgrowth of a larger study in which the Program of Development Studies (PDS) at Rice University has been analyzing the impact of Third World government programs upon income and wealth differentials among communal groups. Communalism has been defined in terms of racial, linguistic, ethnic and religious characteristics. The PDS study noted that educational policies were one of the most salient elements affecting economic inequities in Third World countries. Government activities relating to language regulations, differential expenditures, and quotas on students and faculty have previously been examined by PDS in its effort to understand the impact of educational policies (von der Mehden, 1977). This paper seeks to extend our analysis of what we found to be one of the most important explanatory variables with regard to income wealth differentials: "spatial distortion" or "spatial access" in education.

The issue of access to education based upon geographic setting is of central importance in considering obstacles to the attainment of higher levels of income in the developing world. Spatial access is the ability to obtain equal education based upon the location of the student and/or his family, i.e., maldistribution of quality and quantity of education across geographic areas or administrative units. The relationship of spatial access to income and communalism is based upon three propositions:

1. That there exists a correlation between education and income in the Third World;
2. That a considerable disparity exists in both quality and quantity of schooling among regions and particularly between rural and urban areas; and
3. Where communal groups in plural societies are dispersed geographically, there exist instances of differential access to education.

183

Previous studies have considered the relationship of education to income in the Third World (Anderson, J., 1974; Harbison, 1973; Elliott, 1975; Harbison and Meyers, 1965; Edwards, 1975; Bouden, 1974; Carney, 1967). While recognizing that this is both a complex and a somewhat controversial issue, we can briefly describe this interaction under 1) correlations of income and educational levels, 2) the relation of education to occupation, and 3) the impact of technological development.

1. <u>Correlations of education and income</u>: There have been various studies displaying correlations between higher levels of educational attainment and increased yearly or lifetime income. Studies conducted in Malaysia, Mexico, and Brazil have shown that income increments are a function of levels of education (Carney, 1967: 363; Hoerr, 1973: 256; Sohota, 1971: 440). Simple correlations of this type, however, must be handled with care, particularly within the context of communal divisions in which ascriptive characteristics may disadvantage groups otherwise equally educated. For example, in Guyana, Malaysia, and Sri Lanka, educated minorities have been limited in both teaching and civil service opportunities (Bacchus, 1970). As well, such correlations may hide variations in quality and type of education which also may be tied to communal patterns.

2. <u>Education and occupation</u>: The outside observer might expect that occupation and education would be related, given the necessity of extensive schooling for most higher income jobs. But of equal or greater importance is the factor of widespead illiteracy. At the top of the scale, professors, civil service positions, and technical fields require strong credentials. At the same time perhaps the more pertinent correlations have been at the level of simple literacy. With an 80 percent adult illiteracy in the newly independent states, the literate worker was more likely to obtain the higher paid skilled jobs. As well, the father's occupation can relate to income and education (see Mohd, 1973:10; Foster, 1965:265). This evidence tends to reinforce F. Harbison's comments about LDCs when he stated that, "without any question, formal education is an avenue through which some members of low income groups gain access to the higher income occupations" (Harbison, 1975).

3. <u>Education and Technology</u>: As technology has become more prized in modernizing societies, Western education and particularly advanced scientific training has become more desirable. Thus, traditional religious education as provided in many rural areas may not be relevant to those seeking positions requiring technical skills. A concomitant factor may be the need of European languages to compete for better commercial and technical opportunities (von der Mehden, 1977: 53-57, 100-09). These "modern" languages have rarely been taught in traditional, primarily rural religious schools where Arabic, Pali, and other non-European tongues are used. Thus, the type of education afforded children in different areas can disadvantage them in terms of job opportunities.

The second proposition holds that considerable disparity exists in the quality and quantity of educational opportunities among geographical areas within Third World countries. In analyzing this situation we will concentrate upon two major elements of the problem--the influence of colonial policies and practices and postindependence difficulties in the expansion of the educational infrastructure given previous inequities. Prior to discussing these issues, it is necessary to detail the types and degrees of educational differentiation within LDCs.

Considerable data exists supporting the existence of geographic distortion of educational advantage. These data can be delineated under two divisions, rural-urban and traditional-modern. There are clearly overlapping factors here, and both divisions include variations in both quality and quantity of education. The most obvious distortions have been between rural and urban areas. We have a wide range of data illustrating this situation. For example, in Turkey in the 1960s one-third of the villages had no schools, while in Bolivia 93 percent of urban teachers were certified as qualified and only 39 percent of their rural teachers were qualified. C. Elliott (1975) has gathered statistics from a number of African states showing discrepancies in enrollment between capital cities and rural areas, while H. B. Beebout (1971:37) has detailed variations of teacher qualifications in Malaysia.

Spatial distortion can also be identified between modern and traditional sections of a country. In most states this parallels rural-urban patterns, given the greater impact of modernization in urban areas. Spatial distortion is not always related simply to a rural-urban dichotomy, as evidenced in regions heavily influenced by missionary education, commercial agriculture, and colonial penetration. This is particularly notable along the west coast of Africa where the impact of the European was limited in time and less intense in the hinterlands. Consequently, there exist major variations in educational opportunities as distance increases from the areas of early modernization along the coast. More of this later.

As noted in an earlier PDS study, the duration and quality of traditional or rural education is also of prime concern. The tendency is for students in rural areas to drop out early in their schooling, often prior to achieving functional literacy. As well, schools in outlying areas may not have the same status as their counterparts in the capital city, and their students are disadvantaged when competing for university placement. We illustrated this pattern in Thailand and Malaysia, commenting:

In the Thai case, the vast majority of students left by the end of the fourth year of school. In 1961, 75 percent of those leaving school through the 18th grade had done so by the end of four years; and by that year there were less than half the children attending that started the first year. By the 1970s the majority of students had

185

completed four years, but postprimary education remained for a small minority. However, the problem of spatial distortion is emphasized by the quality, and, particularly, the quality of teaching outside the urban areas. In order to enter one of the country's better institutions of higher learning it is helpful to obtain a secondary education from a good secondary school in the Bangkok or Chiangmel regions. Yet most rural areas only go to the fourth year--with district towns having further primary education and provincial towns comparatively low quality secondary schools. Thus, unless a rural family has money to send its child to a boarding school or has relatives in a provincial town or city, there is no access to higher institutions.

In Malaysia distinct variations in school attendance, dropout, and test scores also exist between rural and urban populations. While 47 percent of urban 15+ youths were enrolled in school in the early 1970s, only 28 percent of rural youths were enrolled. Among Malays the respective percentages were 63 and 28, and Chinese 42 and 31 percent. Even Malaysia, with one of the highest percentages of its budget given to education in the world, shows high levels of attrition throughout the school system (von der Mehden, 1977: 61-63).

This maldistribution of educational opportunities has its roots in colonial attitudes, policies, and practices within an environment of unequal modernization. Prior to discussing the elements of modernization and particular policies affecting inequality, we should note that while considerable variation existed in governmental programs they were not so different in results. There were obvious major differences in overall programs (Furnivall, 1948: 123-30, 371-407; Piper and Cole, 1964; Thompson and Adloff, 1956: 516-56). The Portuguese stressed the "Assimilado" but made little effort at mass education, resulting in 99 percent illiteracy of its African population as late as 1950 (Duffy, 1959: 313-17). In Africa, the Belgians provided the highest level of literacy of any colonial power, but severely limited post-primary education and emphasized "utilitarian" training. The British utilized a variety of programs in different colonies, relied heavily on missionary education in their African colonies, and produced a relatively larger educated elite. The French emphasized assimilation through learning the French language and culture but extended this to a comparatively small portion of their colonial population (Berg, 1965: 232-67; Scanlon, 1954: 118). The Dutch laid little stress on mass education although a small minority achieved advanced training.

What all of the European powers had in common were policies resulting in a small percentage of their charges receiving a minimum of formal education and only a minute number obtaining post-primary training. As the figures in Table 1 show, literacy at the time of

186

TABLE 1

LITERACY AND POST-PRIMARY SCHOOLING IN SELECT COLONIES[a]

Colony	% Literate adults	%Total Population with post-primary education
French West Africa	5-10	0.10
French Indochina	15-20	0.40
British West Africa	5-25	0.27-0.34
Kenya	20-25	0.21
Uganda	25-30	0.37
Malaya	35-40	1.42
Portuguese West Africa	1-2	0.1

[a]Fred R. von der Mehden, Politics of Developing Nations (Englewood Cliffs, N.J.: Prentice-Hall, 1969): 11. Derived from United Nations data.

independence averaged less than twenty percent and post-primary schooling less than one percent. Of particular importance to this study, those who were educated tended to be concentrated geographically in urban settings or other regions impacted by modernization.

These dismal statistics resulted from a variety of factors: relatively short periods of European penetration in some cases, a lack of emphasis on mass education, colonial attitudes towards indigenous peoples, the unequal impact of modernization, and certain policies of colonial administration. While we will be concentrating upon the last two elements, these must be considered against the background of the attitudes of colonial administrators. The colonialists' view of their charges was in part responsible for the general paucity of educational opportunities and for widespread inequities within the colony's population. To many Europeans, formal education of the "natives" was considered unnecessary or undesirable on the basis that they were, for example, uneducable, happy in their primitive state, and/or did not need a formal education for their jobs. Thus, a District Commissioner from Kenya argued that, "...for some years to come he (the African) must be regarded as a child and, as such, not allowed to decide what is best for himself.... It is our duty to educate the native whatever his inclinations may be" (quoted in Sheffield, 1973: 18). A report from pre-war Kenya stated that education should be designed to keep the Kenyan on the farm (Sheffield, 1971: 11). The Portuguese were even more forceful in their view that the African was meant only for work: "It is necessary to inspire in the Black the idea of work and of abandoning his laziness and his depravity if we want to exercise a colonizing action to protect him" (quoted in Duffy, 1959: 318).

If these views helped influence educational policies toward the general population, prejudices against particular groups also led the Europeans to believe that particular groups were less educable than others. Administrators came to believe that groups such as Malays, Moros, southern Sudanese, Amer-Indians, and Dyaks were less capable of absorbing formal education, or were "happier" in their ignorance. For example, peasant Malays and Dyaks in colonial Malaya and Sarawak were to be educated, if at all, only to be better farmers and fishermen. One administrator argued that "the longer he (the Sea Dyak) is kept away from the influences of civilization the better it will be for him, for the good cannot be introduced without the bad" (Gullick, 1967: 202-03; Ryan, 1967: 167-68).

The expansion of European colonialism brought with it economic and social modernization and concomitant demands for education to gain the advantages of this "progress." With the imposition of colonial control came commercial agriculture, exploitation of natural resources, the opening of trading posts, a proliferation of missionary activities, and the development of an infrastructure that included administration, roads, health, and education. Obviously, this process was uneven in its development in terms of period, geographic area, and colonial system, producing modernization of varying intensity throughout the developing world.

It was just this unevenness of penetration that influenced variations in educational opportunities: particular groups within the colony were impacted by modernization more than others. These people might have lived near colonial administrative or trading towns, along lines of transport near roads, rivers, ports or railroads, in regions of commercial agriculture or mining, or in missionary centers.

To understand the relationships among colonialism, modernization, education, and spatial distortion, it is necessary to consider a number of interacting variables. First, as P. Foster, R. Clignet and others have noted, the colonial infrastructure provided an environment conducive to both demands and opportunities for education (Clignet and Foster, 1966; Foster, 1965). The colonialists needed individuals who were skilled in reading and writing in Western languages and who were capable of working in a modern context.

It should be recognized that there were varying reactions among indigenous groups to this new pattern. They ranged from rejection, through apathy, to acceptance, and even demands for more Western education (Yates, 1971; Ranger, 1975). In some cases, a developed trade, widespread support of education, and an educated bureaucratic elite existed before the Europeans arrived. For example, the Buganda already had writing skills and an esteemed educated bureaucracy prior to the arrival of the Europeans, and the missionaries found "a great desire among the younger chiefs and the King's servants to learn to read and write" (Ranger, 1975: 59). In other cases, traditional forces inhibited the acceptance of education (Martin, 1972 and 1975).

Secondly, the colonial regime provided unequal opportunities for education. State supported institutions of high caliber were developed primarily in urban areas where they catered to European children and were available on a limited basis only to the indigenous population. The decision as to where to place missionary schools was often more complex. At times the local leader defined the area of operation--as, for example, in East Africa where missionaries were forbidden to leave Kampala by Mustese I, giving the educational advantage to the Buganda in the area (Richards, 1969: 44-46). Colonial regimes restricted church groups from areas that might be politically difficult. The missionaries themselves sought people who were interested in education, who were vulnerable to proseletyzing, or who were easier to reach (Abernathy, 1969: 35-64). The important point here is that European-supported education was restricted by edict or situation to particular areas: the groups within these regions were, therefore, advantaged over other groups in the colony.

One other impact of the new system of education needs to be considered. Education was normally not free in colonial Afro-Asia. Those living in areas in the money economy could obtain the funds necessary to gain a formal education. A cash income was a prerequisite. Those in traditional rural economies were again disadvantaged (Kilson, 1966: 39).

Aside from the general impact of modernization, specific policies of colonial governments affected educational inequality within areas under their control. While there were a wide variety of policies implemented, we can focus only briefly on a few of the most salient:

1) Decisions to remain out of regions: In a number of cases colonial administrators decided not to expand into particular areas or to actually prohibit Western education from them. For example, Northern Nigeria was "off-limits" to missionary education, and students from that region were discouraged from going elsewhere for education (Lewis, 1965; Williams, 1973). A similar policy was followed by the British in the Northern Territories of the Gold Coast (Ghana) (Thomas, 1975). As well, pre-colonial rulers or traditional leaders under indirect rule often restricted missionary and other forms of Western education, as seen in actions by the Buganda King and Emirs of Northern Nigeria. A different type of limitation was practiced by the French in Algeria: compulsory education was only for those within three kilometers of "native schools" (Heggory, 1973).

Reasons for these decisions varied. Often it was felt that the maintenance of traditional patterns was more desirable than raising conflictual situations by challenging them. This was true in parts of Nigeria, Indonesia, the Philippines, and the Gold Coast. In other cases it was the consideration that people were too isolated or did not need an education given their means of livelihood. Whatever the reason, these decisions effectively disadvantaged groups during and after the colonial era.

2) General development programs: Educational policies were only part of the generally uneven development policies of colonial

governments. While usually not systematically planned, health, transportation, housing, electrification, and other programs developed an urban bias which, in turn, made for demands for opportunities for education. As for the urban dwellers' rural counterpart, G.E.R. Burroughs put it rather succinctly when he noted that in Venezuela those few who could break out of traditional patterns were reluctant to return to their native villages due to a lack of supplies and medical and social services (1974: 8).

3) Aid to Europeans and Pariahs: A basic policy of colonial governments was the establishment of schooling for European children. As early as the eighteenth century, French West Indian schools were almost exclusively European, a pattern followed throughout most of Afro-Asia. In most colonies, expenditures were heavily weighted in favor of these schools. For example, as late as 1959-60, only £2,600,000 were provided for 9,000,000 Africans, but £430,000 were allocated to 100,000 Europeans and Asians (Cameron, 1967: 45). Finally, the best schools were primarily for European children due to a combination of circumstances including the urban setting of the European population, an emphasis on metropolitan languages, costs which could not be met by the local population, and outright segregation.

Ultimately, European schools did provide the foundation for elite schooling of others, first Pariahs and sons of the local aristocracy, and then children of the local urban population. In that sense they augmented the growing gap between urban and rural.

To sum up the impact of the colonial period, it left a legacy of:

a) an urban population with higher levels of education, greater demands for formal schooling, and a larger infrastructure of buildings and teachers than their rural counterparts;

b) high levels of education among children of Europeans and Pariahs, many of whom did not remain after education;

c) a vast majority of illiterates in most colonies, with spatial distortion advantaging those impacted by modernization.

The newly independent states were thus faced with spatial distortion in terms of both those educated and the infrastructure capable of providing opportunities for all. Almost every new elite has publicly subscribed to universal education, to developing literacy campaigns, to expanding school opportunities into rural regions, and to building educational institutions at all levels. However, in spite of good intentions and a general raising of standards, spatial distortion still exists in a manner largely reinforcing the advantageous position of previous centers of modernization. The reasons for the continuance of the colonial pattern are briefly as follows:

1) Power of the colonial structure: The spatial distortions of the colonial period have been extremely difficult to overcome quickly and most Afro-Asian states have been independent less than a generation. Better schools, high demands for education, and employment opportunities have remained in the modernized centers. On the other hand, for example, efforts to get better teachers to rural areas, to keep the educated there to train others, and to

190

develop qualified students to compete for university positions, have all met with difficulty. Equalizing expenditures throughout the nation will not lead to equal education. Thus, PDS studies of the relationship of expenditures to output and outcome have shown that equal financial support cannot overcome past inequities, i.e., levels of expenditures have little correlation among administrative units in terms of literacy, school leavers, etc. (Hill, 1974). This leads to the second point.

2) <u>High levels of necessary expenditures</u>: A key factor in the slow development of rural areas has been the high costs of providing quality education to relatively isolated and often underpopulated regions. The lack of transportation, poor or costly boarding schools, the need to build entirely new plants, the lack of experienced teachers, and the slow systemic development have all compounded one another in discouraging educational expansion. For example, the high cost of upgrading rural teachers has been studied in a number of LDCs which have low levels of income. Even relatively well-off Kenya found the yearly cost of upgrading teachers to be over a million pounds a year, leading one observer to comment:

> It is difficult to avoid the pessimistic conclusion that the mounting cost of teachers as well as capital equipment will not permit large-scale improvement in the quality of primary education over the next five years, even with present fee structure and normal increase in enrollment. Were universal primary education to become a reality, there would undoubtedly be a decline in quality because additional untrained teachers would have to be employed, or costs would rise substantially if more holders of higher qualifications (such as the School Certificate) became available for training as teachers (Cowan, 1970: 29).

3) <u>The ousting of Europeans and Pariahs</u>: Voluntary or forced repatriation of Europeans and Pariahs from urban areas has contributed to a lowering of educational quality, probably temporarily narrowing the gap between rural and urban. However, the ousting of the missionaries from the rural areas, lowering the quantity of teachers and the quality of the educational system, has probably increased the educational gap. Where European languages are the official or commercial form of communication, the expulsion of European teachers has often had a negative effect on the European language proficiency in the area.

4) <u>Prejudicial decisions</u>: While there have been prominent programs of "affirmative action" designed to help previously disadvantaged groups in LDCs (Malaysia and India the most obvious), there have also been cases where governments have sought to limit the educational opportunities of particular communities. Prejudicial policies have been directed more at Pariah communities than at indigenous groups, but we have examples of somewhat similar programs in Sri Lanka, Uganda, and Sudan, among others[1] (Shepherd, 1966: 199).

191

This paper is too brief to describe these factors in detail, but we can state that, in spite of major efforts to expand eduation in LDCs, spatial distortion still exists. There has been only varying success in closing the gaps among indigenous peoples.

III

The third proposition of this paper states that spatial distortion can also account for variations in educational opportunities among communal groups and can thus impact upon income differentials. In attempting to support this proposition we have to recognize severe data problems. PDS at Rice has been wrestling with these for some time, but briefly stated they are as follows. LDCs normally do not collect statistics, at least publicly, along communal lines, which makes it difficult to relate educational levels, expenditures, etc., in terms of ethnic, religious, linguistic, or racial identities. In rare cases such as Malaysia excellent data are available, and in others there have been estimates or partial figures covering Pariah groups, urban areas, etc. If we use administrative units as our basis of measurement, two further difficulties arise: data from subnational units are often scarce and unreliable, and communal groups usually do not concentrate entirely within the boundaries of a particular province or state. District data would be more useful for correlations but these are rarely available. Urban centers which at one time were almost entirely dominated by particular groups have become more heterogeneous as mobility has increased since independence. Finally, some policies or actions of LDCs directed toward communal groups are not publicized for political reasons. With these caveats in mind, we can summarize our findings on the relation of communalism to access.

Spatial distortion has obviously disadvantaged some communal elements, particularly those in isolated regions. Examples include Chins of Burma, Nagas of India, Kurds in the Middle East, Moros of the Philippines, and Taurigs of the Sahal. There are also indigenous communal groups residing in and about urban areas or centered in regions of European commercial activities and who have heavy access to superior education. In Kenya the Kikuyu have taken advantage of this geographic factor, and one study showed that in 1962, 56 percent of the Kikuyu primary school-age group had attained some schooling as compared with 38 percent of the Luo, 34 percent of the Luhyu, and 21 percent of the Kamba (Leys, 1974: 202n). Makerere College enrollments show the fact of tribal dominance in East Africa, with the Kikuyu percentage of Kenyan enrollment at 44.5 percent in 1953, while the Gandian domination was reduced from 78 percent to 50 percent of all Uganda entries into Makerere College (Elliott, 1975: 253). In Sierra Leone the Creole population around Freetown has benefited from good educational institutions. The Sudan is an excellent example of differences according to region with the Arab Moslem north far more advanced in educational terms than the African south, due to a combination of spatial access and government policy. In Ghana, the opposite has

192

been true, with the African advantaged and the Moslim disadvantaged.

Two other studies have attempted to break down educational attainment by tribe. E. Soja has estimated primary and secondary educational levels plus literacy in Kenya (Soja, 1968: 63). A most interesting analysis was made by R. Clignet and P. Foster in 1963 when they interviewed a sample of 80 percent of the post-primary students in the Ivory Coast (Clignet and Foster, 1966). Using a selectivity index which assessed ratios between a group's representation in the sample and its appropriate representation in the total population, they found considerable variation among tribal groups. As well, Moslems with one-third the population had but 15.4 percent of the students. The data also showed our previous emphasis upon urban, modern sector, and colonial influences. As Charles Elliott quite properly notes, no universal statement can be made regarding the future of communal domination, and government policies differ markedly from one country to another. Yet, the combination of pre-colonial and post-colonial forces have severely disadvantaged major elements of the Third World.

NOTES

1. For example, as late as 1965 there were 88 secondary schools in Northern Sudan and 7 in the South, while the figures for Intermediate Schools were 175 and 26, respectively.

REFERENCES

Abernathy, D. (1969). The Political Dilemma of Popular Education. Stanford: Stanford University Press.
Anderson, C. (1964). "Economic Development and Post-Primary Education," in D. Piper and T. Cole. Durham: Duke University Press.
Anderson, J. (1969). "Self-Help and Independency: The Political Implications of African Education in Kenya," African Affairs, LXX (January): 9-22.
Bacchus, M. (1970). Education and Socio-Cultural Integration in a Plural Society. Montreal: McGill University.
Beebout, H.S. (1971). "EPRD Secondary School Survey: Preliminary Report," Kuala Lumpur: Education Planning and Research Division.
Berg, E. J. (1965). "Education and Manpower in Senegal, Guinea, and the Ivory Coast," in Harbison and Meyers: 232-67.
Bouden, R. (1974). Education, Opportunity and Social Equality. New York: Wiley.
Burroughs, J. (1974). Education in Venezuela. Hamden, Conn.: Anchor.
Cameron, J. (1967). "Integration of Education in Tanganyika," Comparative Education Review, XI (February).

Cameron, J. (1970). The Development of Education in East Africa. New York: Teachers College.

Carney, M. (1967). "Rates of Return to Schooling in Latin America," Journal of Human Resources, III (Summer): 359-74.

Clignet, R. and P. Foster (1966). The Fortunate Few: A Study of Secondary School Students in the Ivory Coast. Evanston: Northwestern University Press.

Cowan, G. (1970). The Cost of Learning: The Politics of Primary Education in Kenya. New York: Teachers College.

Duffy, J. (1959). Portuguese Africa. Cambridge: Harvard University Press.

Edwards, E., ed. (1975). Employment in Developing Nations. New York: Columbia University Press.

Elliott, C. (1975). Patterns of Poverty in the Third World. New York: Praeger.

Foster, P. (1965). Education and Social Change in Ghana. Chicago: University of Chicago Press.

Furnivall, J. (1948). Colonial Policy and Practice. Cambridge: University Press.

Gullick, J. (1967). Malaya. New York: Praeger.

Harbison, F. (1973). Human Resources as the Wealth of Nations. New York: Oxford.

Harbison, F. (1975). "The Education-Income Connection," (Mimeographed).

Harbison, F., and Meyers, C., ed. (1965). Manpower and Education. New York: McGraw-Hill.

Heggory, A. (1973). "Education in French Algeria: An Essay on Cultural Conflict," Comparative Education, XVII (June): 180-97.

Hill, K. (1974). "Distributional and Impact Analysis of Public Policy: A Two-Nation Study of Education and Health Policy," unpublished Ph.D. dissertation. Rice University.

Hoerr, O. D. (1973). "Education, Income, and Equity in Malaysia" Economic and Cultural Exchange, II, 2 (January).

Kilson, M. (1966). Political Change in a West African State. Cambridge: Harvard University Press.

Lewis, Z. (1965). Society, Schools and Progress in Nigeria. London: Pergamon.

Leys, C. (1974). Underdevelopment in Kenya. Berkeley: University of California Press.

Martin, J. (1972). "Sociologie de l'enseignment en Afrique Noire," Cahiers Internationeux de Sociologie, VII: 337-62.

Martin, J. (1975). Inegalities regionales y inegalities Sociales: l'enseignments Secondaire au Cameroun Septenrional," Revue Francaise de Sociologie: 217-34.

Mohd, M. B. (1973). Noor, Lapuran. Kuala Lumpur Kementerian Pelajaran.

Piper, D., and Cole, T. (1964). Post-Primary Education and Economic Development. Durham: Duke University Press.

Ranger, T. (1975). "Education in East and Central Africa." Past and Present, XXXII (December): 57-85.

194

Ryan, N. (1967). The Making of Modern Malaysia. Kuala Lumpur: Oxford University Press.

Richards, A. (1969). The Multicultural States of East Africa. Montreal: McGill-Queens University Press.

Scanlon, D. (1954). Traditions of African Education. New York: Teachers College.

Sheffield, J. R. (1971). Education in the Republic of Kenya. Washington: Department of Health, Education and Welfare.

Sheffield, J. R. (1973). Education in Kenya: An Historical Study. New York: Teachers College.

Shepherd, G. (1966). "National Education and the Southern Sudan," Journal of Modern African Studies, IV, 2 (October): 193-212.

Sohota, G. S. (1971). "The Distribution of Tax Burden Among Different Education Classes in Brazil," Economic Development and Cultural Change, 19, 3 (April): 438-460.

Soja, E. (1968). The Geography of Modernization in Kenya. Syracuse: Syracuse University Press.

Thomas, R. (1975). "Education in Northern Ghana, 1906-1940: A Study in Colonial Paradox," International Journal of African Historical Studies, VII: 427-67.

Thompson, V. and Adloff, R. (1956). French West Africa. Stanford: Stanford University Press.

von der Mehden, F. (1969). Politics of the Developing Nations. Englewood Cliffs: Prentice-Hall.

von der Mehden, F. (1977). "Communalism, Wealth and Income in Afro-Asia," Rice University Program of Development Studies. (Mimeo.)

Weeks, S. (1967). Divergence in Educational Development: The Case of Kenya and Uganda. New York: Teachers College.

Williams, G. (1973). "Education and Government in Northern Nigeria." Présence Africaine, 87: 156-77.

Yates, B. (1971). "African Reactions to Education in the Congolese Case," Comparative Education, XV (June): 158-71.

9. Welsh Nationalism and Subregional Inequality

Raymond R. Corrado
Bert A. Rockman

Ethnicity remains a basis for discriminatory treatment in the areas of human, moral, and legal rights. Recruitment to public office and access to political power usually are systematically related to ethnic affiliation. Income, occupation, and education also vary perceptibly according to ethnic affiliation (Porter, 1968; Rose, 1971; Greeley, 1974; Putnam, 1976). These inequalities, in turn, have stimulated ethnic political movements. In this chapter we address the question of how mass support for ethnic nationalism relates to perceptions of political, economic, and cultural inequalities. The answer to this question will be limited to regionally-based ethnic groups in advanced industrial societies with representative political institutions. An analysis of Welsh nationalism, including survey data, will provide the basis for constructing an answer to how perceptions of different types of inequalities relate to support for ethnic nationalism.

INEQUALITY AND DISTRIBUTION OF RESOURCES: COMPETING POLITICAL PERSPECTIVES

Separatist movements threaten the integrity of many nation-states. In Belgium, Canada, and Great Britain, ethnic political parties have gained significant electoral support and, in some cases, control of a regional government through popular elections. Assertions of unequal treatment from authorities and socio-economic disadvantage underlie appeals to ethnic political mobilization. Separatist leaders argue that national political and economic structures are dominated by members of the core region to the detriment of the peripheral ethnic regions and that, specifically, peripheral geographic areas stagnate economically while the core area advances. The leaders of ethnic nationalist movements also emphasize their loss of cultural status; the minority or subordinated ethnic culture experiences a decline while the mass media, the educational system, and economic imperatives enhance the dominant culture (Bertelsen, 1977; Esman, 1978).

While definitions of equality commonly distinguish between equality of opportunity and equality of result, a perspective deducible from the structure and nature of pluralist advanced industrial society is that no one social group should dominate the political and economic systems. Inequalities of human, moral, and legal rights are deemed to be intolerable in pluralistic democracies. But, so long as no one group dominates, limited inequalities in the distribution of wealth, status, and political power seem acceptable (Marshall, 1965; Bottomore, 1966; Runciman, 1966; Titmuss, 1969; Marsh, 1970).

Unequal distribution of economic growth, cultural status, and political power between the core and ethnic periphery constitutes the essence of the debate between the proponents of the political status quo and the proponents of separatism. Ethnic nationalists claim that a lack of economic opportunity, inherent disadvantages in political power, and cultural discrimination characterize the ethnic periphery and core relationship. This "internal colonialism" occurs, in their view, because the core ethnic region dominates the national government whose policies economically exploit the periphery. The economy of the peripheral region often is based upon declining extractive or primary industries or a depressed, non-diversified manufacturing industry. Additionally, the peripheral ethnic culture is demeaned because it is linked to this economic inferiority (Hechter, 1975).

Core group proponents of the political status quo, in turn, argue that the core does not exploit the periphery. In their view, high unemployment in the periphery is related to both natural resource distribution and to the uncertainties of international markets which are not subject to the control of the national government. Defenders of existing political arrangements, instead, argue that the national government encourages investment. It is also argued that far worse consequences will ensue economically if the peripheral region secedes.

Cultural and, most especially, political inequalities also underlie ethnic-regional nationalisms. Policies such as bilingualism, and practices such as ethnically based patronage sometimes have been employed by national governments to temper regional ethnic nationalisms by addressing cultural and political inequalities. Such palliatives, of course, are important but they are unlikely to override a prevailing sense of economic inequality and resentment against core economic dominance. Further, governmental authorities, particularly in unitary states, are likely to be extremely wary toward cultural and political policies that threaten the unity and integrity of the nation-state.

INDUSTRIALIZATION-URBANIZATION
AND SUBREGIONAL INEQUALITIES

Until recently, most theories of development hypothesized that the political repercussions of inequality in advanced industrial societies would be linked to class and occupational differences. The imperatives of industrialization, urbanization, secularization, and nationalism would create organizations, roles, and values that would downplay and eventually extinguish the relevance of the ethnic group (Lerner, 1958; Black, 1967). A competing theoretical perspective, however, foresees the continued importance of ethnicity. The belief that "internal colonialism" characterizes the core-periphery relationship can be a powerful impetus for regionally-based ethnic political movements. Ironically, according to Glazer and Moynihan, the modern social welfare state heightens ethnic awareness since the ethnic group provides a representational base for the struggle over the spoils of social welfare (Glazer and Moynihan, 1975). Finally, in contradistinction to the secularist theories, Walker Connor advances the view that regional ethnic nationalisms are further inspired by the processes of modernization and inter-group interactions (Connor, 1972).

According to the secularist perspective, industrialization and urbanization are key processes that facilitate assimilation. The industrial economy is related to social pluralism, the growth of political parties, and to the welfare state. Urbanization and the growth of secular social and political organization have a profound effect on the erosion of sectarian solidary group supports which in the rural setting play an essential part in the perpetuation of the ethnic group.

From the perspective of ethnic consciousness, however, the rural environment still provides a favorable setting for the preservation of ethnic languages and customs. The exposure to alternative lifestyles--ethnic, and otherwise--is more limited in the rural than in the urban setting and material rewards, occupational mobility, and educational opportunities are less accessible. The former condition perpetuates the bonds of community whereas the latter condition fuels grievance and resentment against the core group.

What is most surprising from the secularist standpoint, though, is that ethnic consciousness can be aroused in the urban setting too. Not only do many leaders of ethnic nationalist movements come from urban areas where they frequently have honed their organizing skills (Smith, 1972), but the most militant mass base in some instances (e.g., Canada) can also be found in the urban areas since the urban setting often accentuates feelings of relative deprivation by exposing people to alternative (higher status) lifestyles. It also provides the means to mobilize discontent more readily through social and political organization. Typically, however, the urban base of ethnic political consciousness is strongest in the case of diasporic ethnic groups rather than regionally based ones.

The industrial and service-oriented economy is largely urban-based and it is directed toward the core region in terms of transportation and markets. The mutual economic advantages of this arrangement usually create strong integrative, cross-regional ties among business groups and among labor unions. Because of such economic interdependence, separatism is thought to threaten a decline in standards of living to a greater extent in the urban areas than in the economically more marginal rural areas of the periphery. Although the coincidence of territory and ethnicity provides a capability for the creation of a separatist nation-state, a capability which does not exist for diasporic ethnic groups such as American blacks, the economic viability of any such state must be questionable. Certainly one indicator of viability is the maintenance of a standard of living not substantially less than that which exists presently.

The preoccupation with economic viability is even more pressing today given the prolonged worldwide recession, the projected slow growth of most advanced industrial economies, and the increased competition from Third World countries of resources and products usually produced in peripheral regions (Strumpel, 1978).

Although there is a pressing need to subject many of these speculations to the demands of a truly comparative analysis of regional nationalisms in advanced industrial societies, our analysis is limited to a single case, that of Wales. While differing in some important particulars (most notably the early industrialization of Britain), the evolution of Welsh nationalism in Britain provides an extremely informative case for the study of inequality, grievances, and the rise of ethnic nationalism. There is, in other words, much in the Welsh case that may be paradigmatic of other territorially based nationalisms occurring within advanced industrial societies.

HISTORICAL OVERVIEW OF INEQUALITY BETWEEN ENGLAND AND WALES

For most of medieval history, the Welsh fought among themselves as much as they did with invading ethnic groups from England. Except for a few brief periods, the Welsh people were not united politically. Still, there is little in their history indicating a desire to be incorporated by the English, and English attempts to win over Welsh territories were met alternatively with strategic compromise and with rebellion. In the 13th century, Edward I defeated the northern Welsh clans and began the process of annexing Wales. This process culminated in 1536 with the Acts of Union, which legally abolished any political, legal, and economic distinctions between Wales and England. While it is difficult to portray the Tudor monarchs (who were part Welsh) as tyrannical warlords, English military dominance remained the ultimate basis of English control over Wales.

But because the English were inattentive to Welsh cultural patterns, Welsh culture survived. Thus, the Welsh language continued to be used widely in rural Wales. Further, the growth of the Nonconformist religions gradually distinguished the majority of Welshmen from the predominantly Anglican English. In the 19th century, however, language became a political issue when the British state expanded its activities and presence to lay the groundwork for universal education and the welfare state. As in earlier periods, the proponents of the Welsh language lost. Notwithstanding the evolution of pluralist democracy, Wales remained numerically inferior to England in parliamentary representation, and, thus, remained a constant loser on most cultural issues.

A critical blow to the Welsh culture occurred when the Education Act of 1870 stipulated that English was to be the sole language of instruction in Wales. By the turn of the century the precipitous decline of Welsh speakers was evident. The preservation of the Welsh nation, particularly the rehabilitation of the Welsh language, was the impetus for the Home Rule movement for Wales. After the defeat of several Home Rule Bills, a handful of Welsh supporters in 1925 formed Plaid Cymru (the Welsh Nationalist Party).

Cultural issues initially dominated the Plaid Cymru platform, but after 1960 economic inequality between Wales and England had become a critical aspect of Plaid Cymru's message to the Welsh electorate. At the onset of World War II, Wales lagged behind England economically. The economic difficulties afflicting Britain after World War II were particularly severe in Wales. The coal and steel industries which dominated the Welsh economy were constricting, while the English Midlands and southeast England, in contrast, grew economically.

Politically, the Labour Party has completely dominated Wales locally and nationally. During the last three national elections, it averaged close to fifty percent of the vote in Wales and occupied nearly two-thirds of the Welsh seats in Parliament.

The strength of the Labour Party in Wales reflects, in part, the population dominance of the industrial and urban south. Two-thirds of the population lives in south Wales where transportation, mass media, and economic ties are directed toward the English Midlands and London. In contrast, central and northern Wales suffered an enormous population drain to industrial south Wales and England over the past century. While the Welsh Nonconformist religions and the Welsh language remain prominent in much of northern Wales, they have declined dramatically in anglicized south Wales. Welsh speakers now constitute only twenty-six percent of the Welsh population.

Plaid Cymru spokesmen maintain that Wales is virtually an English colony. They point to the dominance of the English language and the consistently higher unemployment and slower economic growth in Wales. For Plaid Cymru and the Welsh nationalists, these economic and cultural inequalities are inherent in British society and only the creation of a Welsh nation-state will ultimately adjust these imbalances.

The three Plaid Cymru Members of Parliament support the Labour government's Devolution Bill which, if approved by a referendum in Wales, would create a Welsh Assembly with limited administrative powers. Plaid Cymru views limited devolution as the first step to the establishment of a Welsh state. The party has maintained that it would retain strong economic and foreign policy ties to England while maintaining sovereignty in other affairs. Given the minor electoral support (eleven percent) that it consistently obtained in the last decade, Plaid Cymru has carefully avoided extreme positions on political, economic, and cultural issues (Corrado, 1977). Plaid Cymru is now faced with the prospect that some of the national government's long-standing commitments to

201

revitalizing the Welsh economy will be assisted by North Sea oil revenues and a stronger national economy. The immediate goal of a limited devolution is threatened by the Labour government's strategy of separating the devolution bills for Scotland and Wales and attaching a forty percent favorable referendum vote as a precondition for the Welsh Assembly.

It is problematic whether Plaid Cymru can garner the necessary electoral support to achieve its ultimate separatist goals. In the remainder of this paper, we examine structural and principally attitudinal factors that should clarify the relationship between perceived inequalities and socio-economic attitudes on the one hand, and support for Welsh nationalism on the other.

THE WELSH SURVEY

During 1970 and 1971, Corrado directed a survey in Wales to ascertain the value bases of various forms of nationalism (Corrado, forthcoming). Interviews were conducted with a total of 417 respondents of whom eighty-one percent were of Welsh ancestry, seventeen percent of English heritage, and two percent of other ancestry. Only the Welsh and English ethnic groups, however, are included in our analysis. The sample was stratified along urban-rural lines, but not specifically along Welsh-English lines. Half of the sample (208 respondents) was randomly selected from the rural constituency of South Caernarvonshire in northern Wales while the other half was randomly sampled from the urban electoral constituency of North Cardiff in southern Wales. The urban constituency is more ethnically heterogeneous than the rural one. It is about one-fourth English whereas the rural constituency is only nine percent English. These facts are not unimportant for, as we shall see, ethnic background interacts substantially with the urban-rural distinction in terms of access to material rewards and in terms of attitudinal patterns.

Let us turn now to the survey data in order to evaluate ethnic group and urban-rural cleavages in Wales.

ETHNIC AND URBAN-RURAL CLEAVAGES IN WALES: REWARDS, VALUES, AND CULTURAL AUTONOMY

Although inequalities in the structure of rewards are not a necessary condition for the development of nationalist sentiment, there can be little doubt that material inequalities have helped to give rise to demands for regional autonomy in Quebec, Scotland, and Brittany. There is no doubt, of course, that Wales, as a region, suffers from chronic economic depression and that this sparks a nascent Welsh nationalism. Differences between the material status of the peripheral (Welsh) and core (English) ethnic groups within Wales can provide further sources of discontent. From the data arrayed in Table 1, it is clear that the English who live in Wales enjoy a higher occupational status, higher levels of income, and also perceive themselves as belonging to a higher social status than do

TABLE 1

THE ENGLISH IN WALES ARE BETTER OFF IN SOCIO-ECONOMIC TERMS THAN THE WELSH, BUT THE WELSH IN THE URBAN AREA ARE BETTER OFF THAN THE WELSH IN THE RURAL AREA

(Entries are means based upon ordinal coding categories.)

	Occupation (lowest=1 highest=7)	Education (lowest=1 highest=4)	Income (lowest=1 highest=9)	Subjective Social Class (lowest=1 highest=4)
All Welsh (338)[a]	3.32	1.70	4.37	1.96
All English (69)	3.74	1.80	4.94	2.40
Urban Welsh (151)	3.34	1.91	4.64	2.27
Rural Welsh (187)	3.30	1.53	3.93	1.74
Urban English (51)	3.70	1.76	5.02	2.31
Rural English[b] (18)	3.91	1.98	4.72	2.67

[a]Unless noted otherwise, the marginals in parentheses are applicable to all subsequent tables.

[b]The small number of cases for the rural English sample does not permit reliable inferences to be drawn about this sub-sample. It is disaggregated at this level for illustrative purposes only.

the Welsh. At the same time, when urban-rural differences are controlled, the gap between the urban Welsh and the rural Welsh in most instances is about the magnitude of the raw differences between the Welsh and English. In other words, much of the differential between the Welsh and English in socio-economic status is accentuated by the economic backwardness of the rural environment and the lowly status of the Welsh who live in this environment. While there are material inequalities between the two ethnic groups, these inequalities seem largely to reflect the absence of viable economic opportunities in the rural area.

Material inequalities in the presence of modernizing secular values can lead to attitudes favorable to ethnic militancy and claims for redress of existing inequalities. Aberbach and Walker (1970), for example, show that American blacks became more favorable toward the slogan of black power the more immersed they were in a northern urban environment. Modern social values when combined with perceived deprivation provide a basis for political mobilization. But while the Welsh in the rural environment are the most economically disadvantaged, Tables 2-A and 2-B demonstrate that they hold traditional values more than any other sub-sample. They are least inclined, for instance, to think that a person can be good without religion and they are also the most religious of the sub-samples. This traditionalism may be a conservatizing anchor inhibiting the direct translation of economic grievances into militant political action.

Traditional value structures, furthermore, accompany communal ties based upon cultural solidarity. As we can see from Tables 3 and 4 the rural Welsh think of themselves as Welshmen more self-consciously than do the Welsh in the urban setting and, most especially, they support efforts to preserve and promote the Welsh language as one of the last cultural vestiges of the Welsh nation. Indeed, the differences between the rural and urban Welsh on the language issues are consistently as strong or stronger than those between the Welsh and English ethnic samples. Evidently, resistance to assimilation, at least in its cultural aspects, remains fairly strong in the rural areas, and the cultural basis for Welsh nationalism is clearly rooted there.

Briefly, then, our evidence to this point indicates that the peripheral (Welsh) and core (English) ethnic groups differ in their access to material benefits and in their cultural identities and values. It also directs us to important differences between rural and urban members of the Welsh ethnic group. The urban Welsh are more integrated into the socio-economic system than the rural Welsh, and their attitudes also are more assimilationist than are those of the rural Welsh. But if the urban center represents greater economic opportunity, it also reduces the strength of communal ties. These ties remain stronger in the more depressed rural area but they seem also to be associated with values resistant to radical political mobilization.

In the analysis that follows we probe further the perceptions and attitudes of the Welsh and English ethnic groups in the urban

TABLE 2

THE WELSH HOLD MORE TRADITIONAL VALUES THAN THE ENGLISH,
BUT THE WELSH IN THE RURAL AREA ARE THE MOST TRADITIONAL,

(A)

Can a person be good without religion?
(Entries are percentages answering "no".)

	All Welsh	All English	Urban Welsh	Rural Welsh	Urban English	Rural English
No	33	13	22	41	10	22

Between Welsh and English   Between Urban and Rural Welsh
Yule's Q = -.53[a]   Yule's Q = .43[a]

(B)

Frequency of church attendance
(Entries are percentages answering "never.")

	All Welsh	All English	Urban Welsh	Rural Welsh	Urban English	Rural English
Never	26	36	42	12	35	39

Between Welsh and English   Between Urban and Rural Welsh
Gamma = .23[b]   Gamma = .48[b]

[a]Yule's Q is a monotonic but non-linear measure of association
for 2 x 2 contingency tables.

[b]Gamma is a monotonic but non-linear measure of association for
ordinal contingency tables of greater than 2 x 2 proportions.
It is the equivalent of Yule's Q in the 2 x 2 case.

TABLE 3

THE WELSH ARE MOST AWARE OF THEIR ETHNIC IDENTITY IN THE RURAL AREA

How would you normally describe yourself?
(Entries are percentages.)

	Urban Welsh	Rural Welsh	Urban English	Rural English
Welsh	55	73	0	--
Some Combination or Sometimes Welsh, Other Times British	25	15	20	22
British	20	12	80	78

TABLE 4

THE DESIRE FOR CULTURAL AUTONOMY IS STRONGEST IN THE RURAL AREA

(A)

Is it imporant to preserve the Welsh language?
(Entries are percentages saying "yes.")

	All Welsh	All English	Urban Welsh	Rural Welsh	Urban English	Rural English
Yes	88	70	79	95	71	67

Between Welsh and English   Between Urban and Rural Welsh
Gamma = .50   Gamma = -.66

(B)

Should Welsh be taught in school?
(Entries are percentages saying "yes.")

	All Welsh	All English	Urban Welsh	Rural Welsh	Urban English	Rural English
Yes	77	45	59	91	41	55

Between Welsh and English   Between Urban and Rural Welsh
Gamma = .56   Gamma = -.71

(C)

Should Wales be made officially bi-lingual?
(Entries are percentages saying "yes.")

	All Welsh	All English	Urban Welsh	Rural Welsh	Urban English	Rural English
Yes	79	57	62	92	53	67

Between Welsh and English   Between Urban and Rural Welsh
Gamma = .47   Gamma = -.72

and rural setting toward the economic situation in Wales. We also look at the urban-rural bases of Welsh resentments of the English. These data can help us pinpoint further the sub-regional and attitudinal bases of Welsh nationalism.

ETHNIC AND URBAN-RURAL CLEAVAGES IN WALES: PERCEIVED REWARDS AND ETHNIC RESENTMENTS

One structural feature common to most of the nascent regional nationalisms which have been stirring in recent years throughout many advanced industrial states has been that such regions typically are economically less well-off than the nation as a whole. In some instances, this is due to lagged economic development, as in Brittany. In other instances, such as Wales, chronic economic depression is the result of economic overdevelopment during an earlier era and a subsequent absence of reinvestment necessary to transform an economy heavily dependent upon extractive industries to one emphasizing secondary and tertiary manufacturing. The belief that one's region has been victimized and the belief that the national government is insensitive to the economic well-being of the inhabitants are important ingredients to the development of political nationalism when strong communal ties also exist.

It is true, of course, that there is a pervasive belief among the inhabitants of Wales that the economy fails to provide adequate job opportunities (Table 5-A). In accordance with their generally lower socio-economic standing, the Welsh appear to be more sensitive to the economic problems of Wales than are the English who live in Wales. But what is particularly significant about the data in Table 5-A is that the division across urban-rural lines is even greater than that which exists across ethnic lines.[1] Dissatisfaction with the economic situation in Wales is clearly most pervasive in the rural area, and this accords with the objective differentials in socio-economic status between inhabitants of the rural and urban areas in Wales. Although the present analysis does not permit a definitive statement, economic disenchantment in Wales seems more a product of objective deprivation than of rising expectations.

Yet too much can be made of the nationalist potential stemming from economic grievances. For instance, another question which elicits responses to how well the national government takes care of people such as the respondent (Table 5-B) shows (a) satisfaction levels to be reasonably high; (b) only very modest (and statistically unreliable) differences between Welsh and English respondents in their reported level of satisfaction, and (c) no differences between the rural and urban Welsh in reporting satisfaction. Thus, while there exists substantial grievance regarding the economic prospects of Wales in the rural areas, the rural Welsh are no less dissatisfied by the British government's handling of their personal welfare needs than are the urban Welsh. Indeed, the Welsh sample, in general, is not fundamentally less satisfied with the British welfare state than is the English sample. Whatever the level of grievance about economic stagnation in Wales, the effective penetration of the British social

TABLE 5

ECONOMIC GRIEVANCES ARE LARGEST IN THE RURAL AREA,
BUT SUPPORT FOR THE BRITISH WELFARE STATE IS PERVASIVE

(A)

Are there adequate job opportunities in this area?
(Entries are percentages saying "No.")

	All Welsh	All English	Urban Welsh	Rural Welsh	Urban English	Rural English
No	75	61	52	93	51	89

Between Welsh and English   Between Urban and Rural Welsh
Gamma = .32   Gamma = -.82

(B)

How well does the national government take care of people like you?
(Cell entries are percentages.)

	All Welsh	All English	Urban Welsh	Rural Welsh	Urban English	Rural English
Well	50	62	50	50	63	62
Pro/Con	23	15	23	23	14	17
Poorly	27	23	27	27	23	22

Between Welsh and English   Between Urban and Rural Welsh
Gamma = .18   Gamma = .00

welfare state surely must act to dampen the prospects of active support for a political nationalism that would cut Wales adrift from London.

Nevertheless, as the evidence in Table 6 shows, Welsh resentment against the English is certainly not insubstantial, but this resentment exists to any significant degree only in the rural setting. In fact, as Table 6-A reveals, many more of the urban Welsh believe, in spite of objective evidence to the contrary, that the Welsh rather than the English obtain the best jobs in Wales. Further, while the Welsh feel that the English have too much power in Wales (Table 6-B), only the rural Welsh give majority support to this notion. Indeed, only on the social distance measure--whether the English treat the Welsh as if they were inferior--does any difference emerge between the two ethnic groups that is not otherwise a function of urban-rural differences among the Welsh. Further, not only are the Welsh-English differences relatively moderate, but even a majority of the English are willing to admit that the Welsh are sometimes treated by them as inferiors.

We can conclude, then, that grievances stemming from the stagnant character of the Welsh economic situation are more strongly associated with sub-regional differences than they are with ethnic identity and, for the most part, whatever ethnic resentments exist are also largely a consequence of these differences. But even these grievances and resentments must be weighed against the attachments that have developed toward the British welfare state and tempered by the feeling among Englishmen that the Welsh sometimes have been subjected to socially discriminatory treatment. Not only is it that the attitudinal basis for Welsh nationalism is not particularly vigorous, but such attitudes are basically confined to the rural areas where the population holds to rather traditional values--a factor that inhibits support for mass-based political organization which simultaneously employs nationalist and stridently redistributive symbols and appeals.

Ultimately, however, we can best gauge the political significance of Welsh nationalist sentiment by examining feelings of loyalty and allegiance to the British nation-state, assessments of the political and economic aftermath of a hypothetically independent Wales, and support for particular political options. To this analysis we now turn.

ETHNIC AND URBAN-RURAL CLEAVAGES IN WALES:
POLITICAL ALLEGIANCES, PROSPECTS, AND OPTIONS

Whether more cosmopolitan as in the urban area of Wales or culturally isolated as in the rural area, the Welsh consistently exhibit less ultimate loyalty to the British state and less pride in the symbols of British statehood than do the English (Table 7). Still, except for one's willingness to die for the United Kingdom (7-C), the differences between the urban and rural Welsh are also quite consistent. The message of these data seems clear: Welsh nationalism is largely a rural phenomenon. Perhaps nowhere is this

TABLE 6

WELSH RESENTMENTS AGAINST THE ENGLISH ETHNIC GROUP
TYPICALLY ARE STRONGEST IN THE RURAL AREA

(A)

Who gets the best jobs in Wales?
(Cell entries are percentages.)

	All Welsh	All English	Urban Welsh	Rural Welsh	Urban English	Rural English
English	21	--	5	34	--	--
Equal	55	61	66	47	73	28
Welsh	24	39	30	19	27	72

Between Welsh and English   Between Urban and Rural Welsh
        Gamma = .49   Gamma = -.48

(B)

Have the English been trying to gain too much power in Wales?
(Entries are percentages saying "yes.")

	All Welsh	All English	Urban Welsh	Rural Welsh	Urban English	Rural English
Yes	45	20	37	52	22	17

Between Welsh and English   Between Urban and Rural Welsh
        Gamma = .46   Gamma = -.31

(C)

Do the English treat the Welsh as equals or behave as if they were superior?
(Entries are percentages claiming that the English at least
occasionally treat the Welsh as inferiors.)

	All Welsh	All English	Urban Welsh	Rural Welsh	Urban English	Rural English
At least Occasionally Welsh are Treated as Inferiors	63	51	62	64	57	33

Between Welsh and English   Between Urban and Rural Welsh
        Yule's Q = .25   Yule's Q = -.04

210

TABLE 7

THE ENGLISH ARE MORE ALLEGIANT TO GREAT BRITAIN THAN THE WELSH,
BUT THE RURAL WELSH ARE LESS ALLEGIANT THAN THE URBAN WELSH

(A)

When you hear "God Save the Queen" (British national anthem) does
create in you a feeling of belonging?
(Entries are percentages who say "yes.")

	All Welsh	All English	Urban Welsh	Rural Welsh	Urban English	Rural English
Yes	50	75	61	41	76	72

Between Welsh and English   Between Urban and Rural Welsh
Gamma = -.49   Gamma = .39

(B)

Does being a citizen of Great Britain make you feel proud?
(Entries are percentages who say "yes.")

	All Welsh	All English	Urban Welsh	Rural Welsh	Urban English	Rural English
Yes	79	97	86	73	96	100

Between Welsh and English   Between Urban and Rural Welsh
Gamma = -.87   Gamma = .36

(C)

Is this country (U.K.) worth dying for?
(Entries are percentages who say "no.")

	All Welsh	All English	Urban Welsh	Rural Welsh	Urban English	Rural English
No	36	19	33	39	18	22

Between Welsh and English   Between Urban and Rural Welsh
Gamma = -.29   Gamma = .04

(D)

When there is conflict between national economic and political
interests and those of Wales, on which side do you usually stand?
(Entries are percentages choosing Welsh interests.)

	All Welsh	All English	Urban Welsh	Rural Welsh	Urban English	Rural English
Welsh Interests	44	17	28	58	20	11

Between Welsh and English   Between Urban and Rural Welsh
Gamma = .54   Gamma = -.44

more sharply etched than on the question which pits loyalty to the interests of Wales against loyalty to the interests of the United Kingdom (7-D). The rural Welsh quite clearly favor Welsh interests over British interests.

If Wales were to become independent, however, differences between the Welsh and English ethnic groups assume even more importance in assessing the prospects for Wales in the aftermath of such an event. Members of the English ethnic group are especially apt to believe that an independent Wales would bring with it more division than presently exists and also a lessening of their personal standard of living (Table 8).[2] Certainly the advantaged economic position of the English in Wales makes them more cautious with regard to substantial alterations of the political status of Wales. But the urban Welsh who are economically better off than the rural Welsh are no more skeptical of the socio-political and economic consequences of independence than are the rural Welsh. And, indeed, on the socio-political divisions question it is the rural Welsh who are more apt to believe that independence actually would bring about increased division within Wales. Oddly, then, while the rural Welsh generally show less political allegiance to the United Kingdom than the urban Welsh, the urban Welsh show no more fear about the consequences of Welsh independence than the rural Welsh. The allegiance questions, in other words, evoke two types of cleavages which typically have run through our data: first, there is a persistent difference across the two ethnic groups, and second, there are differences between the rural and urban Welsh with the latter usually holding attitudes more closely in accord with those held by the English. But when we look at the perceived economic and socio-political prospects for an independent Welsh state, we see that the differences are largely of a Welsh-English nature and the cleavage between the rural and urban Welsh is much less prominent. Moreover, all of the samples seem more troubled by the socio-political aspects of Welsh autonomy than by its economic aspects. Uncertainties over socio-political divisions could be a more restraining element in defining the political options of the Welsh nationalist movement than could economic uncertainties. In this respect, perhaps, British political culture with its emphasis upon moderate social and political conflict assumes considerable importance. The price of socio-political division may be perceived as too great to warrant large political change even if the risks of economic nonviability are not perceived as inordinate.

Finally, what are the political options for Wales favored by the Welsh and English ethnic groups and the urban and rural Welsh? One option that is almost unanimously rejected by all groups is political violence on behalf of separatism, even that which is not directly threatening to human life.[3] As we can see from Table 9-A, however, the Welsh ethnic group clearly is more supportive of a change from the political status quo toward giving Wales increased political autonomy. Four times as many Welshmen as Englishmen support a policy of separatism, but still only sixteen percent of the Welsh favor independence. Larger proportions of Welshmen favor the

TABLE 8

THE ENGLISH ARE MORE PESSIMISTIC THAN THE WELSH ABOUT THE FUTURE OF AN INDEPENDENT WALES

(A)

Would Wales be more divided after independence?
(Entries are percentages saying "yes.")

	All Welsh	All English	Urban Welsh	Rural Welsh	Urban English	Rural English
Yes	59	80	51	65	76	89

Between Welsh and English   Between Urban and Rural Welsh
Gamma = -.45   Gamma = -.20

(B)

If Wales became independent would your personal standard of living fall--
ten years after independence?
(Entries are percentages saying "yes.")

	All Welsh	All English	Urban Welsh	Rural Welsh	Urban English	Rural English
Yes	42	54	44	40	49	67

Between Welsh and English   Between Urban and Rural Welsh
Yule's Q = -.23   Yule's Q = .05

TABLE 9

THE RURAL WELSH SUPPORT THE WELSH SEPARATIST PARTY TO A GREATER DEGREE THAN THE URBAN WELSH BUT THEY DO NOT FAVOR A SEPARATIST OR REGIONAL POLITICAL ENTITY TO A SIGNIFICANTLY GREATER EXTENT

(A)

Which of the following would you like to see happen for Wales?
(Cell entries are percentages.)

	All Welsh	All English	Urban Welsh	Rural Welsh	Urban English	Rural English
Separate Nation	16	4	12	20	6	--
Regional Government	30	23	30	30	22	28
Status Quo or More Integration with U.K.	54	72	58	50	72	72

Between Welsh and English
Gamma = .39

Between Urban and Rural Welsh
Gamma = -.17

(B)

If a general election was to be held today, who would you vote for?
(Cell entries are percentages.)

	All Welsh (303)	All English (60)	Urban Welsh (132)	Rural Welsh (171)	Urban English (45)	Rural English (15)
Plaid Cymru (Welsh Separatist Party)	24	--	14	37	--	--
Labour	42	32	42	42	36	20
Liberal	5	10	2	9	9	13
Tory	29	58	42	12	55	67

214

more moderate course of regional devolution. Although this would provide a limited form of self-government, it still would subject Wales to the superordinate powers of the British national government. Welsh sentiment, however, is clearly divided, for a majority of the Welsh oppose any change in the political status quo and as Table 9-A further indicates, the differences between the urban and rural Welsh on the political future of Wales are weak. The English-Welsh differences are more sizeable but there also is a substantial minority body of opinion among the English (about one-fourth) supporting increased autonomy for Wales. In sum, neither the Welsh nor the English ethnic groups greatly support more political autonomy for Wales, and attaining the forty percent support necessary for London to grant a Welsh Assembly is by no means assured. Yet, clearly (and obviously) more support for these options can be found among the Welsh than among the English. At the same time, a surprisingly sizeable minority (twenty-seven percent) of the English support some additional political autonomy for Wales, nearly all of these favoring a moderate course of devolution rather than separatism. A minority of the English in Wales, then, either sympathize with aspirations to achieve greater autonomy from London (though these fail to receive majority support from the Welsh as well), see devolution as a defusing option, or think of Wales as a region rather than a nation or ethnic group and therefore see themselves as Welshmen in the regional if not the ethnic sense. What is most surprising of all, however, is that in spite of the fairly sizeable differences in economic status and in attitudes on many matters, there is little rural-urban difference insofar as views on the future political status of Wales are concerned. And as we shall now see, this lack of difference in urban-rural views toward the political options is all the more curious in light of the urban-rural differences that exist in expected voting behaviors.

Support for Plaid Cymru in Wales has never been particularly great. In the 1970 general elections held prior to this survey, Plaid Cymru received only twelve percent of the vote. Its support was derived principally from rural constituencies. When asked how they would vote if a general election were held today, a much larger proportion indicated support for Plaid Cymru than could be shown by the party's previous fortunes at the polls and, even more to the point, by its subsequent record of electoral performance. An urban-rural cleavage in Plaid Cymru support persists, however, and this is reflected in our survey evidence.

The inflated figures for Plaid Cymru support may be a result of at least two factors. First, it could be that the particular constituencies employed as sampling sites have been stronger bastions of nationalist sentiment than other areas. But since no other evidence sustains this possibility, it is more likely that mass sentiment for Plaid Cymru was at a high water mark during the period of the survey and receded subsequently. Even more probable is that an oral commitment to a vote in an election that had yet to be called is a simple form of protest which probably would not have to be acted upon. Nevertheless, even if it was to be acted upon, it may still be thought of as a protest vote rather than as a commitment to a program of separatism. In this regard, it is striking that nearly twice as high a proportion of the rural Welsh voice a preference for Plaid Cymru than support separatism as a policy option.

The survey data imply, therefore, that the Welsh nationalist party is tapping a much more diverse constituency than is warranted by the amount of support offered for the separatist option. As indicated previously, Plaid Cymru strategically has done much to mask its appeal to a straightforward separatist option. It has come to support both devolution and separatism and by doing so allows electors to selectively perceive their own preferences in the party's position. The growing fuzziness of the appeals of Plaid Cymru is designed to enable it to attract votes beyond the electorate's support for its separatist aims.

The flow of North Sea oil at least temporarily has vitiated the bases of support for Welsh nationalism through the promise of substantial injections of capital. Politically, however, the status of Wales remains unresolved. Labour continues to be divided on the wisdom of devolution and thus has not really been able to control the issue as yet. A Tory accession to power, however, may further fuel the issue if Mrs. Hatcher's staunch line of opposition to devolution dominates. The ascension of Mrs. Hatcher's point of view could result in a more substantial electoral base for Plaid Cymru (even if not greater support for its ultimate aims) especially if hopes for economic recovery are dashed. For now this is only speculation. What is not speculation, however, is that a willingness to voice support for the party of Welsh nationalism far exceeds the policy support for it among the Welsh electorate.

CONCLUSION

It is clear that state nationalisms in Western Europe have eroded sharply since the end of World War II. But as commitments to the nation-state have grown less intense, the emergence and re-emergence of ethno-regional nationalisms in contemporary Europe have been notable.

A prime force producing such territorial nationalisms is the status of these regions as economic laggards. Economic discontents are often bonded together with traditional communal ties providing a potential mass base for some form of political autonomy. Communal ties and economic discontents both are likely to be strongest in those parts of the "periphery," typically rural sectors, which are least linked to the core economy or culture. Objective inequalities tend to be linked also with feelings of social inferiority and discrimination at the hands of the "core" ethnic group. It is not surprising, therefore, that mass support for nationalist political movements within the periphery tends to arise in these rural areas.

The Welsh case that we have examined here fits such a pattern although we think that, in general, support for political nationalism in Wales is fairly tepid. Because discontents often are rooted in economic grievances, the questionable economic viability of a separatist entity is often a factor inhibiting support for such an option. Surprisingly, we found no greater skepticism among those in the urban area than among those in the rural area toward the prospects for an economically viable Welsh nation-state even though economic grievances certainly are larger in the rural area. A more inhibiting factor seems to be rooted in the fear of social and political uncertainty.

The future of the Welsh separatist party undoubtedly depends upon its capability to manipulate its appeals in such a way that it can attract broad-based support. To do that may mean abandoning the ultimate goal of separatism for the less ambitious objective of greater regional self-government under the ultimate control of Westminster. For the time being the party has manipulated appeals both to devolution and to separatism despite the fact that there is not very great support for the latter option. As in the case of Quebec, however, it is possible for a party to come to power espousing more ambitious separatist objectives than are supported by its electors. Unlike Quebec, Wales is not a province in a federal system and it has virtually no capacity to break away from the core state.

Ultimately what happens in Wales, as through much of its history, will depend upon decisions reached in London. A major economic transfusion in Wales, which the British economy now has a greater capacity to undertake, should have a significant impact in eroding support for Welsh political nationalism.

NOTES

1. A somewhat more ambiguously phrased question asks the respondents whether too many "Welshmen" are forced to find work in the United Kingdom outside of Wales. Ethnic and urban-rural differences are of similar magnitude here. Sixty-six percent of the Welsh ethnics agree contrasted with forty-five percent of the English. And while over three-quarters of the rural Welsh agree, a more modest fifty-four percent of the urban Welsh do so.

2. A similar question asks the respondents whether they think they would suffer a drop in their personal standard of living immediately after hypothetical independence from the United Kingdom. Overall, a slightly larger percentage of respondents thinks there would be a decline in their personal fortunes than when they are asked about their standard of living a decade after independence. Most importantly, though, the differences between the Welsh and English are of the same magnitude as the responses of the ten years later question. Fifty-one percent of the Welsh and sixty-two percent of the English believe that they would suffer economically immediately after independence. Responses to the ten years later question are shown because we think this is a better measure of perceived prospects for the economic viability of an independent Welsh nation-state.

3. Some Welsh nationalists had taken to blowing up water mains. Thus a question posed to the survey respondents asked them if they approved of political violence, such as the blowing up of water mains, if done in the interests of Wales. Only seven percent of the rural Welsh, the maximum support group, indicated acceptance of such activities.

REFERENCES

Aberbach, J. D. and Walker, J. L. (1970). "The Meanings of Black Power: A comparison of White and Black Interpretations of a Political Slogan." American Political Science Review 64:367-88.
Bertelsen, J. (1977). Non-State Nations in the International Context. New York: Praeger.
Black, C. E. (1967). The Dynamics of Modernization. New York: Harper.
Bottomore, T. B. (1966). Classes in Modern society. New York: Random House.
Connor, W. (1972). "Nation-Building or Nation-Destroying?" World Politics 24 (April): 319-55.
Corrado, R. (1977). "The Welsh Non-State Nation," ed. Judy Bertelsen. Non-State Nations in the International Context. New York: Praeger.
Corrado, R. (forthcoming). The Politics of Ethnicity. New York: Marcel-Dekker.
Esman, M. (1977). "Perspectives on Ethnic Conflict in Industrialized Societies," ed. M. Esman. Ethnic Conflict in the Western World. Ithaca, N.Y.: Cornell University Press.
Glazer, N. and Moynihan, D. (1975) Ethnicity. Cambridge: Harvard.
Greeley, A. (1974). Ethnicity in the U.S. New York: Wiley.
Hechter, M. (1975). Internal Colonialism. Berkeley: University of California Press.
Lerner, D. (1958). The Passing of Traditional Society. New York: Free Press.
Marsh, D. C. (1970). The Welfare State. London: Longman.
Marshall, T. H. (1965). Class, Citizenship and Social Development. New York: Anchor.
Putnam, R. D. (1976). The Comparative Study of Political Elites. Englewood Cliffs: Prentice-Hall.
Porter, J. (1968). The Vertical Mosaic. Toronto: Toronto University Press.
Rose, R. (1971). Governing Without Consensus. Boston: Beacon.
Runciman, W. F. (1966). Relative Deprivation and Social Justice. London: Routledge and Kegan Paul.
Smith, A. D. (1972). Theories of Nationalism. New York: Harper.
Strumpel, B. (1978). "The Changing Face of Advanced Industrial Economies: A Post-Keynesian View." Comparative Political Studies 10:299-322.
Titmuss, R. (1963). Essays on the Welfare State. Boston: Beacon.

Part IV
Strategies for Change

10. Strategies for Change: A Classification of Proposals for Ending Inequality

E. Thomas Rowe

Most discussions of inequality eventually come to the questions of whether or not and how changes can be produced. How can inequalities be reduced or ended? What alternatives are there for seeking change? To begin to answer these questions requires an overview of the types of strategies which have been proposed for attacking inequalities. Before that overview can be attempted, however, there is another issue, logically prior to a consideration of strategies for change. That is whether moving toward greater equality is even desirable.

THE DESIRABILITY OF EQUALITY

Studies of inequality usually contain the underlying assumption that lessening or eliminating the inequality being discussed would be desirable. The inequalities between rich and poor countries, and within countries between racial, ethnic, gender, or age groups, are identified partly to describe and analyze reality. In addition, however, implicitly or explicitly, the inequalities are usually viewed as inequitable, as unjust features which should be changed. There may be differences on whether change is possible or how it might be brought about, or how desirable or undesirable various byproducts of change might be; but the inequalities themselves are likely to be viewed as unjust.

Even many proposals which call for unequal treatment are based upon an underlying commitment to equality. "Affirmative action" measures, for instance, involve special attention to groups deprived because of a history of discrimination and unequal treatment.[1] The special or unequal measures favoring such groups are supposed to help overcome the inequalities resulting from the past, and to create a new situation of eventual equality. Simple equality of treatment in the present would perpetuate the status quo.

Similarly, some aspects of the "New International Economic Order" might be viewed as a kind of affirmative action program at the international level.[2] Preferential trading arrangements with poorer countries, for instance, are seen as a means of overcoming the inequalities of the present international system arising from the unjust and unequal treatment of the poor in the past. After a

221

period of preferential treatment, the products of the poor will be able to compete on an equal basis with those of the rich.

Both the New International Economic Order and affirmative action involve preferential treatment for the historically deprived. However, the apparent violation of the normative commitment to equality is true only in the short run. The short-term preference is designed to ensure greater equality in the long run. Similarly, providing special facilities for the physically handicapped is designed to ensure that these individuals can act or compete on an equal basis with others. From a broader perspective, equity again involves equality.

The central notion in most commitment to equality involves the inequity of inequalities resulting from conditions over which the individual has no control or choice. Categories from which individuals cannot escape--such as race, ethnic group, gender, or age--or which are unrelated to the performance of tasks for which individuals receive rewards, ought not to serve as the criteria by which benefits are distributed. The accompanying assumption here, of course, is that none of these categories is a reliable means for classifying individuals in terms of abilities, performance, etc.

Many writers would challenge the normative commitment to equality. Also, many have argued the inherently superior capabilities of particular racial, ethnic, or other groups. Despite the persistence of racist, ethnocentric, or other exclusive ideologies and behavior, however, the evidence available discredits such views.

My assumptions in this discussion of strategies for change include the notion that inequalities are an indication of inequity and that a lessening of inequalities is desirable at both domestic and international levels.[3] In what follows, then, I will not be concerned with justifications for change. My only aim is to identify and discuss various strategies by which change might be brought about.

CENTRAL DIMENSIONS DISTINGUISHING
PROPOSALS FOR CHANGE

Two dimensions are central in distinguishing various proposals for change. One is whether the basic causes of the inequalities are viewed as rooted in the internal characteristics of the deprived groups or in characteristics and relationships external to the deprived (including exploitive relationships between the privileged and the deprived). For example, the problems of Blacks in the United States sometimes have been explained in terms of weak motivation, poor job habits, inadequate education, etc. If these are seen as the major causes rather than as symptoms of the problems, they are explanations internal to the deprived. On the other hand, the real causes may relate to racial discrimination, systematic degradation and denial of respect for Blacks, denial of educational and economic opportunities, or exploitation of Blacks by Whites. These are clearly a type of explanation quite different from the first and hence call for very different policies if one seeks change.

The second dimension in distinguishing proposals for change has to do with the basic nature of the solution proposed: whether the solution envisages assimilation of the deprived into the existing system as equals or if it requires fundamental changes in the existing order. Using the example of U.S. Blacks again, for instance, one might argue that once they adopt White behavior patterns, or are educated, or are no longer subject to discrimination, Blacks will escape their present deprivation and eventually achieve equality. However, some would contend the capitalist system itself is the cause of the condition of Blacks in the U.S. If so, the basic problems could be met only by changing the economic system as a whole.

The two major dimensions are illustrated in Table 1, along with the four main types of proposals which result from combining the two. I have labeled these isolation, socialization, integration and revolution.

The isolation category involves rejection of the existing system but looks for change in the attitudes and characteristics of the deprived rather than in those of the overall system. Some Black nationalist and separatist movements in the United States might fit in this cell of the table. Socialization proposals also seek to change the characteristics of the deprived, but for the purpose of enabling the deprived to participate effectively in the system. To some degree, justifications for Head Start programs could be classified in this category. The integration category also accepts the basic nature of the existing system, but seeks simply to end those features of the system which prevent equitable participation. The civil rights movement and affirmative action programs would be classified here. Finally, the category labeled revolution sees the problems as so deeply rooted in the system that fundamental change is required. Marxist analyses of racism in the U.S. would generally fall in this category.

There is an additional distinction useful in grouping proposals for change. In each of the four main types listed in Table 1, there are those proposals which emphasize subjective elements (i.e., values, attitudes, and ideas) and those which emphasize objective elements (i.e., institutions, basic structures, and relationships). While difficult to identify with clarity, this subjective-objective dimension is important. Proposals involving acceptance of the existing system--socialization and integration in Table 1--may mean acquisition of the values and attitudes of the dominant system or acquisition of the skills, training, and other objective characteristics of the privileged. Similarly, rejection of the system--isolation and revolution in Table 1--may relate to such things as the basic values, on the one hand, or major economic institutions and relationships on the other.

Whether subjective or objective elements are the central focus, most writers explicitly or implicitly see changes in the one following changes in the other. Hence, the real difference here is in cause and effect--i.e., whether basic values, attitudes, and ideas determine the character of institutions, structures, and

223

TABLE 1

FOUR TYPES OF PROPOSALS FOR CHANGE

	Basic Nature of Solution:	
	Acceptance of the Existing System	**Rejection of the Existing System**
Basic Source of Problem: Internal to Group: Group/Individual Characteristics	**SOCIALIZATION:** Deprived must acquire the values and behavior that bring rewards to the more privileged in the dominant system. With self-help and aid from the privileged, the short-comings of the deprived must be eliminated.	**ISOLATION:** Deprived must reclaim or develop the values and behavior necessary for the good life. These may have been held and lost, or may simply be future goals to be sought. In any case, the values and behavior derived from the dominant system are inherently destructive and must be rejected.
External to Group: Relationships with/ Characteristics of Others	**INTEGRATION:** Deprived must be allowed to participate as equals in the system. Exclusive attitudes and behavior of the privileged and dependent and exploitative relationships between deprived and privileged must be broken.	**REVOLUTION:** Exclusive attitudes and behavior of the privileged, and dependent and exploitative relationships between deprived and privileged, must be broken. However, these are inherent in the system. Hence, escape from inequalities requires fundamental change in the dominant system. Even autarky can only work in the short run, since the dominant system will eventually intrude.

relationships, or vice versa. In other words, the distinction has importance in determining where initial efforts at change are directed. Whatever the initial efforts, the assumption is always that the end result will be changes in both values and behavior.

TYPES OF PROPOSALS FOR CHANGE

The classification system put forward here for proposals for change can be applied both to inequalities at the international level and to those at the domestic level, as shown in Table 2. In reality, of course, actual proposals tend to involve some mixing of the types given in the table, but the schema is useful in identifying central elements.

Isolation

Analyses of inequality that fall in what I have labeled the isolation category attribute deprivation to the values and behavior of the deprived, but reject the values and behavior in the dominant society or international system as inappropriate and undesirable.[4] Many traditionalist movements, such as the Muslim Brotherhood in Egypt or the Ram Rajya Parishad and the Rashtriya Swayamsevak Sangh in India, could be considered in this category. Most frequently, the deprived are viewed as having been damaged or corrupted by those characteristics acquired as a result of the impact of the society or in efforts to emulate that society. The loss of real or mythical historical virtue is often seen as the source of problems, and proposals then call for the reassertion of traditions.

Isolation proposals rarely attract more than a few adherents from outside the deprived group itself, since the proposed solutions are usually designed for the deprived rather than for the society or international system as a whole. Among the deprived, such proposals are not likely to receive much support unless the barriers to participation in the dominant society are strong and the possibilities for overall change remote or nonexistent. Moreover, some group identification among the deprived and a persisting subculture are probably prerequisites for support. Even under all of these conditions, however, the long-term attractiveness of these types of proposals is likely to be limited. Too many desirable things are controlled by the dominant society or international system and are distributed in accordance with criteria determined by that society or system. To get those desirable things, it is necessary either to meet the criteria or to change them for the society as a whole. In addition, isolating the deprived from the dominant society--in order to change values and behavior or to reassert traditional virtue--is difficult under the best of circumstances and perhaps impossible under most. Hence, over time, attempts to implement proposals involving isolation or separatism tend either to fail or to be transformed into efforts to build the pride and self confidence of the deprived so that they can compete more successfully with the privileged. In short, they sometimes end up combining group pride

225

TABLE 2

CLASSIFICATION OF PROPOSALS FOR CHANGE

Basic Nature of Solution: Acceptance of the Existing System

Vertical axis — SOCIALIZATION (left) / INTEGRATION (right)

Basic Source of Problem: Internal to Group / External to Group

	SOCIALIZATION — Subjective	SOCIALIZATION — Objective	INTEGRATION — Subjective	INTEGRATION — Objective
Domestic (Internal to Group)	a. Deprived must abandon their unproductive and self-destructive values, ideas, and attitudes, and adopt the values, ideas, and attitudes of the more privileged in society. (Examples would include teaching "responsible" behavior and self-confidence.)	b. Deprived must abandon their unproductive and self-destructive behavior and acquire the skills and behavior of the more privileged in society. (Examples would include job training programs.)	a. Society must view the deprived as equals, welcome equal participation, and reject past and present attitudes which have allowed exploitation of the deprived. (Examples would include education of whites to end prejudice.)	b. Society must end the practices which have brought discrimination and exploitation, ensure equal participation, and help the deprived overcome the disadvantages arising from past and present inequalities. (Examples would include affirmative action programs.)
International (External to Group)	c. Poor countries must abandon the traditional values which prevent development, and acquire the values, ideas, and attitudes of the rich, industrial societies. (Examples would include "westernization" or "modernization" of culture.)	d. Poor countries must abandon the traditional behavior and institutions which prevent development, and acquire the skills and behavior of the rich, industrial societies. (Examples would include technical assistance programs to bring western skills and technology.)	c. Rich countries must recognize the poor as equals, welcome equal participation, and reject past and present attitudes which have allowed exploitation of the deprived. (Examples would include international efforts to condemn racism and apartheid.)	d. Rich countries must end the practices which have brought discrimination and exploitation, ensure equal participation, and help the poor overcome the disadvantages arising from past and present inequalities. (Examples would include most aspects of the New International Economic Order.)

ISOLATION

REVOLUTION

Basic Source of Problem:

	Domestic		International	
	Subjective	Objective	Subjective	Objective

ISOLATION

a. Deprived must reject self-destructive attitudes of helplessness and inferiority derived from the dominant society, and adopt more productive attitudes and values of self-respect and pride. Appropriate values can only be found in the group, not from the dominant society. (Examples would include some cultural nationalist movements among ethnic and racial groups.)

b. Deprived must reject unproductive and self-destructive behavior and institutions derived from the dominant society, and adopt those fitted to the character of the group. These can only be found in the experience of the group, not from the dominant society. (Examples would include some separatist movements.)

c. Poor countries must reject self-destructive attitudes of helplessness and inferiority, develop attitudes of self-respect and pride, and find areas and values more productive and more suited to their needs than those coming from the rich, industrial societies. (Examples would include traditionalist nationalism based on religious beliefs.)

d. Poor countries must reject unproductive and self-destructive behavior and institutions, and adopt those fitted to their societies. These can only be found in the experiences of the poor countries, not from the unsuitable systems of the rich. (Examples would include traditionalist nationalism emphasizing traditional institutions.)

REVOLUTION

a. Deprived must be viewed as equals and exploitation must be rejected as wrong. However, the central values of modern society justify inequality, and exploitation of one individual or group by another. Hence, the basic culture requires fundamental change before equality can be achieved. (Examples would include some calls for a new internal system based on cooperation and mutual concern.)

b. Deprived must be treated as equals and exploitation must end. However, the social, economic and political systems are based upon inequality and exploitation and cannot operate successfully without them. Hence, fundamental change is required. (Examples would include some internal revolutionary movements.)

c. Poor countries must be viewed as equals and exploitation must be rejected as wrong. However, the central values of the present international system justify inequality and exploitation. Hence, the basic values require fundamental change before equality can be achieved. (Examples would include calls for a new world order based on cooperation and mutual concern.)

d. Poor countries must be treated as equals and exploitation must end. However, the international socioeconomic and political systems are based upon inequality and exploitation and cannot operate successfully without them. Hence, fundamental change is required. (Examples would include some world revolutionary movements.)

Rejection of the Existing System

Basic Nature of Solution

and identity with a degree of socialization or integration into the dominant system. This seems to have happened, for instance, to some Black nationalist groups in the United States.

Socialization

Proposals for solutions which fall in what I have labeled the socialization category in Tables 1 and 2 tend to be especially convenient and attractive to the more privileged countries, groups or individuals in any system of inequality.[5] In the first place, the system from which the privileged benefit is accepted as legitimate and fair. In the second place, the causes of inequality are seen as rooted in the shortcomings of the deprived.[6] Moreover, to escape their inequality, the deprived must seek to become more like the privileged. The privileged owe their privileges to their own virtues--the values, attitudes, skills, and behavior they exhibit. If the deprived acquire these same virtues, they too will benefit. These conceptions of the causes of inequality have an attractiveness to the privileged, not necessarily as hypocrisy or simply self-justification, but as expressions of real belief in the systems from which they benefit.

Proposals adopted as government policy at domestic and international levels have often fallen in the socialization category, probably because of their attractiveness to the privileged. Various observers have identified the basic causes of domestic inequalities as inhering in such features as the family patterns of the deprived, their attitudes and lack of motivation, or their inadequate skills and training. Government programs have then been designed to try to broaden experiences of the deprived, to change their attitudes and values, and to teach them new skills. In addition, various social welfare programs, created ostensibly to ensure minimal conditions of life, are frequently combined with rules and regulations designed to impose officially espoused norms and values on the program recipients.

The same features are clearly evident in foreign aid programs at the international level. The early development literature is replete with explanations of poverty focusing on the problems of "traditional" cultures which made economic development difficult or impossible, and arguing the necessity for "westernization." Foreign aid programs, at least in their explicit justifications, were designed to transfer the values, skills, and technology from the rich, industrial societies to the poor countries. Once these and other characteristics had been acquired by the poor societies, they would develop toward equality. Similarly, grants and loans, whether bilateral or multilateral, have frequently been tied to the recipients' adoption of economic and financial policies considered "sound" or "appropriate" by the governments or multilateral agencies making the decisions.

In recent years, after a long period of frustrating and seemingly unsuccessful experiences with these socialization proposals, there have been growing criticisms and some disillusionment at both

228

domestic and international levels. More assertive and self-confident elements among the deprived are unwilling to accept that their deprivation is the result of their own shortcomings. Among the privileged, the apparent failure to bring significant change has led to skepticism and reassessment. Proponents of major programs argue that time has been too short and efforts too small to be a real test; but they appear, at the moment, to be losing the argument to critics.

Some of these critics see no possibility for change. They argue the inevitability of inequalities, and sometimes contend that the conditions of the deprived are rooted in their own unchangeable defects. As I stated at the outset, I will not attempt to discuss these arguments. Suffice it to say that there appears to be some revival in the popularity of these views among the privileged in the United States.[7]

Integration

There is also growing popularity for proposals falling in what I have called the integration and revolution categories. Integration involves acceptance of the basic features of the existing domestic or international system, while revolution calls for fundamental changes in those features. However, both attribute the causes of inequality to factors external to the deprived themselves--the values, attitudes, institutions, and behavior of the privileged--and the relationships between privileged and deprived.

Proposals in the integration category, and even government policies based on those proposals, are not uncommon at either domestic or international levels.[8] Laws barring discrimination, for instance, clearly fall in this category. The same is true of a wide variety of other measures designed to ensure equal treatment and equal opportunity, including affirmative action legislation. Affirmative action is a logical outgrowth of earlier anti-discrimination concerns. It is designed to help overcome the effects of past discrimination and to create a new situation in which real equality is possible. At the same time, it arouses hostility and resistance because it requires active efforts to eliminate inequality rather than passive acceptance of whatever situation develops when current discrimination ends. Such passive action tends to mean perpetuation of the status quo and some continued privileges for those already benefiting from the system. Affirmative action, if implemented, would mean some real sacrifice of privileges.

In many respects, formal-legal equality at the domestic level--i.e., the end of officially sanctioned, legal discrimination--is similar to the end of traditional colonialism at the international level. Both involve an end to subordinate and second class status in the legal system. Domestically, legal discrimination on the basis of racial, ethnic, gender, age, or other groupings continues; but there has been real movement toward formal-legal equality. Internationally, some traditional colonial relationships continue, more semi-colonial relationships exist, and a large number of groups which

229

would like to participate in the international system as sovereign and equal units are prevented from doing so. Nevertheless, it is still true that most of the traditional European empires have now collapsed. Only vestiges of these earlier empires remain, and most colonies have now become legally sovereign states. In practice, of course, legal equality in domestic law has not meant real equality in domestic practice, which is one of the reasons for affirmative action measures. Similarly, sovereign equality at the international level has not produced real equality in international practice. The parallel to affirmative action here, I think, is the New International Economic Order.

Because of its label, the New International Economic Order may be viewed as a rejection of the existing international system. In fact, however, it is not. It is a series of proposals designed to integrate the "Third World" countries more equitably into the international system and to ensure that they acquire an equitable share of the benefits of that system. As with affirmative action, the proposals are intended to overcome the effects of a long history of unequal treatment and exploitation, not to overthrow the basic system itself.[9] This is evident in the calls for increased foreign aid, regulated but also more extensive private investment by the rich in the poor countries, preferential access to the markets of the rich by the products from the poor, and increased transfers of technology from the rich to the poor. These may involve redistribution of some benefits, but no redesign of the system. In fact, they imply that with moderate intervention and regulation, the system can be made to operate equitably for the equal benefit of all.

Revolution

Proposals in the revolution category do not accept that the existing system can undergo minor reforms and then operate equitably.[10] The fundamental structures and values in the system produce and justify inequalities and exploitation.[11] Unless those structures and values are changed, the system will continue to produce unacceptable results.

Many views falling in this category are Marxist and semi-Marxist. The capitalist economic system inevitably produces domestic and international inequalities, which can only be stopped with the end of capitalism. Various reforms may bring temporary relief, or may change some distribution patterns so that the identity of who is privileged and who is not may be altered, but the basic inequality and exploitation would continue.

Another viewpoint argues that the problems inhere in the competitive and exploitative values and attitudes of the system. In this view, changes in the legal system, in institutions or in similar aspects of domestic and international society, will not change the real character of behavior and relationships. Instead the new laws and institutions will simply operate in the usual competitive and exploitative ways, consistent with the fundamental values that pervade the present system. Capitalist, socialist, and communist

230

institutional arrangements have all produced inequality and exploitation, and will continue to do so as long as the underlying values remain unchanged. Humane, supportive, compassionate, and inclusive attitudes towards others must replace competitive, exploitative, and exclusive attitudes as the fundamental determinants of behavior. Until they do, legal and structural changes are not likely to have a significant impact on inequality.

The dilemma is a difficult one. Structural changes may be undermined by the persistence of earlier attitudes and values, with the result that there is little real change in behavior. On the other hand, attempts to change values and attitudes may be frustrated by the existence of structures within which those values and attitudes seem inappropriate. The obvious solution of simultaneous change is certainly remote. More importantly, the methods most likely to bring about structural changes may not be conducive to the development or survival of appropriate values. Perhaps, as Mahatma Gandhi or Martin Luther King argued, the methods chosen for bringing about change are of central importance.[12] The same values and attitudes which should govern relationships in a changed society must govern the methods used in creating that society. Otherwise the values underlying the means chosen will corrupt the new society and create new or simply revised inequities.

At the same time, many would argue that Gandhi and King were wrong in supposing that their methods, and the values upon which those methods were based, could bring about fundamental change. Humane, compassionate, inclusive attitudes may prevent a successful confrontation with the structures and values of existing society. If so, the values necessary for the creation of more equitable domestic and international systems may be unable to survive because of the methods necessary to bring an end to existing systems.

CONCLUSIONS

What conclusions can be drawn from all of this? While I do have preferences, my purpose has not been to suggest that one type of proposal is superior to others. Rather, the schema here has been designed to clarify alternative strategies for change and to present a few thoughts with regard to each. At the same time, some proposals seem more viable than others.

Those of the isolation variety appear doomed to frustration in an era of increasingly intense communications and interchange of goods and services across group or national lines. Truly autonomous values, institutions, and behavior are likely to be even more difficult to maintain in the future than in the past. The value to be gained here, however, may be in the development of a sense of identity, self-respect, and pride, rather than in creating actual autonomy. This is likely to stimulate more dissatisfaction with inequalities and to intensify demands for change by the deprived. In turn, the results may contribute to other efforts for change, even though the original aim of isolation is lost.

Proposals in the socialization category have had and will continue to have some popularity. However, the absence of clear evidence of the success of government policies based on these proposals presents difficulties. There has been amelioration of specific problems, e.g., in some educational and technical assistance programs, but the overall inequalities, domestically and internationally, seem to remain or even to become worse. In addition, substantial evidence supports the thesis that various groups are likely to be excluded from the benefits of domestic and international systems even if their members have or acquire the attitudes, skills, and behavior of the privileged. Moreover, the more self-confident and assertive the deprived, the less acceptable are proposals which contend their deprivations result from their own presumed shortcomings. As a result of these combined circumstances, declining popular enthusiasm among the privileged for government policies based on socialization proposals has been accompanied by increasing resistance to those policies among the deprived. Hence, there has been a substantial shift to proposals of the integration type.

In the integration area there has been visible progress in formal-legal equality. This is evident in the successes of the anticolonial movements, the collapse of the traditional European empires, and the emergence of "new" states from former colonies. It is evident in the widespread movement toward elimination of officially sanctioned, legal inequalities in domestic law. Legal equality has not yet been achieved, of course; but changes here have been far more dramatic than changes in other aspects of inequality.

The failure to achieve more rapid progress in dealing with these other aspects is an important explanation of affirmative action at the domestic level and the New International Economic Order at the international level. In a sense, each represents a last attempt to affirm the possibilities of achieving equity within the existing order. They each involve reform, but not fundamental change. If they fail, it may well be that rejection of the existing domestic and international systems is the only remaining alternative.

Proposals in the revolution category, whatever their ultimate truth, are easier to espouse than to implement. Moreover, as I noted earlier, there may be an irreconcilable conflict between necessary means and chosen ends. If fundamental change is perceived as necessary, however, that conflict between means and ends will not be accepted as an inevitable or fatal flaw. Revolutionary measures will be attempted. At the same time, these are likely to be so costly as to be seen as actions of last resort. In short, if the deprived feel there is any real possibility for equity in the existing domestic and international systems, the revolutionary alternatives are not likely to be chosen.

NOTES

1. Discussions of the nature and implications of affirmative action can be found in, e.g., Lucy Sells (ed.), Toward Affirmative

Action (San Francisco: Jossey-Bass, Inc., 1974); Thomas Conrad, "The Debate about Quota Systems: An Analysis," American Journal of Political Science, 20:1 (February 1976), 135-149; Judith Jarvis Thomson, "Preferential Hiring," Philosophy and Public Affairs, 2:4 (Summer 1973), 364-384; Robert Simon, "Preferential Hiring: A Reply to Judith Jarvis Thomson," Philosophy and Public Affairs, 3:3 (Fall 1974), 312-320; George Sher, "Justifying Reverse Discrimination in Employment," Philosophy and Public Affairs, 4:2 (Winter 1975), 159-170; George Sher, "Groups and Justice," Ethics, 87:2 (January 1977), 174-181; Gertrude Ezorsky, "On Groups and Justice," Ethics, 87:2 (January 1977), 182-185; Thomas Nagel, "Equal Treatment and Compensatory Discrimination," Philosophy and Public Affairs, 2:4 (Summer 1973), 348-363; Paul Taylor, "Reverse Discrimination and Compensatory Justice," Analysis, 33:6 (June 1973), 177-182; Michael Bayles, "Reparations to Wronged Groups," Analysis, 33:6 (June 1973), 182-184; Daniel Bell, "Meritocracy and Equality," The Public Interest (Fall 1970), 29-68; Rose Laub Coser, "Affirmative Action: Letter to a Worried Colleague," Dissent, 22 (Fall 1975), 366-369; Morton Tenzer and Rose Laub Coser, "A Debate on Affirmative Action," Dissent, 23 (Spring 1976), 207-210; and Nathan Glazer, Affirmative Discrimination: Ethnic Inequality and Public Policy (New York: Basic Books, 1975).

2. Discussions of the nature and implications of the New International Economic Order are extensive. See, e.g., K. Brunner, "New International Economic Order: A Chapter in a Protracted Confrontation," Orbis, 20 (Spring 1976), 103-121; T. De Montbriad, "For a New World Economic Order," Foreign Affairs (June 1975), 61-78; Nathaniel Leff, "The New International Economic Order--Bad Economics, Worse Politics," Foreign Policy, 24 (Fall 1976); Jan Tinbergen, et al., Reshaping the International Order, A Report to the Club of Rome (New York: E. P. Dutton, 1976); Richard Cooper, "A New International Economic Order for Mutual Gain," Foreign Policy, 26 (Spring 1977), 66-120; Fred Hirsch, "Is There a New International Economic Order?" International Organization, 30:3 (Summer 1976), 521-532; B. Gosovic and J. Ruggie, "On the Creation of a New International Economic Order: Issue Linkage and the Seventh Special Session of the UN General Assembly," International Organization, 30:2 (Spring 1976), 309-346.

3. I do not mean to minimize the serious difficulties in attempting to define equality or in applying those definitions. Nor do I wish to imply that there are no real problems in a normative commitment to equality or in joining the notions of justice and equality. Rather, my aim is simply to avoid those difficult issues in order to discuss the question of strategies for change.

4. For discussions of nationalist and separatist movements, see, e.g., Alphonso Pinkney, Red, Black and Green, Black Nationalism in the United States (Cambridge: Cambridge University Press, 1976); Eric Lincoln, The Black Muslims (Boston: Beacon Press, 1961); E. U. Essien-Udom, Black Nationalism (Chicago: University of Chicago Press, 1962); James S. Coleman, "Nationalism in Tropical Africa," American Political Science Review, 47:2 (June

1954), 404-426; Ralph Linton, "Nativistic Movements," American Anthropologist, 45 (April-June 1943), 230-240. There are some elements of this isolation category in Kwame Nkrumah, Consciencism: Philosophy and Ideology for Decolonization and Development (London: Heinemann, 1964), in his emphasis on the traditional "African personality." The same is true of Leopold Senghor, On African Socialism (New York: Frederick Praeger, 1964).

5. Examples of writings I would place in this category include Nathan Glazer and Daniel Moynihan, Beyond the Melting Pot (Cambridge, Mass.: Harvard University Press, 1963); W. W. Rostow, The Stages of Economic Growth: A Non Communist Manifesto (Cambridge, Cambridge University Press, 1960); Daniel Lerner, The Passing of Traditional Society (London: Free Press of Glencoe, 1964); Fred Riggs, "Agraria and Industria: Toward a Typology of Comparative Administration," in W. Siffin (ed.), Toward a Comparative Study of Public Administration (Bloomington: University of Indiana Press, 1957); Richard Bendix, "What Is Modernization?" in W. Beling and G. Totten (eds.) Developing Nations: Quest for a Model (New York: Van Nostrand Reinhold, 1970); Max Millikan and Donald Blackmer (eds.), The Emerging Nations: Their Growth and United States Policy (Boston: Little, Brown, 1961).

6. An important distinction must be drawn between those analysts who see characteristics of the deprived as symptoms or consequences of their situation, and those who see those characteristics as causes of their deprivation. Theotonio Dos Santos, "The Structure of Dependence," American Economic Review, 60 (May 1970), 231-236, stresses that seeing underdevelopment as a result of inadequate education, scarcity of skills, etc., mistakes the symptoms for the disease. Similarly, when Irving Horowitz, Three Worlds of Development, The Theory and Practice of International Stratification (New York: Oxford University Press, 1966), discusses the "mental set of developing man," he notes that he is talking about the "psychological consequences of colonialism." Also see O. Mannoni, Prospero and Caliban; The Psychology of Colonization (New York: Frederick Praeger, 1964). At the domestic level, those seeing the characteristics of the deprived as causes of their condition include Glazer and Moynihan, op. cit.; Franklin Frazier, The Negro Family in the United States (Chicago: University of Chicago Press, 1966); Edward Banfield, The Unheavenly City, The Nature and Future of Our Urban Crisis (Boston: Little, Brown, 1970). On the other hand, those emphasizing characteristics as consequences include Kenneth Clark, Dark Ghetto (New York: Harper and Row, 1965); Thomas Gladwin, Poverty USA (Boston: Little, Brown, 1967); and Elliott Lebow, Tally's Corner: A Study of Negro Streetcorner Men (Boston: Little, Brown, 1967).

7. See, e.g., Steven Goldberg, The Inevitability of Patriarchy (New York: William Morrow, 1973); George Gilder, Sexual Suicide (New York: Quadrangle Books, 1973); Arthur Jensen, Educability and Group Differences (New York: Harper and Row, 1973); Arthur Jensen, "How Much Can We Boost IQ and Scholastic Achievement?" Harvard Educational Review, 39 (Winter 1969), 1-123; Richard

Herrnstein, "I.Q.," Atlantic Monthly (September 1971), 43-64;
Richard Herrnstein, "More About I.Q.," Atlantic Monthly (December
1971), 101-110; Richard Herrnstein, I.Q. in the Meritocracy (Boston:
Little, Brown, 1974); Irving Kristol, "About Equality," Commentary
(November 1972), 41-47; and Daniel Bell, "Meritocracy and Equality,"
The Public Interest, 29 (Fall 1972), 29-68.
    8. See, e.g., Dorothy James, Poverty, Politics and Change
(Englewood Cliffs, New Jersey: Prentice Hall, 1972); Charles
Fisher, Minorities, Civil Rights and Protest (Belmont, California:
Dickenson, 1970); Lester Thurow, Poverty and Discrimination
(Washignton, D.C.: The Brookings Institution, 1969);
Pierre Uri (ed.), North-South: Developing a New Relationship
(Paris: Atlantic Institute for International Affairs, 1976);
Jack N. Behrman, Toward a New International Economic Order
(Paris: Atlantic Institute for International Affairs, 1974); and
Betty Friedan, "Our Revolution Is Unique," in Mary Lou Thompson
(ed.), Voices of the New Feminism (Boston: Beacon Press, 1970).
Friedan's earlier work, The Feminine Mystique (New York:
W. W. Norton, 1963), tended to emphasize that the training of women
and their resulting attitudes prevented them from achieving equality.
This type of analysis would fall more in the socialization category.
Friedan's subsequent analyses, however, have given more attention
to the legal and institutional barriers to equality.
    9. Even if one believes fundamental redesign of the system is
necessary, however, one may still favor certain types of more limited
reform. Denis Goulet, The Cruel Choice, A New Concept in the
Theory of Development (New York: Atheneum, 1973), 294-298, 329,
makes a useful distinction between "palliative" and "creative"
incremental change. He argues that fundamental change is
necessary, but some small changes may move usefully in the right
directions while others will be obstructions to adequate overall
change:

> Palliative measures obstruct basic change because they lull
> people into believing that gradual amelioration is an
> adequate response to fundamental problems....Creative
> incremental measures, on the other hand, breed new
> possibilities for subsequent radical change, although at the
> moment they appear quite modest (295).

    10. See, e.g., Evelyn Reed, Problems of Women's Liberation
(New York: Pathfinder Press, 1969); E. Altbach (ed.), From
Feminism to Liberation (Cambridge, Mass.: Schenkman, 1971); Anne
Koedt, Ellen Levine and Anita Rapone (eds.), Radical Feminism
(New York: Quadrangle Books, 1973); Shulamith Firestone, The
Dialectic of Sex (New York: Bantam, 1970); James Foreman, The
Making of Black Revolutionaries (New York: Macmillan, 1972);
Julius Lester (ed.), The Seventh Son, The Thought and Writings of
W.E.B. DuBois (New York: Random House, 1971);
Andre Gunter Frank, Capitalism and Underdevelopment in Latin
America (New York: Monthly Review Press, 1967); Johan Galtung, "A

Structural Theory of Imperialism," Journal of Peace Research, 8:2 (1971), 81-117; K. T. Fann and Donald C. Hodges (eds.) Readings in U.S. Imperialism (Boston: Peter Sargent, 1971); Halge Hveen, "The Global Dominance System: Notes on a Global Theory of Political Economy," Journal of Peace Research, 10:4 (1973), 319-340; James Cockroft, et. al., Dependence and Development: Latin America's Political Economy (New York: Anchor Books, 1972); T. E. Weisskopf, "Capitalism, Underdevelopment and the Future of the Poor Countries," in J. Bhagwati (ed.), Economics and World Order (New York: The Free Press, 1972); Joyce Kolko, America and the Crisis of World Capitalism (Boston: Beacon Press, 1974); and Susanne Bodenheimer, "Dependency and Imperialism: The Roots of Latin American Underdevelopment," Politics and Society, 1:3 (May 1971), 327-357.

11.   Many of these critics would argue that at least some measures in the socialization and integration categories may be worse than no action at all.   Foreign aid, for instance, may simply help to sustain inequitable regimes and to enmesh more fully the poor societies in the economies of the rich.   See Teresa Hayter, Aid as Imperialism (Middlesex: Penguin Books, 1971); and Denis Goulet and Michael Hudson, The Myth of Aid: The Hidden Agenda of the Development Reports (New York: IDOC North America, 1971).

12.   For   Mohandas   Gandhi's   views,   see   his   Non-Violent Resistance, Satyagraha (New York: Schocken Books, 1951) and his Satyagraha in South Africa (Stanford, California: Academic Reprints, 1954).   Also   see   Joan Bondurant,   Conquest   of   Violence--The Gandhian Philosophy of Conflict (rev. ed.; Berkeley: University of Calfornia Press, 1965); and Erik Erikson, Gandhi's Truth, On the Origins of Militant Nonviolence (New York: W. W. Norton, 1969). For Martin Luther King's views, see his Stride Toward Freedom, The Montgomery Story (New York: Harper and Row, 1963) and his The Trumpet of Conscience (New York: Harper and Row, 1967).   Also see Hanes Walton, Jr., The Political Philosophy of Martin Luther King, Jr. (Westport, Connecticut: Greenwood, 1971).